REBUILDING
WITH
CHRIST

RADIO MESSAGES OF THE SECOND PART
OF THE TWELFTH LUTHERAN HOUR

REBUILDING WITH CHRIST

By WALTER A. MAIER, PH. D., D. D., LL. D.

PROFESSOR OF OLD TESTAMENT INTERPRETATION
AND HISTORY, CONCORDIA THEOLOGICAL SEMINARY
SAINT LOUIS, MISSOURI

CONCORDIA PUBLISHING HOUSE
SAINT LOUIS, MISSOURI

COPYRIGHT 1946
BY CONCORDIA PUBLISHING HOUSE
SAINT LOUIS, MISSOURI

PRINTED IN THE U. S. A.

To

EDMUND KUHLMAN

". . . who bestowed much
labor on us."

Romans 16:6

FOREWORD

WITH the close of the Twelfth International Lutheran Hour, we can begin to survey the results and continue the praise of God for His blessings on our radio crusade for Christ. Despite the restrictions limiting our live broadcast to the morning and prohibiting even a vague suggestion of financial contributions, this season of broadcasting stands as a miracle of the Almighty. During these twelve months we have received 340,000 letters, the largest number in our radio history. One might well expect that the people of our country, hearing fundamentally the same messages for more than a decade, would lag in their response. Yet the Holy Spirit has permitted us year after year to witness a steady increase in the number of listeners' letters.

Again while the new policy adopted by the Mutual Broadcasting System forbade any reference to the financial support of Bringing Christ to the Nations, the gifts for the Twelfth Lutheran Hour were unquestionably the greatest in our entire broadcasting experience. Let this marvelous truth be a strengthening reassurance to everyone of us! God keeps His promises.

The letters, more than a third of a million, came to us from these countries and districts (asterisks represent the nations or territories in which we have broadcasting stations):

Admiralty Islands
Alaska
Algeria
Argentina *
Austria
Australia *
Bahama Islands

Belgium
Bermuda
Bolivia *
Brazil *
British East Africa
British Guiana *
British Honduras

British West Indies *
Canada *
Canal Zone
Chile *
China
Colombia *
Costa Rica *
Cuba *
Dominican Republic *
Dutch Guiana *
Ecuador *
England
France
Gold Coast of Africa
Guatemala
Haiti *
Hawaii *
Honduras *
Iceland
India
Italy
Jamaica
Mexico
Mozambique *
Natal
Newfoundland
New Guinea
New Zealand
Nicaragua *
Nigeria
Northern Rhodesia
Panama *
Paraguay *
Peru *
Philippine Islands
Puerto Rico *
Salvador
Southern Rhodesia
Transvaal
Union of South Africa
United States *
Uruguay *
Venezuela *
Virgin Islands

The increase in our mail was reflected also in the growth of our station list. While we began the twelfth season with 540 stations, we were privileged to close it with 609, the highest all-time figure we have ever recorded. Once again we state with humble gratitude to the Almighty that the Lutheran Hour represents the most widespread broadcasting system in radio.

Notable progress during the past year was made chiefly in the following fields:

First: The addition of frequency modulation stations.

Second: The addition of four outlets in Quebec, Canada.

Third: The increase to more than 100 small government broadcasting stations which use Lutheran Hour transcriptions.

Fourth: The increase in the number of Spanish programs along the Mexican border in our country.

Fifth: The first invitation to broadcast from a European station.

Foreword

Sixth: The resolution of the Lutheran Laymen's League which, we trust, will lead to the establishment of our own long- and short-wave broadcasting stations in Europe.

When we present on the following pages the addresses delivered from February to May, 1945, the second half of our portion in the twelfth broadcasting season, and when we print in this foreword letters from people in various sections of the world who have been blessed by our mission of the air, we must repeat what we say at every Lutheran Hour Rally concerning our broadcast: Please give us personally no credit whatever for these startling blessings. If it were not for our heavenly Father's love, the Savior's compassion, and the Holy Spirit's enlightening, sanctifying help, the broadcast would have been off the air years ago. What a merciful and wonderful God He is to take us, frail and faulty as we are, and to use us for His mighty purposes! How we ought to praise Him daily for the magnificent outpouring of His benedictions by which the Lutheran Hour stands as a miracle of modern missions!

SAVED BY GRACE

It is our privilege simply to proclaim the Gospel of the crucified Savior. The Holy Spirit must give the blessing. How can we sufficiently thank the Lord for the tremendous benediction of His enlightening guidance by which our broadcast has brought multitudes to the faith? During the twelfth broadcast Dr. Bertermann, radio director of the Lutheran Hour, sent questionnaires to a small group of those who have listened to the Lutheran Hour, approximately 2 per cent of the people who have written to us. They were asked: "Have you or others in your household accepted Christ as your Savior through listening to the Lutheran Hour?" and, "Do you know of others (not of your household) who have been brought to Christ the Savior through listening to the Lutheran Hour?" Altogether about 7.5 per cent of those who received this questionnaire have answered. According to their own statements these listeners replied that they knew of 1,737 conversions in their own family, 913 outside their family, a glorious total of 2,650 reported as coming to the

Redeemer through the broadcast. Their letters, of which the following are typical, and unsolicited statements by others, give us much reason to thank God. They write:

Arizona — My husband and I have become Christians through your radio mission.

Ohio — By the grace of God, Mrs. —— of Defiance has joined a Lutheran church of the Missouri Synod through your broadcasts.

Minnesota — The Lutheran Hour has had a very effective part in leading us to Christ.

Wisconsin — Mr. and Mrs. —— and their daughter have been brought to Christ through the Lutheran Hour. They are now taking instructions at Grace Chapel.

Connecticut — The Lutheran Hour has been one of several factors in shaping my faith and bringing me to the Church of Christ.

Texas — An invalid whom our pastor has visited and instructed has come to Christ through the Lutheran Hour. Her child also attends our Sunday school.

Michigan — Several have listened to the Lutheran Hour at my home and become interested in church and religion. Two of these have joined a Lutheran church.

Wisconsin — My husband joined a Lutheran church by listening to your broadcast and by going to church with us.

Massachusetts — One of our household has accepted Christ and joined the Finnish congregation through the work of your radio mission.

Michigan — My husband came to Christ through the Lutheran Hour. He had had no religious training at home, neither as a child nor when he was older.

Wisconsin — Mrs. —— and her two daughters are now members of the Lutheran Church, thanks to the influence of your radio mission.

Ohio — Mr. and Mrs. —— and their family have joined Concordia Lutheran Church in Cincinnati through the influence of your radio mission.

Illinois — Five members of my family have joined Zion Lutheran Church through the direct influence of your radio mission.

Michigan — Mrs. ——, a former neighbor, who used to spend Sunday afternoons with us, was confirmed through the Lutheran Hour. Later her two children followed her example.

Foreword XI

South Dakota — My husband used to turn the radio off at each broadcast. He has now become a regular listener and has joined the Church.

Missouri — My daughter and her children have become members of Concordia Lutheran Church through the influence of the Lutheran Hour.

Minnesota — Our entire family has now joined the Lutheran Church, by God's grace, after hearing your radio messages.

Minnesota — A family of five has been gained here through the Lutheran Hour. Our pastor is instructing both parents, and they will join our Lutheran Church soon.

Louisiana — Your radio messages helped my husband, now in the Army overseas, to become a member of the First English Lutheran Church.

New York — My husband never went to church before. Now he comes with me to the Lutheran church every Sunday and regularly listens to the Lutheran Hour. He has not yet joined, but he has taken adult instruction since last winter. A friend was listening to false religion, when I encouraged her to tune in the Lutheran Hour. She has now joined our Lutheran Church.

Pennsylvania — Our stepson was converted this past summer through the work of your radio mission.

Michigan — Mrs. ——, a cripple, who cannot leave her home, was brought to faith by hearing your programs.

Michigan — Miss —— of State School for the Blind has now become a member of Christ Lutheran Church after hearing the Gospel proclaimed on the Lutheran Hour.

Missouri — A number of people I meet in business have told me that they have seriously turned to religion since listening to your program. While I was shopping, a salesgirl recognized my Lutheran Hour cross, stating that she had one and had joined one of our north-side churches through this broadcast.

Illinois — Three members of our family have become affiliated with the Lutheran Church through the Lutheran Hour.

Illinois — My husband, who did not belong to any church before, became blind nine years ago. Since then he has become a Christian, partly through listening to your broadcast.

Illinois — Mrs. —— and her three children have become members of Trinity Lutheran Church through the Lutheran Hour.

Kansas — Mr. ——, a member of my congregation, who is now

deceased and whom I buried, was won for the Savior through the Lutheran Hour.

Wisconsin — I know three, two young ladies and a gentleman, who have come to the faith after hearing broadcasts of the Lutheran Hour.

California — Mr. and Mrs. ——, the former of whom passed away a month ago, were first brought to Christ through your radio mission.

Illinois — Two of whom I know have become affiliated with St. John's Lutheran Church through the Lutheran Hour.

Michigan — Before his death my husband was brought to faith by the Lutheran Hour.

Kansas — My neighbor, who was unchurched, listened to the Lutheran Hour with me. Now she is a church member.

Wisconsin — I first listened to the Lutheran Hour one Sunday in 1942, in Illinois. Then I started to go to church, and I have now joined a Lutheran congregation. Whenever I have a radio near, I always listen to the broadcasts of the Lutheran Hour.

Illinois — Mr. —— and his family have joined our Lutheran congregation as a result of your work on the radio.

Michigan — I was born a Lutheran. My husband was baptized on what we then thought was his deathbed. He lived, thanks to God, was later confirmed and became a voting member of my church, thanks to you, God's messenger.

California — My uncle was baptized and confirmed last year, through the Lutheran Hour, and joined the Lutheran Church of the Wisconsin Synod.

New York — One member of my family was converted to Christ through the Lutheran Hour.

Indiana — My husband listened to the Lutheran Hour and then joined St. Paul's Lutheran Church.

Connecticut — Four members of my household joined Emmanuel Lutheran and Salem Lutheran Churches as a result of the Lutheran Hour.

Missouri — I know of one young man who definitely and positively was brought to Christ through the Lutheran Hour. He was confirmed with my brother and joined St. Matthew's Lutheran Church.

Ohio — After hearing your sermon "The Key to the Kingdom — Rebirth in Christ," I began thinking and shortly thereafter joined First Lutheran Church.

Michigan — I have accepted Christ as my Savior through listening to the Lutheran Hour.

Wisconsin — Mr. and Mrs. —— and their son have found salvation through faith in Christ as a result of the message of the Lutheran Hour.

Minnesota — I have come to faith through your radio mission and joined Emmanuel Lutheran Church.

Minnesota — Four members of my family have found Jesus as their Redeemer and become members of Bethany Lutheran Church.

Wisconsin — There are three in our family who have joined Resurrection Evangelical Lutheran Church through the work of your radio mission.

Texas — Mr. and Mrs. —— attend our church because of the Lutheran Hour.

Wisconsin — My brother in California, formerly a Mason, died last winter, a true Lutheran through the Lutheran Hour.

Ohio — Two in our household have joined St. John's Evangelical Lutheran Church after hearing your challenging messages over the air.

Nebraska — A seventeen-year-old boy whom we had taken into our home accepted Christ through the Lutheran Hour. He is now in the Navy.

Washington — My son and his wife as well as my daughter and son-in-law have been led to faith in Christ through the work of the Lutheran Hour.

Missouri — My brother, who departed this life in Christ in 1941, was gained for life everlasting through the work of your radio mission.

Iowa — Mr. and Mrs. —— have been brought to faith in Jesus through the ministry of Bringing Christ to the Nations. They are old and cannot attend divine worship.

Minnesota — As a fruit of your radio mission Mr. —— was confirmed in the Lutheran faith at the age of sixty-five years.

Minnesota — My wife and I accepted Christ after hearing the Lutheran Hour.

Oregon — Every now and then, when I am giving out Bible tracts, I run across someone who has been led from death to life through the work of the Lutheran Hour.

Michigan — My brother-in-law found his Savior after hearing a Lutheran Hour sermon.

South Dakota — Two friends here in our community have found faith through Bringing Christ to the Nations.

Illinois — Through your ministry the six children of our family have embraced the Lutheran faith and become members of Trinity Lutheran Congregation.

Wisconsin — My son, daughter-in-law, and their two children, as a result of your broadcast, have come to faith in Christ.

Maryland — Through your program we know Christ is our Savior.

Nebraska — Through the help which the Lutheran Hour has given, our oldest boy is now in confirmation class at Trinity Lutheran Church.

Texas — A member of my congregation has been won for Christ through your ministry on the radio.

Wisconsin — Mr. —— and family have joined the Lutheran Church through the ministry of the Lutheran Hour.

Ohio — Miss ——, now deceased, a former resident at a Roman Catholic Home for the Aged, came to the knowledge of her salvation by grace through faith in Christ as a result of the Lutheran Hour.

Pennsylvania — Faith Lutheran Mission in this city was begun through the instrumentality of the Lutheran Hour.

Missouri — I know of two who have joined Zion Lutheran Church through the work of the Lutheran Hour.

Ohio — Two young people here have already joined the Lutheran Church, and four are considering it, thanks to the ministry of Bringing Christ to the Nations.

Pennsylvania — The entire —— family has joined the Lutheran Church. They were brought to this faith through the Lutheran Hour.

Ohio — It might interest you to know that a girl, a very dear friend of mine now, was sitting home alone on a Sunday afternoon about four years ago, and while you preached, the Holy Spirit convicted her; she was saved right there. She comes from an ungodly home and is the only one in her family who is Christ's. Before entering the service as a WAVE, she was our Sunday school superintendent and was very active in our church. She knows the Lord as her personal Savior.

Ohio — I thank God over and over, for it was you and your broadcasts that brought my family and me to God. We haven't missed one Communion since we went into the church. I pray that God will give us the strength and health to attend every service. I have a guilty conscience even to think of an excuse for not going to services. I regret that I didn't find the Lutheran Hour sooner. I am humbly happy that my family and I are an inspiration to our congregation. I'm giving God and you the praise for it all.

BROUGHT BACK TO CHRIST

Besides calling sinners to repentance, the broadcast was mightily used by the Holy Spirit in recalling backsliders. It often seems that the hearts of those who once knew the Savior but then rejected Him become harder than those who never confessed Him as their Lord. Yet the Holy Spirit was able to overcome all this opposition, and some who were brought back to the Lord, or others who knew them, wrote us letters like these:

Tennessee — Mrs. ——, an ardent listener, was renewed in the faith by your Gospel broadcasts. She had been confirmed in the Lutheran Church as a child but had not returned to the church until she heard you.

Ohio — I drifted away. But after listening to the Lutheran Hour, my children and I have again accepted Christ.

Pennsylvania — I had fallen away from church. I have, however, again accepted Christ through the Lutheran Hour.

South Dakota — Mr. and Mrs. ——, who were baptized years ago, but who fell away, have been converted to Christ through your ministry on the radio.

Ohio — Mother took instructions a second time last winter. This year Mother was confirmed in the Lutheran Church. Now we are one, thanks to God and the Lutheran Hour.

California — After listening to your service, I felt the urge to let you know how much that message meant to me. You see, today for the first time in my life I have come to know God as the true Friend and unfailing Companion, who is capable of lifting my soul from the depth of sin and despair. I am twenty-five years old and have been married for only three years. My early life was happy enough, because I went to church and as a child was able to place my confidence and trust in Christ. For more than several years I have lived in mortal fear that God had taken away from me the ability to know and love Him as the result of my sins.

I have never in these past several years had less to be happy about than I have at this moment, but because I have found Christ, I have everything in life that I want. I sincerely hope that I may someday help someone else to know my heavenly Father as I know Him now.

ROMAN CATHOLIC SUPPORT

Although the name of our broadcast, the Lutheran Hour, might be expected to keep Roman Catholic friends from our broadcast, the number of listeners in that Church steadily increases. Roman Catholic newspapers, while criticizing some of our utterances, have nevertheless enthusiastically endorsed the broadcast. Listeners in this group continue to write letters like these:

New York — I am a Roman Catholic, but I am so much in agreement with your sermons that I am writing you to ask you to send me *Beautiful Savior.*

Minnesota — My husband is a Catholic, and he certainly enjoys your sermons. He has learned to love and know Jesus since he listens to your sermons every Sunday. I say, "Thank you, Jesus."

Michigan — I listen to you every Sunday and wonder why more people don't go back to God. Being a Catholic doesn't stop me from hearing you, and I would not miss your God-fearing voice.

New York — If souls can't be saved by your fine way of preaching the Gospel, then there is no hope for them. We are Catholic, but we are for every good worker out to save souls with the great message. May you continue in God's great service!

Indiana — I enjoy your broadcasts very much. I listen to them every Sunday and sometimes twice. I am a Catholic, but I get as much good out of your sermons as I do from those in my own church. I want to thank you for the work you are doing for Jesus, our wonderful Savior. I will keep on helping and praying for you for Jesus' sake.

Pennsylvania — Enclosed is a gift to help a little in Bringing Christ to the Nations. Would you be kind enough to send me some copies of your last Sunday's address? I think, if these were distributed, it would be a great help in awakening the people to the dangers which are confronting our nation and our people today. I am a Catholic, and my only son has died in this war.

New Jersey — I heard your broadcast on Sunday, and I enjoyed it very much. My aunt and uncle, with whom I live, are

Foreword XVII

Roman Catholics also. I wish to become a minister. Will you please send me the address of a Lutheran boarding school which isn't so far from where I live? Perhaps one in Delaware or Philadelphia? I will appreciate this very much.

California — You will be interested to know that recently a Roman Catholic told me (I am a chaplain) that his mother was a regular listener to your program, and that he tunes in frequently also.

Wisconsin — Enclosed is a thankoffering for the best radio program on the air. We work for the highway department and must work on some Sundays. Last Sunday we had to work, but we called all the boys into the office and listened to you. You could hear a pin drop. One of them was a Catholic, and he said, "He surely tells the truth." Thanks be to God for your most wonderful broadcasts! God's richest blessing to you!

CHRISTIANS
OF PROTESTANT DENOMINATION WRITE

During the Twelfth Lutheran Hour thousands of letters were received from friends who were not members of our Church. Although they realize that the Lutheran Church proclaims principles which contradict their creeds, they wrote their endorsement of our program in glowing terms like these:

Nebraska — Will you please send me as many of your Sunday morning radio sermons as possible, as I would like to use some of them in the men's class of the Baptist Church in this city?

Kentucky — I want to thank you from the bottom of my heart for the way you have made me think since listening to your service. I am a member of the Free Will Baptist Church. In my opinion you have the greatest ability of ministering the Gospel of any man or woman that I have ever heard speak.

Ohio — Last week I was talking to a lady of the United Brethren Church. Her son is a consecrated boy. Word was recently received that he is missing in action. She feels very bad about it. Every Sunday you give her courage and hope in your messages, to which she is a regular listener.

New Jersey — Enclosed find our gift as a help for your radio expenses. We can hardly express our thanks for being able to listen to your most inspiring sermons. We know and pray that God will bless every word you preach, that many souls will be brought to the decision to accept Christ as their Redeemer. I am a Presbyterian pastor.

Ohio — I enjoy your programs so very much, when I cannot get to Sunday school and church. I am a member of the Brethren Church, live alone on a farm, and it is not possible for me to get out every Sunday. So your sermons, hymns, and prayers mean much food for my soul. My prayers are with you.

Rhode Island — For some time I have been inspired by the wonderful sermons delivered by your speaker. Although I am a Baptist, I feel that Dr. Maier is doing much to spread the Gospel of Christ. May God prosper him in his good work!

Indiana — We enjoy your messages over the radio so much. My husband is superintendent of one of the United Presbyterian churches here in Gary. But quite often we listen to your sermons. They are so inspiring. My mother is eighty years old and in fairly good health. She always tunes you in. We are quite sure you are doing a wonderful work in bringing souls to Christ.

Michigan — I am a member of the Christian Reformed Church, and I must say that I never miss one of your broadcasts. Many are the words of comfort and peace that you have spoken, and I sincerely hope your broadcasting helps many, as it does me.

Minnesota — I have listened to your Sunday radio hour many times after coming home from church and have always been greatly helped. It is the kind of preaching I long for, which we do not get at our —— church here.

Maine — Praise the Lord for your good message today on "Christ, the Light"! I, a member of the Apostolic Mission House, would like to have five copies for my unsaved relatives. Would you please send a copy to my friend in service? May God richly bless you in your fearless preaching of the Word! We advertise your program far and near.

SICK AND SHUT-IN LISTENERS

More than 17,000,000 Americans went to our hospitals last year. No one knows exactly how many cripples and shut-ins are confined to their homes, unable to attend church services. The radio has been a signally blessed instrument for bringing the Gospel directly to the invalids, the incurables. Few letters we receive are more grateful than those, like the following, from our shut-in audience:

Foreword

New York — I agree with you wholeheartedly, but then I would, because I love the Lord and everything He stands for. I am handicapped; I have never walked and cannot use my hands very well, but God has shown me how to help myself in many different ways, like typing. I type with a stick tied to my right hand and have to do almost everything with that hand, but I am thankful that I can do as much as I can. Jesus called my dear mother home seven years ago, leaving Dad and me alone. It was hard to lose her, but I know that someday we all shall be together forever.

Connecticut — Some time ago I called at a home in which was an aged man, an invalid. He lived with his daughter and family. As I came to his bedside and told him I was a Lutheran pastor, he asked if I knew about the Lutheran Hour. You know my answer. Then he told me that the Lutheran Hour messages were the only food he was receiving for his soul. He was a firm believer in Christ and was a Lutheran. I was able to minister to him but for a few weeks, as he was then called to heaven.

Pennsylvania — I have just listened to your sermon. May the Lord bless mightily the message today! Our family here at our Old People's Home are eager to listen in, week after week.

Arizona — We are sending an offering to help, for we enjoy the broadcasts, as we are shut-ins and don't get to attend our church here. We are victims of T. B., have been confined to bed for many months. Your services over the air are inspiring to us. We enjoy the singing, too.

Pennsylvania — Your sermons mean a great deal to me. My illness in the past years is cancer. I have had operation, radium, and deep therapy. My doctor said the only help I can have now is morphine to make me a little more comfortable. I would like to write more, but I am not strong enough right now.

Michigan — From the bottom of my heart I thank you for making the evening of my life so beautiful. I am eighty-one years old and appreciate more than ever the unfailing comfort of God's holy Word that you bring to us in your messages. With a prayer in my heart, I'm enclosing a gift. May God bless and keep you and your ministry!

Colorado — I am a wheel-chair invalid in a convalescent home, where there are six other patients besides myself. Your program is certainly a blessing to all of us.

Washington — I heard your sermon tonight, and I should like to have it in print. I am an old man living in the Masonic Home here, where there are about 165 members, all old, from seventy to ninety-seven. Many of them are members of some cult; no new birth, no blood of Christ. I wish you could send me a few tracts that might be helpful.

BROADCASTING TO OUR FIGHTING FORCES

Since the beginning of the war a little more than four years ago, the Lutheran Hour has found one of its most important fields of activity in broadcasting the message of Christ, the Prince of soul peace, to the men and women in our armed forces. For this purpose every available station near our military camps has been secured; more than 100 small Army transmitters in various places throughout this country and abroad feature the Lutheran Hour; Lutheran Hour music has also been beamed abroad in special broadcasts entitled Hymns from Home; and military hospitals feature the Lutheran Hour over their amplification systems. Battleships have likewise used transcriptions for Protestant services. An important supplement to our radio work was the distribution of literally hundreds of thousands of Lutheran Hour sermons, prayer books, pamphlets, and New Testaments. From various parts of the world come appreciative acknowledgments like these:

"U. S. S. Gunston Hall," c/o Fleet Post Office, San Francisco — Thank you for your encouragement of my attempts to be of aid physically and spiritually to our people aboard ship! Your sermons have arrived regularly throughout this last year and have been a very important help to the success of our church services. Although help has come to me from many sources, most of the material for sermons was taken from your sermons. Because of their excellence and universal appeal they frequently filled the bill perfectly also for our needs. The enclosed orders of service are examples in which the sermons were drawn chiefly from the messages previously broadcast by you. It was gratifying to hear and see (in letters censored) several of our "regulars" contrast our services with those of other ships, enthusiastically favoring ours. Although this may have been done just "to please the doctor," I like to believe that such comments are sincere manifestations of a genuine appreciation of a truly Christian sermon and church service; all credit, of course, to God, to our Church at large, and

you! After my experience with hundreds of people from all walks of life who have attended our services aboard ship, no one can ever tell me again that "you've got to be modern," religiously speaking, to have a successful church service. These men *want* the "pure milk of the Word" and come away hungry if they don't get it. An enthusiastic "Amen!" to your "the American people want, not fancy, goody-goody talk, but Scriptural messages," and again to your answer to the pastor who wrote you, "Why do you always preach the same thing?" . . . May God continue to give you life and vigor and opportunity to preach "the same thing," the unchanging message of the Holy Spirit, to preach Christ, and Him crucified! Recently my orders came aboard, and I am now waiting for my relief. After twenty months and nine invasions I look forward, with God's help, to that for which everyone out here dreams and hopes and prays — home, loved ones, security, and also an opportunity to worship in a real church again, and, Dr. Maier, to sit with my family and listen to one of your broadcasts. — Surgeon in the U. S. Navy.

Illinois — Our son is overseas in the armed forces of our country. He is in the 7th Army in southern France. He informed us in one of his letters that he was quartered with a German family — a Lutheran family of the *Freikirche*. They were very happy to learn that our son and one of his "buddies" were also Lutherans, especially of the Missouri Synod. They knew all about the Lutheran Hour and Dr. Maier, praising and thanking God, hoping and praying that this war would soon be over so that they too could enjoy and join us all in worshiping Christ and in listening to your wonderful sermons over the Lutheran Hour.

Hollandia — I should like to be placed on your mailing list for copies of your Sunday sermons, also any literature which you may be able to spare for our men over here in Hollandia will be greatly appreciated.

Nancy, France — Being so far from home and unable to hear your broadcasts, I very much appreciate your sending me your sermons. After thoughtfully reading them, I pass them on to others, and likewise the tracts you enclosed. I would appreciate your continuing in sending them to me. — Army nurse.

Texas — This is a request from a sailor who fought at Guadalcanal and Tarawa. There were a lot of men in our outfit who were Lutherans, and they were certainly a wonderful group of men. I wonder whether you would send me your picture of Christ that you mentioned over the radio? It would be most deeply appreciated.

XXII   *Rebuilding with Christ*

c/o Fleet Post Office, New York — I have just received your very nice letter of May 25, and I appreciate your taking the time out of a very busy life to write a personal letter. I have also gratefully received the literature which you have sent me. My mother listens attentively to all your programs and has written me about the great work which you are doing. — Commander, U. S. N. R.

Luzon — Yesterday I received two of your messages. Thank you very much! I surely do appreciate them a lot. I get a lot of good from them, especially when it isn't possible to attend services on Sunday. We are working seven days a week around here, but whenever we are close enough to where there are church services on Sunday morning, I always quit work and attend services. I am very thankful they can't keep a fellow from attending services. There are places on this island of Luzon where the temperature gets up to 130 degrees and over, and the way it feels to me this is one of them.

Aboard a Pacific Troop Transport — I featured the Lutheran Hour transcriptions which you sent me on our ship, bound for the Pacific battle zones. The program was carried over the ship's loudspeaker system, and everyone on the boat was able to hear. I had given the Lutheran Hour appropriate advance publicity, and I feel sure that there was much interest in this undertaking. Afterward, I received some fine comment. I shall continue to use the Lutheran Hour recordings in other places as opportunity will allow.

Georgia — I tuned in on the Lutheran Hour today. During the time Dr. Maier was speaking, I looked behind me, and there was a corporal. He immediately stated that he would like to hear the sermon. I asked him if he was Lutheran. He said he wasn't, but he wanted to hear the sermon, anyway. He stayed until it was over. I personally cannot praise it highly enough.

c/o Fleet Post Office, San Francisco — It is a comfort to hear and read the promises from our only Savior Jesus Christ, and of the riches of His blessing through Bringing Christ to the Nations. Oh, what comfort and joy in these days of war! I am stationed at an air base sixteen miles from Eureka, California. Enclosed is a portion of our good Lord's blessing. All praise, honor, and glory to His holy name! God bless you!

Central Pacific — I received copies of the Lutheran Hour addresses and enjoyed them immensely. We are stationed in the Central Pacific, and radio broadcasts are very limited out here. Would it be possible to send recordings of the broadcasts, since

Foreword

we have access to phonograph machines on this base? Anything that your office could do in sending these weekly addresses of the coming season will be greatly appreciated.

Alaska — I am writing you these few lines to tell you that I am surely glad to hear your program when I get a chance to. I am located in Alaska.

West Indies — We now have a radio among us and enjoy a lot of programs from the States. It surely makes a fellow feel closer to home. We heard the Lutheran Hour the other Sunday. It is just as forceful as always.

Hawaii — Here it is Sunday morning, and the fellows and I who are here in the barracks just finished listening to your weekly Lutheran Hour program. I can't begin to tell you and all the members of the Lutheran Hour how much we enjoy listening to your program each and every week. No matter what we have to do Sunday morning, we always manage to tune in to your inspiring broadcast. You can't possibly imagine the pleasure we get from hearing your weekly sermons.

c/o Postmaster, New York — I am enclosing a check as a donation to the Lutheran Hour from Chaplain S—— and me. I don't know what we would do without the program, and it is so good to know that it is so far-reaching.

Saipan — Your letter a short time ago was very welcome. Thank you very much for sending me the Lutheran Hour literature! I have not read all of it yet, but what I have read, I have enjoyed very much; and when I am finished with it, I will pass it on to others so that they too can benefit from your wonderful message. I will be more than pleased to have any other literature that you wish to send, for there is no Missouri Synod chaplain here. Reading your literature is the only way I have of enjoying the many lessons of the Scripture.

China — I have just finished reading the three sermons my father had you send. I appreciated them very much as we are a small unit and don't have a chaplain. Now I am going to ask you to send some more of them, if you will. Before I came over here the Lutheran Hour was a regular Sunday program for me, and it still is for the folks back home. Do you still have the small gold crosses that you had a few years back? If so, could I get another one, as I haven't mine here? Thanks so much for the *Wartime Prayer Guide!* I am using it now.

Indiana — For the last few Sundays I have listened to your program. I think your sermons are very, very fine. More people

XXIV   *Rebuilding with Christ*

in this spoiled country should listen to these sermons. They are true facts in every respect. Recently I have returned from the Italian campaign. My division had a very high casualty rate, which can be expected in the infantry. An incident happened which I'll never forget. My sergeant and I lived in the same pup tent. One morning we had a service on the field before moving toward the front. I went and returned in time to pack up. My "sarge" was very angry with me. I told him it was his last chance for services, before facing the enemy. Well, he only let out a silly grin. He was too busy reading jokes to his squad of men. Today I am the only one of my platoon back in America. The rest of them are either buried or out of their minds. If this world was more God-conscious, I'm sure this awful war would end much sooner. My family tunes in your broadcasts.

Arizona — We are seventy miles from town. Your sermons on the radio inspire me each Lord's Day. I do need your help. Our only child was killed on Iwo Jima. He had been a Christian for years. Won't you please tell me what you think happens to Christians when they die?

Oklahoma — For a long time I've wanted to write and tell you how much your sermons mean to me. My husband is in the Navy, in the South Pacific, but, thank God, he is on one of our finest battleships, and not in a foxhole, as so many of our boys are. He writes that some time ago he was in the ship's library and discovered some of your sermons, and he was so happy. He told some of the boys about you and how much he enjoyed hearing you while he was home; so they began reading, too. It means much to them to be able to read good material. I shall try to do more to help spread God's Word. Thank you for your inspiring messages, and may God bless you!

c/o Postmaster, New York — I certainly enjoy reading the grand sermons you sent. There is nothing more comforting on the front lines than God's Word. May the dear Lord bless you in your daily work!

New York — I want to take this opportunity to acknowledge receipt of your welcome and appreciated copy of the New Testament. It came at a very convenient time, as I am now recovering from wounds received in France. It is at times like these that a man realizes what the grand old Book means to him. Let me once again express my appreciation and thanks for your thoughtful gift!

Foreword

Nebraska — In gratitude to God for returning me safely from the battle fronts of Africa, Sardinia, Corsica, and Italy, I want to help spread the Gospel of Christ.

Ohio — I was again very fortunate in hearing your broadcast today, and sincerely I can say it was simply grand, making me feel as if a "bit of heaven" was very close. You are indeed a blessing for our present time, and I pray God may give you many, many years in your work, so that others too may benefit from your truly heartfelt inspirational messages.

France — Your message by mail surely was a blessing to me, and I would like it if you would send me all your messages. If possible, I should like to receive "Christ, Set the World Aright," "The Mothers America Needs," and "Guide Us, Good Shepherd."

France — Thank you, Dr. Maier, so very much for your thoughtful personal note which just reached me, along with several copies of your sermons! It was indeed a real feast for my soul to read of the love of God and His boundless mercy as man's only recourse from the eternal penalty of sin. Last night's mail brought word from my wife that she had remembered your work regularly while I have been overseas. It was my lot to be with our boys who landed on the Normandy beaches on D Day. Its memory, as well as many scenes that have made history since, have indelibly inscribed themselves upon my mind. Some were of matchless horror, some of supreme sacrifices, some of joy unbounded on the part of those liberated, but through it all, sin. In a very real and very personal way we found our defense, our strength, and one chief joy in Christ Jesus, and in Him alone, for He never fails us. Out there in the darkness, under aerial or artillery fire, always came the still, small voice, "I will never leave thee nor forsake thee." What a wonderful Savior is Jesus, our Lord!

Dutch New Guinea — Greetings in Jesus' name from Dutch New Guinea! I was one of your regular listeners to the Lutheran Hour while in the States. The wife of one of the boys sent him three of your sermons, trying to get him saved; he passed the sermons on to me, and I enjoyed them so much. It gave me an idea how I could enjoy your preaching here in New Guinea. In this area spiritual food is as scarce as hen's teeth. It seems as if those that stand behind the sacred desk don't know my Jesus and have no concern about the souls of men. Please send me your weekly sermons!

Bermuda — I heard your inspiring sermon over the radio last Sunday, and I enjoyed it very much. Since I have been stationed down here, this is the first Lutheran service I have heard in a long, long time. I can't begin to tell you how it lifted up my spirit and filled my heart with joy. I hope I can pick up your sermon again this Sunday. It would please me very much if you could send me a Testament and some Lutheran literature. I know it will give me many hours of comfort and joy.

Texas — When I went home on furlough in February, my mother told me about the Lutheran Hour. She had written letters to me previously, but somehow I never found time to listen to the radio to hear you. When I went home, she told me so much about you that I made it a point to hear you. I heard you today, and I feel so different. I am glad that I am one of the very fortunate ones to hear you. You are all my mother said. I shall try from now on to listen to you.

Ohio — I know several young men now with the armed forces overseas who were brought to faith through the Lutheran Hour.

Wisconsin — Mr. ——, now in the armed forces, has been gained for Christ through the messages he heard in Bringing Christ to the Nations.

Colorado — Prior to the war we here at home had been for many years regular listeners to your broadcasts. But shortly after the outbreak of hostilities, I was with one of the first contingent of troops to be sent to the SWPA, and it was there, while still on the mainland of Australia, that I realized I needed Jesus Christ more than ever. And so, a few months before my hazardous assignment up in the island of New Guinea, I wrote to you asking for your prayers, at the same time purchasing a good many of your books and other reading material. I was in desperation to find complete salvation in and through Christ, my Savior. With the aid of your books and other reading material made available, plus the experience of my training (Army), I was given renewed courage and strength for the trials ahead, but it really wasn't until I had received a letter personally from you and had gone through the hell of war that I really found the reality of God in Christ, and went through these various acid tests and experiences which served to strengthen me in my convictions. And it is by His grace that I am here today. Recently I have returned to the States on furlough status, after having served more than two and one half years in the Pacific.

Foreword XXVII

THE RADIO'S PENETRATING POWER

The radio is a God-given means for spreading the Gospel, particularly because it can bring the promises of Christ when distance, isolation, inclement weather conditions, make it impossible for worshipers to reach their churches. We thank God for being able to render the service acknowledged by the following letters.

Twillingate, Newfoundland — We do enjoy your broadcast, especially your plain speaking of the Word. I thank God for such men as you who are not afraid to attack evil as we see it today among our nations. As you say, we cannot leave God out and expect a better world. I'm living on an island far out at sea. We are now cut off from all navigation for five months. It is so nice to have you come into our homes through the radio. God bless you!

Vermont — How comforting it is to have our God come to us in His blessed Word through the Lutheran Hour, to assure us that day by day He will give us strength to meet our responsibilities! Since we have no Lutheran church near us in Vermont, we look forward with eager hearts to the Lutheran Hour every Sunday. We pray that God in His mercy will help us to remain true members of the Church by sincere faith in our Lord Jesus.

South Dakota — I am a sheepman, and I listen to your sermons out on the prairie. We cannot get help to take care of our sheep; so I herd them myself with the pickup. I have a radio in the car. This gives you an idea just how far out your sermon reaches. We are a long way from a town and have a large herd of sheep. I am thankful to God and thankful to you. Keep up the good work!

Texas — The Lutheran Hour is helping our family very much. We are about seventeen miles from our nearest church, but because of gas rationing it is impossible to go to church. We listen to the broadcast over KTRH and KTHT, Houston, on Sunday mornings. In the evenings we listen to KWBU, Corpus Christi.

South Dakota — I am writing to let you know how much the Lutheran Hour means to us as we live so far from church and have poor roads, especially in winter. We get much comfort from your sermons. We wish you success and pray daily that you may continue to stay on the air. May God bless your good work always!

New Zealand — I should have written long ago to tell you how much I appreciate your broadcasts through HCJB. I would gladly send a small donation toward the cost of your work, but our government does not approve of money leaving the country. I live with my parents (aged 91 and 83) in a little country village in far-away New Zealand. The attendance at church is often very poor; fourteen is looked upon as a good congregation. Ormond is a Presbyterian Home Mission Station, with eight other small preaching stations around it. At the service on the first Sunday of last month the organist did not come, and when I went to the organ, it left only three people in the seats besides the minister's family. I felt sorry for him. I have a little undenominational Sunday school in the public school. My address has to be very simple for the sake of the children. It gives me a great thrill to see how the dear Lord provides me with material for my address, often through the radio. I would be glad to accept your offer of a copy of "Lord, Teach Us to Pray" if you have a copy to spare, please.

California — I finally had my radio fixed and heard your program last Sunday. I am glad I did, for it is very lonesome here. I am getting old, and I live away off up here in a little mountain village. I am not able to get out very much; so I am glad that I can now have my radio once more to hear the blessed Word of God; praise His dear name! God bless you in your wonderful work!

New Mexico — Perhaps your name is not spelled correctly; but if so, you will forgive me. I have only heard it today. I listened to your broadcast on our little local station in preference to Toscanini's interpretation of Debussy, and I am glad I did. Your message was heart-warming and soul-healing. Just to hear you speak of our precious Savior was enough. He is so precious, and it warms the heart to hear Him so designated — going out over the air. . . . It was easy to see that you too have that blessed hope in Christ — of His coming again. What would we do without it nowadays? I have not seen my husband for twenty-six months. He, a Scotsman and civilian, was five years away in the last war — Gallipoli, etc., on Lord Allenby's staff, later the Palestine campaign. This war, in the American Army, he has been in two invasions and commanded successively the great parts of Casablanca, Naples, and now Marseilles. He has been six times decorated by four different countries! God has kept him so far. I send a small contribution ($25) toward your work. God bless you, and may His Spirit fill both you and your message!

Colorado — Please send me a copy of your sermon of May 6. It was comforting to hear such a good message. As we live high up in the mountains, near Longs Peak, many of our church mes-

Foreword XXIX

sages come over the radio. Yours came at a time of day when we had opportunity to listen to the good Gospel.

Pennsylvania — We in western Pennsylvania are badly snowed in, and this fact gave us an opportunity to listen to your broadcast last Sunday afternoon, which we very greatly enjoyed. I am enclosing a small offering to help in continuing your valuable radio ministry.

Indiana — Since we have been completely snowbound since Christmas and therefore unable to go to church, I have had the opportunity to hear your Sunday morning sermons and want you to know how very much they have been appreciated.

California — Your voice has finished the Spirit-filled message. Today, away up in the mountains, I have the joy of joining you in worship by hearing your broadcast. God bless you and yours in every plan for His glory, especially reaching the lost in their native tongue. Here is my tithe.

OTHER RACES AND COLORS

In emphasizing universal grace, our broadcast exerted a special appeal to black, yellow, red listeners. In this connection we receive letters like these:

Michigan — A colored friend accepted Jesus as his Savior after tuning in your broadcast.

Missouri — I am a soldier here in Camp Crowder and live off the post with my wife and baby. I wish I could tell you in words how much I am blessed when I hear you over the radio, preaching Christ. It is truly nourishment for our souls. My wife and I are both Korean and hope that someday the doors will open for the Gospel in Korea. Enclosed is a small gift from our hearts. God bless you in your service for Jesus, our Lord!

Georgia — I am a colored man, a weak Christian, a veteran of World War I. I listen to your sermons every Sunday, and they have helped me so much. Would to God that we had the Gospel preached in our churches as you preach it! You are a man of God; I can feel your sermons as I never did any other ones. They strengthen me so much. May God keep you healthy and strong until the Gospel that you are preaching will reach every heart, as it has mine!

Missouri — I, State supervisor of Negro schools, enjoyed your religious broadcast on faith. I should like to receive a copy of this address.

Kansas — I am a shut-in. I was badly burned a year ago and am unable to attend church services. I never realized how much one needs God until the accident happened to me. But it is certainly a joy to be able to hear God's Word delivered by you. I have a problem, and I am sure you can help me. I am a Negro woman, but know this will make no difference to you since God created us all.

Missouri — I, an assistant State supervisor of Negro schools, have listened to your program over the air for two years, and I shall never be able to express how much it has helped me.

California — I am writing to let you know that we, a colored family, listen to your program every Sunday and that we really enjoy it to the utmost. We never miss a Sunday in hearing you, and you don't know how it fills our souls with joy to receive the Lord's holy Word. We are all Christians from my husband down to my smallest son.

Illinois — I am a veteran of two wars, the son of refined German Jewish parents. I became a member of a Christian church many years ago. Since Hitler came into power, Jews have been singled out more than ever. Many times my friends discuss Jews in my presence in an unfavorable light. I stayed home Easter morning for this reason and accidentally tuned in your broadcast from 11:30 to 12:00 and received consolation from your broadcast of the Master Christian, Jesus Christ.

Ohio — I have listened to your radio program for some time and have been very much encouraged by your sermons. I have been here in the hospital and in bed for a year. Since I have been through trials and tribulations, with death all around me, I will say that it all has brought me closer and closer to God. I am a colored girl, twenty-two. I have faith and trust in God and know that someday soon He will ease burdens, heal me, and send me home. All I ask for is that God will give me one more chance and try me one more time. I want to be a Sunday school teacher when I leave here. Do you think God will answer my prayers?

Michigan — I mentioned the Lutheran Hour to the colored cleaning help of the office, and they have been listening in and like the program. I have referred one to our colored mission in Detroit.

Ohio — Many of our colored help listen to the Lutheran Hour regularly. While they still attend their own services, they also come to the Lutheran church.

Pennsylvania — Many colored people in our city have been won for the Savior through the Lutheran Hour.

Pennsylvania — One of the men in my Bible class made the following statement, which I know is true. He said that a week ago yesterday he had occasion to need two helpers on a large poultry farm with which he is connected, but could not get the help in the neighborhood; so sent to a Japanese relocation camp, and in a short time two Japanese men (prisoners of war) came over to the farm. My friend explained what was necessary to be done — it was about 12:30 P. M., and these men said, "All right, we will do the work for you, but we must stop to hear a sermon." With that my friend remonstrated and said, if he was paying them, he did not want them to stop until they finished the job. The two men looked at each other, and one finally said, "Well, we'll start, but will stop for the sermon just the same, even if you deduct it from our time." My friend inquired why they were so determined to hear this sermon over the radio, and their reply was that they had been prisoners of war in this country for eighteen months and that they had never failed to hear the Lutheran Hour on Sundays. When your Lutheran Hour came on the radio, they stopped their work to listen, and my friend said he listened with them. My congratulations are to you when I think of two Japanese prisoners of war being so determined to hear your message.

SPANISH AND PORTUGUESE BROADCASTS

Convincing evidence of the Holy Spirit's power to overcome spiritual ignorance may be found in the blessings that follow our Gospel messages, especially in our Spanish and Portuguese programs. While we are still barred from broadcasting in Mexico, and while we are prevented from using our outlets in Argentina, we have, thank God, been able to maintain our Gospel front in Latin America. Despite the thousands of miles which separate us from our listeners, we have enjoyed an encouraging correspondence with many newly found friends of the Savior. This Spanish and Portuguese work, under the direction of Pastor A. Melendez, must be increased. We need radio offices in Rio de Janeiro and Buenos Aires to avoid the months of time consumed in answering correspondence. From the mass of letters sent by our neighbors to the south we present a few to impress our readers with the warm welcome the Gospel has received in these distant areas.

Montevideo, Uruguay — I am a fervent Catholic. But I listen continually to the Lutheran Hour with my family. I also invite my neighbors to listen in. I shall appreciate your writing to me.

Santiago, Cuba — The more I listen to the Lutheran Hour, the more I wish and pray that the Lutheran Church be established in our country. If I can be of any help in this respect, please let me know! I shall be very glad to serve wherever and with whatever I can.

Montevideo, Uruguay — In my name and that of my family I thank you for the wonderful messages of the Lutheran Hour. It brings us spiritual blessings because the messages are based on the Bible only and you preach nothing but Christ crucified. May they always remain that way!

Alameda, Chile — It was a blessing to me to have become acquainted with the Lutheran Hour. The Spanish literature you sent me has been a source of spiritual edification. Although I have been educated in another religion, I feel that I am now part of yours. How I wish I could go to your country to study what you teach in your sermons! If you can in any way help me in this respect, I shall be eternally grateful. Again I thank you for the privilege of having heard about Christ's teachings through the Lutheran Hour.

Manati, Puerto Rico — I have a vivid interest in the radio work which you are carrying on. I have listened to other radio preachers, but they are dry and hollow compared with the messages you deliver. Please inform me about the stations which carry the Lutheran Hour in this country! I should also like to get better acquainted with your Lutheran literature. I would like to get your theological monthly. Although I am a graduate of a Reformed seminary, I should like to widen my knowledge of the Scriptures. Please help me!

Valparaiso, Chile — I am very grateful to you for your messages of the Spanish Lutheran Hour. I am only fifteen years old, but I come in contact with so many who do not teach what the Bible teaches that I should like to be better informed concerning the true Bible teachings. Please send me all the information you can concerning the right doctrines!

Las Vinas, Cuba — I am thankful for the fact of having heard your message through the Spanish Lutheran Hour. I shall be very glad to receive your literature. My greatest ambition is to win souls for Christ, and I am sure your literature is going to help me.

Placetas, Cuba — I praise God for the work you are doing. I have studied here in a Bible school, but I should like to go to your seminary and study your theology. There is another young man here who would also like to study with you. I shall appreciate your guidance in this matter.

Huancayo, Peru — I had the pleasure yesterday of listening to your sermon. The singing was also beautiful. The whole family listened to the program, and all were very much pleased. I shall continue listening to your program.

Montevideo, Uruguay — I have been bedridden for a number of years. I am unable to move and therefore cannot attend church. My only spiritual food is the reading of my Bible and your Bible-based sermons. Your messages are uplifting, and the good Lord has led me to hear them. They are my comfort every time I listen to them.

Atahona, Uruguay — My sincere congratulations on your wonderful messages! May the seed of God's Word find fertile soil in this country! I do not only listen to your programs but I also invite my relatives and friends to listen to them.

Montevideo, Uruguay — I take this opportunity to express in my humble way the immense happiness which is mine through listening to the Lutheran Hour, in which the love of God in sending His only Son to die for us sinners is stressed. Now I also know that He died to save my soul.

Havana, Cuba — May God bless and keep you in His love so that you may continue preaching the wonderful Gospel of salvation through Christ alone! I am a young man eager to bring the Gospel to those in my country who are ignorant of it. My great desire is to study for the ministry in the Lutheran Church. Please pray for me so that I may accomplish my wish with God's help!

BRINGING CHRIST TO AFRICA

Our work in Africa proceeds encouragingly. Besides the powerful station in Lourenzo Marques, Portuguese East Africa, we also use the facilities of smaller stations on the Gold Coast and in Eritrea, chiefly in connection with our own military forces. Missionary groups in Africa are showing keen interest in using the transcriptions locally over public address systems. Letters like these reflect the welcome with which our messages are received in Africa:

Kano, Nigeria, West Africa — How I wish you could have been here last evening to sit in a circle of some forty white people out in front of our main mission house here at Kano! About half of them were servicemen from various countries, the rest of them being missionaries. It was the first try-out of the Lutheran Hour radio transcription records which you sent me last year. Dr. Helser tells me that they were getting the Lutheran Hour on their radio direct from America by short wave Sunday afternoon; the broadcast reaches here at five o'clock, Kano time. This was direct transmission from the Mutual Network's short wave. We thank God for the world-wide testimony you are now bearing for the Gospel of our Lord and Savior Jesus Christ. We pray for you in the great work and trust that you will see increasing fruitfulness from it.

Karino, East Transvaal, South Africa — Tonight I have decided to write to you. I have been tuning in and listening to your services quite often, and always there was something new for me. I am no good in expressing myself, but I can assure you I am looking forward to them. There are a lot of shortcomings in my life, and hard as I struggle, lately I seem to be slipping away from the Cross. What is wrong in me? We need your prayers, my husband and I. I pray God that my hubby might repent, too. He does not know anything about repentance and does not understand it. Oh, help me! I am looking forward to your next broadcast.

Pennsylvania — Some time ago you sent us some transcriptions of the Lutheran Hour messages, which our missionary took with him to Eritrea. Word has been received that these have been widely used in Army camps in Eritrea and have been deeply appreciated. We have other missionaries sailing for Eritrea within the next three weeks. If you have other transcriptions for which you have no further use, our missionaries will be glad to take them along. You can be assured that they will be as widely used as our missionaries find it possible.

Kranskop, Natal, South Africa — This evening I switched on my brother's wireless set and found myself listening to a Gospel message (the service had already started), "Why Does God Permit Suffering?" I thoroughly enjoyed the service. I gratefully accept your offer of a picture of Christ Jesus and a copy of the message. Our next-door neighbor is the Reverend Doctor Astrich of the

Foreword   XXXV

American Lutheran Church. Both Dr. Astrich and his wife are great friends of ours. Mrs. Astrich and my mother used to spend many happy afternoons together. Mother went "home" in July, 1934, and I have stayed with my brother and his wife since then. I know from personal experience what the love of God means day by day. I enclose an account of what God did for me the day I went blind on a train. God moves in a mysterious way. May God's blessings be with your work at all times!

Durban, Natal, South Africa — I have just finished listening to one of your broadcasts and have enjoyed it immensely. You mention in your sermon that you will send free of charge a picture of Christ. I shall be very glad to have one. I wish you all the good you deserve.

Krugersdorp, Transvaal, South Africa — We listened to your broadcast service tonight, relayed through Lourenzo Marques station. Please send us some of your literature, which was advertised at the end of your service. We enjoyed your sermon very much indeed and are praying for you and your wonderful work.

Maritzburg, Natal, South Africa — I have been listening to your broadcast from Lourenzo Marques every Sunday evening, and I am very glad to say we get a good reception and look forward to it. Will you please send me one of your pictures? I shall be so pleased to have one. I don't know what amount to send you, but if you will please let me know, I shall send it with great pleasure. I have three brothers and three sons in the forces, and I hope your prayers will also reach them. God bless you!

Berea, East London, South Africa — I am eleven years of age and longing for a luminous cross you offered; so if you would send me one, my mother and I would be pleased. Will you please pray for us, as my father is not a Christian and has left us. God bless you! We so enjoyed your sermon.

Gold Coast, Africa — How strange and surprising it should be to receive these few lines of appreciation from an unknown boy who is enjoying his life under the tropical sun, somewhere on the Gold Coast! I am working as assistant librarian. On Sunday afternoons, when the library is in its utmost state of tranquillity, our staff sergeant turns on the radio to Station WAGI. The radio furnishes a beautiful program, attractive and charming songs, which might quench the sorrows of a tortured soul. The cool African wind, which freshens both whites and blacks, blows from the ocean through the south end of the library. It projects the sweet song from the office throughout the hall. The whole hall is filled with a spiritual mildness and happy prosperity. You can perceive some of the soldiers humming, their faces illuminated with looks of delight as if they were assembled in front of an altar. With eagerness and keen ears, I too have had opportunities to dedicate my leisure minutes to listen to this program. One day, in my curiosity, I asked the sergeant from where this program was broadcast. He made me understand that it was the Lutheran Hour, broadcast by the Church of which he is a member. Without any hesitation I can say that when what we are praying for has come to pass — and I have saved enough to provide me a building on the Gold Coast — I shall not forget to tune my radio to the Lutheran Hour, enjoy its precious words and beautiful hymns, and accompany the choristers in singing "Beautiful Savior."

Kano, Nigeria, Africa — We have been playing your records to British soldiers and airmen, to some American boys, and to many Africans. We are sending you two pictures taken while your broadcasts were being heard in a section of Kano, Nigeria. The man to the left of Dr. Ter Meer is the president of this section of Kano and has some 10,000 people in his section of the town. He speaks English well and thoroughly enjoyed the broadcast. We have a big conference out here, where more than 100 missionaries gather. We also have churches where you could speak to 1,000 to 1,500 at a time. Would you consider coming out for a month or six weeks of lectures? The air service is getting better all the time.

Darnall, Natal, South Africa — I have had the privilege of listening to a few of your messages and was led to pray for you in the work you are doing. May God bless you in His precious service and may you be a blessing to many who hear you!

Venterspost, Transvaal, South Africa — I cannot put into words how much I enjoy your sermons every Sunday and always look forward to the next.

Durban, Natal, South Africa — Early in December my niece, a young sailor, and I managed to get through by radio to your station which broadcasts a religious program called the Lutheran Hour, and I am writing to tell you how impressed we were by the minister who preached that night. It was a message given with sincerity and power, and his prayers also came right from his heart. His text was "What Have They Seen in Thine House?" I was overjoyed to see the two young people so interested. I am quoting a portion of the sailor's letter to me. He feels that he has strayed from the path in a way, but really only needs the help of a true disciple of Christ. His letter reads in part: "Maybe the fault now lies entirely with me, but all the padres I have come across in the Navy are of little help. Their prayers are read and automatic, and spoken with no apparent meaning attached to them; the same applies to their sermons. If only they were like that American we heard over the radio on the last Sunday I spent with you, I would be interested again."

Matopo Mission, Bulawayo, Southern Rhodesia — We have just listened to your broadcast, relayed through Portuguese East Africa. We enjoy the singing and the messages every Sunday evening. We are inspired anew as we hear the Gospel of the Lord Jesus preached. The program strengthens us, cut off, as we were, from European services. God bless your services! We appreciate them. We are a group of American missionaries under the auspices of the Brethren in Christ Church, headquarters at Harrisburg, Pennsylvania.

PROBLEM MAIL

One of the least known but most effective parts of our Lutheran Hour services is found in the counseling we can give to many thousands who, without any spiritual guide of their own, urgently need help in many vital issues. We are happy to say that this part of our activity, by the Holy Spirit's blessing, has helped lead many to the Lord. The questions for which our answers are desired often touch on acute personal problems, as the following letters show:

Minnesota — Will you please advise me what to do? I'm a white American girl. Is it wrong to marry a Filipino boy? I am twenty-one, and he is thirty-five years old. We both love each other and want to get married. I have known him for eight months and never had any arguments. He can give me a nice home, and we can both go to our Lutheran Church. He has a good steady job. But is it wrong for white to marry dark?

Iowa — I am a first-year student here at the State University of Iowa, and some doubt has arisen in my mind in regard to the creation of man. This doubt is quite natural, I believe, after studying some of the textbooks, for they teach evolution. According to the social science textbook, man's existence on earth can be attributed to evolution. Man is the highest form of animal life. Quote: "Man is a social animal." One of the first forms of animal life was the amoeba; as time went on, animal life became more complex until at a late date in the world's history, man, having the highest mental powers of any animal, came into the world. Man, they say, is very closely related to the monkeys and apes. Quote: "Mammals may be classified as nonprimates, the primates including monkeys, apes, and man." I'm not saying that I believe or don't believe either theory, but as I said before, some doubt has arisen in my mind concerning the "how come" of man's existence on earth. I am a confirmed Lutheran and have no intention of becoming an atheist unless I see no other alternative. Can you help me?

Michigan — My husband had a stroke sixteen months ago that left him speechless and paralyzed on the right side, although he seemed to have his right mind. He doesn't go to church, nor does he listen to you over the radio. What would your advice be?

California — Some time ago I received a card which showed that you remember for a long time those who have called on you for help through prayer and advice. I wrote you a long time ago when I was most deeply distressed and didn't know if I could live through it all, and your letters comforted me beyond words to express. It is about a year now, and things seem more permanent. My husband has indeed changed for the better; though he has never said he was sorry, he is very different and goes to church regularly, is kinder and more thoughtful at home, and rarely flies into a rage now. I want to thank you from the bottom of my heart for your prayers, for all that you have done for us, and for the continual inspiration your broadcasts are.

Illinois — Would you please give me some advice as to whether or not it is wrong to marry a man who is divorced from his wife because she was running around with another man? He has evidence, photostatic copies of letters written to his wife by the other man, to whom we now think she is married.

Ohio — I live in a troubled home. My husband is not a Christian and will not allow me or my two children still remaining at home to go to church. My daughter is twelve and my son nine, and it's a terrible thing to me that they are not getting any religious training. My husband doesn't even like the sermons and will not listen to them. Sometimes he shuts off the radio or the current. Any advice you give will be appreciated.

Quebec, Canada — My oldest child, a boy, will be twelve years old in July. The boy has never been normal since birth, and when I say I have had twelve years of worry, it's only putting it mildly. There are times when I think I cannot keep up much longer. He does not walk very well and cannot talk plainly. He is not deformed, just isn't bright. He tears books and breaks things belonging to the other children. In summer time he runs away continually and gets hurt. . . . Would it be a sin to try to place him in an institution? I know it will almost break my heart to part with him.

Ohio — I am writing to you about a terrible tragedy to see whether you can give me a few words of comfort. Some nights I cannot sleep, and when I do sleep, I awake several times during the night with this on my mind. They are going to electrocute my brother. I will tell you a little about the case. My brother married; he was a Protestant, his wife a Catholic. They had ten children — he was a soldier of World War I. Three years ago his wife went to a defense plant to work, and she traveled to work and back in a share-a-ride group, and she had papers served on him so he couldn't come home nor see his children. . . . He is not a drunkard, but he drank some liquor and killed his wife and one son, who tried to take the gun away from him, and also shot a daughter, who did not die. He also shot himself, but did not die. He wanted to die. He is sentenced to die, and told his attorney not to get a new trial. When the judge asked him if he had anything to say, he said he was well satisfied with the sentence. Will you pray with me that the heavenly Father will save his soul? Please advise me what to do, and do you think his soul will be saved, doing what he did and dying like this?

Ohio — I ask for your prayer help at once. A dear friend was very jealous of me and got drunk in a beer place and got in a fight and cut the bartender, so that it was necessary for the doctor to use four stitches to sew the wound together. Now my friend is going to be tried and may be sentenced to the penitentiary. He has learned his lesson and asks you to pray at once that he receive probation to prove it. We want to be married and settle down; we both will love Jesus and do all in our power to serve Him. Please give us prayer help now, before it is too late! Please ask Jesus to be with all judges and those who are connected with the case, so that my friend will receive probation!

Pennsylvania — It seems as though my cross is too heavy to carry. Seven months ago I lost the dearest friend in the world, my mother, who died suddenly of a heart attack. It was a shock to the family to lose her that way. One month ago, we got a telegram from the War Department informing us that my brother, who was only twenty, the baby of the family, had been killed on the Italian front. These were two loved ones taken within seven months. Don't you think that is too much for one to face? What I want to know is, why did God take them both at one time? Why do the believers suffer?

Ohio — I have a spiritual problem that I would like to ask you about. A minister who preached at our church told me that he had read the Bible in the original Greek, and that it is much different from our Bible that we have now. I hope this is not true, for I want to believe our Bible as it is. Also, is the Hebrew Old Testament the same as we have today? I hope it is. I am partially blind.

Wisconsin — I need help and some Christians to pray for my husband. I have had heart trouble six years, and I just don't see how we can live through the next few months without somebody praying and helping us. My husband is held on a serious Federal charge. The trial comes up soon. Can you help us to pray for him to show justice and mercy? We were always faithful Christians, but have fallen away. My husband is trying to work hard and pay back $300 he took. He has repented, and I know God will have mercy. He was a faithful and an honest and true husband to me for twenty-three years. He is not the type to do such things, but time and money pressed us very hard, and on the spur of the moment this happened. Will you please send him a letter to keep faith and not lose hope that God will not let him down? He needs many, many words of comfort and condolence from the Christians who are left in this world to help those who are down. I am depending on you, as you are the only one to whom I can bring my heavy load besides God.

Wisconsin — Your letter came today, and I went right out. It's six miles from here. The man is a Dutch Reformed, and the woman Baptist. The man, temporarily employed in the post office, took $300 out of envelopes, was caught, returned the money, but is told by his lawyer that he most likely will have to serve one year. The woman, having a weak heart, cannot work. The daughter, a soldier's wife, living with her, has one child. The house is not paid for. So there is at least a financial setback to be expected. Both the man and the woman are not without Christian knowledge and are to all appearances really penitent. They received the comfort I could give them with thanks; they also invited me to come again. I shall see what I can do to help them. A woman in their neighborhood comes to my adult class.

Foreword **XLI**

WITH SINCERE THANKS

As the years of our broadcasting increase, the number of those to whom, under God, we are indebted, steadily grows. Our thanks go out, first of all, to the vast listening audience, particularly to those who have prayed and worked and given in behalf of our broadcast. We will never see most of those who worshiped with us, but how glorious the hope that we shall be united in heaven! Particularly do we acknowledge the help generously given by the many pastors who have repeatedly called the broadcast to the attention of their members and have secured many contributions for our cause. Besides, they have co-operated in visiting unchurched members of the radio mission who have written for help. Christian day school teachers have also consistently stood by us. Especially are we grateful to the Lutheran Laymen's League for its continued sponsoring of the broadcast. We know of no laymen's organization that has ever undertaken so vast a missionary program as that represented by Bringing Christ to the Nations. This year I feel especially indebted to the Lutheran Laymen's League, because at a time when my physician ordered me to rest in a warmer climate, the Board of Governors of our laymen's organization generously provided the funds for a month's stay in Florida and arranged for the broadcast to originate there. The affairs of the Lutheran Hour are conducted by the Executive Board, the Board of Governors of the Lutheran Laymen's League, and by an operating committee, a group of St. Louis men who spend long hours in solving our problems. To them (Oscar P. Brauer, chairman; John Fleischli, Alfred T. Leimbach, T. G. Eggers, Dr. Eugene R. Bertermann) I give a hearty "Thank you!" The Lutheran Hour announcers: Reinhold W. Janetzke, the Reverend Elmer J. Knoernschild, the assistant, and Louis Menking, the transcription announcer, have executed their important part of the program with great fidelity, yet without salary. We are deeply indebted to the Lutheran Hour Chorus of Concordia Seminary, Harold Buls, director; the Valparaiso University Chorus, Dr. Theodore Hoelty-Nickel, director; the Springfield Seminary Chorus, Prof. Fred L. Precht, director; the St. Louis Choral Group, Homer Gruber and E. W. Schroeter, directors; and all other choruses that have furnished the musical framework for our messages.

The thousands of radio technicians who help broadcast the Lutheran Hour deserve grateful mention, particularly Carl Meyer, chief operator of station KFUO, and his assistants.

Among those who have assisted the broadcast from a distance, we should mention W. C. Hutchings, Chicago manager of the World Broadcasting Company, where our transcriptions are made; Arthur A. Kron of the Gotham Advertising Company, New York City; Pastor C. T. Wetzstein of Waterloo, Ontario, in charge of the Eastern Canada office, and the Reverend W. A. Raedeke of Calgary, Alberta, in charge of the Western Canada office.

The clerical and technical staff of the Lutheran Hour itself now embraces eighty-five employees. Their willingness to work overtime, especially during the rush periods, has been a decisive factor in the success of our office work, an unseen and often unrecognized aspect of our work. I am deeply indebted to my own office staff, headed by Miss Harriet E. Schwenk, who again has helped in preparing these radio addresses for the printer and otherwise given valuable service; and to two volunteer workers, Mrs. Bernard Keiser, and Miss Lucille Biehl, who each week give time without any compensation.

Dr. William Arndt, of Concordia Seminary, whose office adjoins mine, has not only read each message before delivery and after printing, but has also generously served as personal adviser in many problems.

I would not be fair if I were not to signalize the outstanding services rendered by Dr. Eugene R. Bertermann, radio director of the Lutheran Hour. No task has been too great for him, no personal sacrifice of time and inconvenience too large, if only the cause of Bringing Christ to the Nations could be advanced. Without his unfailing energy, foresight, and leadership it would have been difficult to have completed this twelfth broadcasting season.

Again my wife has not only assisted me in proofreading these pages but helped me meet the many problems and responsibilities in the detailed issues of the Lutheran Hour.

Foreword

To our great and good God, however, I give all glory and honor. It has become a regular obligation for me to mention in public gatherings that the personal and human element in the Lutheran Hour must fade entirely into the background. Christ must increase as we must decrease. Instead of praise, I need prayer; and earnestly I request my readers and the radio audience to intercede before the Throne of Mercy for me, that the Father would give me strength; the Son, His love; and the Spirit, wisdom, guidance, and understanding.

Rebuilding with Christ has been selected as the title for this volume, the fourteenth in the series of our radio messages, because it is our firm and Scripture-founded conviction that unless the Gospel of the Savior slain for the sins of an evil world is widely proclaimed and accepted in the ruins of our postwar world, we cannot without Him build a new age that has the promise of His blessing. It is our prayer that through the Holy Comforter's enlightenment these pages may help to enthrone the crucified but everliving Christ in many more hearts.

WALTER ARTHUR MAIER

Concordia Theological Seminary
New Year's Day, 1946

"Brethren, pray for us, that the Word of the Lord may have free course and be glorified." — II Thessalonians 3:1.

CONTENTS

	PAGE
THE SWEET POWER OF PRAYER	1
Exodus 15:24, 25	
CHRIST IS MY LIGHT	22
Saint John 12:46	
WAKE UP, AMERICA!	39
Saint Matthew 26:43, 44	
A NEW TRIAL FOR CHRIST	59
Saint Mark 14:57-62	
HOW DO YOU BEHOLD THE MAN?	80
Saint John 19:5-7	
DON'T GAMBLE YOUR SOUL AWAY!	98
Saint Matthew 27:35, 36	
"I THIRST"	116
Saint John 19:28	
STAY WITH THE CRUCIFIED CHRIST!	135
Saint Mark 15:40, 43-45	
THE DAY DEATH DIED	153
II Corinthians 4:13, 14	
LOVE THAT WILL NOT LET YOU GO	171
Saint Mark 16:7	
JESUS CHRIST — OUR LIFE IN DEATH	192
Saint John 3:36	

XLVI *Contents*

	PAGE
THEY CAN'T TAKE CHRIST AWAY!	211
Saint John 20:13-16	
WITHOUT CHRIST WE FAIL	229
Isaiah 7:9	
THE VICTORY IS THE LORD'S	246
I Chronicles 29:11	
FAMILIES OF AMERICA, STAND BEFORE THE LORD!	260
Deuteronomy 29:9-12	
COME, HOLY SPIRIT!	277
Acts 2:1, 4, 41	
GOD BE WITH YOU!	294
II Corinthians 13:14	

THE SWEET POWER OF PRAYER

"The people murmured against Moses, saying, What shall we drink? And he cried unto the Lord; and the Lord showed him a tree, which when he had cast into the waters, the waters were made sweet." EXODUS 15:24, 25.

STRENGTHENING SPIRIT OF GOD: How true it is in this world of war and woe that men have not because they ask not! Therefore, teach us to pray, first of all, with faith-filled hearts, which look to the Lord Jesus and His cross at Calvary, for the assurance that our petitions in His name will be heard! Then guide us to plead, not selfishly, but with compassion for our sorrowing, sin-burdened neighbors; to petition Thy strength, not only in hours of deep despair, but daily seek Thee in contrite confession of our sins, yet in victorious confidence that Thou, who dost change the hearts of believers, canst also change masses of our fellow men. We pray that Thou, with whom nothing is impossible, wouldst send the country's youth back to the pathways of peace and give the world, sobered by the lessons of past struggle, an opportunity to recover, rebuild, and return to Thee. Take away our guilt for Jesus' sake, and daily draw us close to Him who is the only and last Hope for every one of us, as for our world! So fill our souls that we may live our faith and daily "show forth the praises of Him," our blessed Savior, who hath called us "out of darkness into His marvelous light"! We pray with assurance because we plead in His saving, reassuring name. Amen!

A Minnesota mother writes me: "My greatest blessing and joy was my only son. No one knows the tears I shed when the government called him and he had to leave home to kill people, just as no one knows the hours I spent on my knees, begging God to bring my boy back safely. But he was killed and lies buried in the South Pacific. What can life ever give me now? I am sure of one thing, however: the God you talk about every Sunday does not hear our prayers. I am even beginning to doubt whether there is a God." — Her words, typical of letters from many American mothers of different social levels, show that at a time when prayer should be a particularly powerful refuge and strength, increasing numbers, even within the churches, are beginning to doubt the value and the victory of personally petitioning the Almighty.

On the other hand, many American young men learned the blessing of communion with God in the heat and hardship of battle. Private Ferris of Washington, D. C., with a medical detachment in western Europe, writes: "We had to go to a section where the Germans were laying down a heavy barrage of artillery, to get some casualties. . . . I prayed that the shelling would stop long enough for us to go in and get the injured men out again. As true as I'm writing this, the shelling stopped for about twenty minutes, and we had no sooner gotten out of the area than they started throwing shells again."

Private Hollinger of York, Pennsylvania, lost in a South Pacific jungle, finally, after foodless days and nerve-racking nights, came through to safety. How? Ask him, and he replies: "Well, we just prayed and kept moving. And believe me, we did a lot of praying."

The Sweet Power of Prayer

An Edinburgh church paper told of three Scotch soldiers and their corporal, hidden in a Belgian village which the Germans were systematically destroying. As the enemy drew closer to their hiding place, the corporal suggested prayer, adding that this would probably be their last petition to God. After reading the Savior's words from the New Testament: *"Fear not them which kill the body but are not able to kill the soul. . . . Are not two sparrows sold for a farthing? And one of them shall not fall on the ground without your Father. But the very hairs of your head are all numbered. Fear ye not therefore; ye are of more value than many sparrows"* — they knelt, committing their way unto the Lord and asking strength to face their end like men. In the midst of this pleading a German officer entered, cried out exultingly as he first beheld his cornered enemies, but gasped in surprise when he realized that they were on their knees. While the Scotch corporal calmly concluded his intercession, and as the doomed soldiers repeated the Lord's Prayer, the German officer suddenly clicked his heels, stood at attention, and then closed the door softly, never to return. In the evening the four fighting men found a roundabout way back to their own lines. — You see, when soldiers are saved by the same miraculous love that rescued Daniel from the lions' den, they know the power of prayer and pay no attention to atheists who blasphemously belittle the value of personal pleading.

May the Holy Spirit give us all the same assurance! If communion with our heavenly Father is the priceless privilege of faith at all times, it is a double gift of God's grace in the harrowing, heavy-laden, heartbreaking hours of sorrow, affliction, bereavement, which may suddenly come upon any American home. More than any of us realize, our petitions to the Almighty can bring us light, comfort, guidance, strength, victory, teaching us — and this is today's message of sustaining promise —

THE SWEET POWER OF PRAYER,

its marvelous turning of sorrow to joy, life's agonies to spiritual advantages, each day's fear into new fortitude of faith. All this is shown by our text, the divinely inspired words of Exodus, chapter fifteen, verses twenty-four and twenty-five: *"The people murmured against Moses, saying, What shall we drink? And he cried unto the Lord; and the Lord showed him a tree, which when he had cast into the waters, the waters were made sweet."*

I

PRAYER CAN CHANGE LIFE'S BITTERNESS TO BLESSING

It was only three days after the Almighty had performed one of the most thrilling miracles in history, the dividing of the Red Sea, the freeing of Israel from Egyptian slavery, and the destruction of Pharaoh's hosts, when God's people were thrown into danger which almost destroyed them. In the heart of the bare, blistering desert they were without water. The day before yesterday they had praised the Lord for His marvelous deliverance; but today their water bags empty, their lips parched, their tongues heavy, the earth baked and cracked beneath their feet, they wonder whether they have been led out into the desert to perish in its trackless wilderness. — So it often is with us in the quick changes of this earthly life: one day our hearts are high in hope and rejoicing; but the next they are suddenly crushed in grief. Thirty-two parents in Augusta, Maine, began last Wednesday as any other day, but ended it with unspeakable grief, when fire burned their children to death. A hundred families and more in Mexico started last Thursday in much the same way that they began the first of the week, but before sunset they screamed in piteous anguish, because a railroad accident had killed their loved ones.

The children of Israel, marching on through the waterless waste, finally came to Marah; and it is hard to overestimate their joy when they there beheld inviting wells. Yet, can you imagine their despair and utter misery when, as they frantically drew up the water and pressed their swollen lips to the drinking bags, they could not swallow it, thirsty as they were? It was bitter beyond endurance. — People today often have similar experiences. A girl goes through many years without finding a husband, only to realize, soon after the wedding, that marriage has brought her measureless misery. Others slave and save to heap up wealth, yet discover that money has destroyed their domestic happiness, separated husband and wife and led to the divorce court.

Too often, likewise, people thus frustrated, do what Israel did — they blame some utterly innocent person. We read: *"The people murmured against Moses, saying, What shall we drink?"* Three days before he had been a national hero; seventy-two short hours later he had become a public enemy, responsible for leading his followers to their destruction in the desert. Have men not always shown this ingratitude and repeated a similar indictment? Recall the Jerusalem mob crying, *"Hosanna!"* on the first day of the week and, *"Crucify Him! Crucify Him!"* on the sixth! Remember Peter telling Christ on Thursday night, *"Though all men shall be offended be-*

cause of Thee, yet will I never be offended," then denying the Savior and cursing as he rejected Him early Friday morning! Think of the infidel Tom Paine, printing brutal attacks on George Washington during the darkest hours of the Revolution! He showed that from the very beginning of our country atheists have never been good Americans. But think of yourself and the instances in which you have passionately blamed innocent people! How often has not a faithful pastor been falsely charged with causing some of the setbacks which his members have suffered! How frequently people seek to make the Lord responsible for their sins and failures! Many a weakling has tried to excuse himself for his lustful transgressions by declaring, "If I had not been born with these desires, if God had not created these longings within me, I certainly would not have fallen into crime."

When Moses heard the sullen, resentful murmuring of the masses against him, he did not wash his hands of the whole Exodus program for liberating his people and in deep-rooted disgust resign as national leader. Neither did he give a snarling, sarcastic reply of rebuke, nor did he institute a WFA, a Water Finding Authority. He did what every national leader should do in any crisis, *"he cried unto the Lord."* First of all, he fell on his knees before the Almighty, raised his voice in earnest entreaty, laid the whole difficulty before his God, and pleaded for His guidance. If only our generation had been blessed with *Fuehrers,* kings, emperors, prime ministers, and leaders who, before they decided to call their countrymen to arms in bloody conflict, had likewise knelt in soul-deep prayer, beseeching divine guidance for peace! Do you not agree that if seven and eight years ago, before this brutal bloodshed began, the head of each of the fifty nations involved had humbly and persistently bowed before the Almighty, this struggle could have been averted? And do you not likewise see that unless those charged with shaping the policies for the postwar world contritely recognize the Lord, we must face a future filled with fear and terror? The pathway to true peace is still the pathway of true prayer. Therefore may the Holy Spirit give us prayer-minded public officials who know personally that all our blessings come from God, and who persistently appeal for Heaven's direction, men after the measure and manner of Moses, who will cry unto the Lord with all their soul!

Our heavenly Father, merciful and mighty, will not fail them, as He did not fail Moses. We read: *"The Lord showed him a tree, which when he had cast into the waters, the waters were made sweet."* Chemists have made many conjectures as to which wood might have this purifying, sweetening power, and many conflicting, contradictory suggestions have been proposed. Preachers sometimes spend much of their sermon arguing these technical points, just as one of you recently reported that you heard a pulpit debater, discussing the miraculous feeding of the five thousand, devote one-fifth of his sermon to the theory that the fish must have been herring and the loaves crackers. Personally, I do not care what species of tree God provided. I am entirely satisfied that the Lord could have used a Joshua tree, a palm tree, a cactus bush, even a stone or a dead stick, to sweeten Marah's bitter waters. As in a thousand other miracles, we do not understand how He performed this wonder, but we know that He did. Our assurance rests not on emotions, on signs, on our ability to understand, on our scientific training, but on God's unbreakable Word. The Almighty heard Moses' prayer, and the people were saved. That is fact, not fancy.

Many of you find yourselves burdened with afflictions similar to those which tortured Israel. The cup you must drink is blackest bitterness itself. The war brought you a succession of deep and deadly sorrows. You are alone; your dearest ones far overseas. You are sick, weak in body, and sad in soul. You are frustrated and fearsome. Despite greater income you have less happiness. Your heart is heavy with the weight of growing worries, your conscience crushed by a sense of guilt and unremoved sins. Your peace of mind has been destroyed by the seething unrest of war within you.

Now, where in all this besieging bitterness can you find help and hope? Certainly not in the pursuit of sin, the hell-born mistake that drives many people to drink and vice, as they try to drown their difficulties and stifle their grief! Sin at first appears attractive and alluring, but, as your letters reveal, all too soon it becomes a terrifying nightmare. Nor can you find freedom from fear and the sweetening of your bitter sorrows in yourself, by your own ability, however remarkable that may be. Health and knowledge cannot grant happiness. Only a few days ago in Kansas City a nationally known physician, who wrote and lectured to large audiences on physical culture, slashed himself to a suicide's death. Have you heard the story of the man who five years ago was called the "Wizard of Wall Street"? He made and lost four fortunes, one of more than three million dollars. Finally, alone in a saloon, he wrote a note containing the confession, "I am a failure," and then killed himself. His millions could not save him from misery; nor can you change the ugly taste of an embittered life by any of these new, sugar-coated brands of religion which boldly advertise the promise of peace, but actually lead to increasing conflict.

We must rather believe with our whole heart that, as Jehovah gave Moses a tree with which to sweeten the brackish waters of Marah, so in the wilderness of our lives He has given each of us a tree which, through faith, can sweeten every bitter moment. I mean the accursed but ever-blessed tree of Calvary. There the Son of God offered His own body, shed His own blood, sacrificed His own life, to free us from all fears and afflictions. There, enduring the indescribable burden of every human transgression, He paid with His agony and death for *"the iniquity of us all."* There He, *"who knew no sin,"* became *"sin for us."* There He, whom men hated, betrayed, blasphemed, belied, and brutally killed, was thinking of you, pleading for you, giving Himself for you, of whatever race, region, or religion you may be. On that cross He died for your life. At Golgotha He suffered the torture of the damned to grant you heaven's hallowed bliss. On the skull-shaped hill He fulfilled the demands of God's Law for you, atoned fully and finally for your transgressions.

Now when you accept Christ — but "accept" is a weak, unworthy word; when your heart, crushed and contrite, cries out, "O Jesus, You suffered, died, and rose again for me"; when you believe every word He spoke is the truth of truths; when you trust Him though He slay you; when you forget yourself and build your hope on nothing less than His blood and righteousness, then, by that faith you are restored to your heavenly Father and assured of His constant companionship. Oh, if it were not the Almighty Himself who promises this salvation, it would be too good to be true, this priceless pledge of justification by faith; too good for us who have deserved nothing but condemnation, rejection, and punishment; too good for a world that has hated Christ and hastened from Him; far too good for an age that systematically ridicules the Savior's redemption. But, thank Heaven! it is not too good for the God of love and mercy and compassion. Here is the crown and climax of our Christian conviction: *"While we were yet sinners, Christ died for us."*

Now, whenever sinners, fortified by this trust, glory in the Cross, looking only to Jesus, they can have the assurance that life, even in its bitterest moments, can be sweetened for them. They know that, because in the Crucified they have no sin, God will never punish them. His Son has fully paid their indebtedness, and the Lord does not demand payment twice. If you owe $5,000 on a mortgage, and a friend generously pays that full amount, you need not pay it again; similarly, since our Redeemer completely removed all our iniquities, *"there is therefore now no condemnation to them which are in Christ Jesus."* The believer recognizes that the heaviest sorrows are mercifully designed by our loving Father to cleanse, purify, refine us, bring us closer to Him, increase our reliance on His redemption, make us more willing to give the Holy Spirit mastery over our lives and more sympathetic with our suffering fellow men. By Calvary's tree, bitterness becomes blessing. *"Whom the Lord loveth He chasteneth.*" That is why tried and true Christians can actually thank God for adversity; why the faithful can bravely face a series of war's hardships which drive scoffers to suicide; why humble Christians who have had five sons in the armed services abroad enjoy more peace of mind than wealthy families with their only son at home; why true disciples of our Savior can suffer from amputation, cancer, consumption, and still smile, or even die with real rejoicing, while infidels often scream in unrelieved terror. The redeemed of Christ know, beyond debate or doubt, that His cross always changes the bitterness of death into the sweetness of eternal triumph. Through personal, penetrating, powerful, Spirit-blessed prayer they cry to the Lord for even stronger faith and more triumphant trust.

Many of you, however, including some of the most wealthy, influential, and intelligent members of this radio audience, continue in your resentfulness, because you do not know this sweet power of prayer. Your souls are famished when they might be fed in overabundance. Your lives are empty, fear-burdened, narrow, dismal, when they might be brimful, courageous, rich, and radiant. Talk about soldiers who die though only a few feet from safety, of sailors who drown because they do not know how to use their life belts, of airmen hurled to death because they fail to pull the rip cord of their parachute! This is tragic enough; but what can we say of the far deeper sorrow which destroys souls when men refuse to recognize "what a privilege it is to carry everything to God in prayer" and spurn true intercession, by which bitterness is banished from their lives?

II
IT MUST BE TRUE PRAYER TO PRODUCE THIS CHANGE

How important, then, that everyone of us learns not only to pray but to approach our Father in the right way, with the promise of His answer! For this too we can discover necessary lessons in our text. Thus, for example, we are not told how long Moses *"cried unto the Lord";* and the length of a prayer does not count in God's sight, although America today is in no danger of pleading too long. If General Henry Havelock, British hero, could spend the first two hours of each day in communion with his Savior, arising at four in the morning when in camp; if Martin Luther declared: "When I fail to spend two hours in prayer each morning, the devil gets the victory through the day. I have so much business I cannot get on without spending three hours daily in prayer" — then certainly we, who are not burdened with the world-moving affairs which confronted these men, should find much more time consecrated to sacred pleading with our God. Yet it is not merely the many minutes consumed that make our pleading acceptable. The hastily spoken "Lord, help me, for Jesus' sake!" requiring only two seconds, has been answered by Heaven's omnipotence, while the mouthings of empty, wordy phrases in pagan temples for two days or two weeks or two years have ended unfulfilled, in failure.

Again, the important thing in your intercession with God is not the language you employ. The Lord paid little attention to the rhetoric and oratory Moses may have used. Even if you cannot speak English correctly; even if you do not know the meaning of long, hard words which some men like to use, the all-knowing, and all-loving Father understands every language, overlooks errors in grammar and pronunciation.

Don't think for a moment that God has reserved special, exclusive places where you must meet Him if you hope to be answered! Many of you connect your prayers with your church; and where, indeed, can we more appropriately come before our Lord than in the temple of His truth, which, according to His own Word, is to be *"a house of prayer"* for all people! Yet too many churchgoers restrict their communion with God to Sunday and the sanctuary; too many churches are open only two or three hours on the Lord's day and closed for the remaining 165 hours each week. Have you ever stopped to realize that few buildings in our country are used less than our churches? The courtrooms, the pool halls, the night clubs, the taverns, the theaters, are open practically every day; but many churches are bolted. Protestant America must learn to keep its churches open, before atheist Communists try to tear them down as economic losses. Believe, however, that God can hear your prayers at any place! His direct and pointed instruction reads, *"I will, therefore, that men pray* EVERYWHERE." You need no special shrine or sanctuary, no goal of pilgrimage, to gain the assurance of Heaven's reply. On your way to work, in the factory, the office, the shop, the schoolroom, in the midst of an overbusy, whirling world, wherever you may be, you can find your way to the Throne of Mercy. Moses came before God in the dry, crackling wilderness; Saint Paul knelt before Him in the Roman prison; Washington sought His counsel in the blood-stained snow of Valley Forge; and if today all over comfortable, richly blessed America men would penitently seek His face, the nation would be covered with blessings never before experienced.

God's Word sets no specific time for prayer, and Moses recognized none; yet men who think themselves wiser than the All-knowing have claimed that special hours have special blessings. The Bible recognizes nothing like that. Instead, it offers this schedule for our supplications: *"praying* ALWAYS *with all prayer."* The war showed us that many people reserve their petitions as a last, desperate resort; but what an insult to the Almighty this eleventh-hour petition may be! How often, too, have men in the armed forces, miraculously rescued from ruin, confessed that they soon forgot God! Israel cried unto the Lord when they had no water; but read on in Hebrew history, and you will see that in periods of prosperity this same people forsook Him, forgot His grace and guidance. Our country has been guilty of the same ingratitude. World War II did not bring all our people penitently before God; instead, its quick and easy money, its luxury and lust, pleasure-madness and drunkenness, shocking immorality and undisguised blasphemy, featured on the stage, glorified in best sellers, and practiced in the private lives of multitudes, make them scoff at prayer and ridicule reliance on Jesus. In protest, and for individual and national blessing, may Christians learn to start and close each day with fervent pleading to our country's and our fathers' God! If in your home, members of the family leave for work at different, conflicting hours, don't give the devil his easy way and say, "We would like to have prayer together, but we simply can't find time!" Deep in your hearts you know that this excuse is dishonest. If the parents and children in your household were each paid five dollars for joining in worship, alarm clock or no alarm clock, you would all be on time every morning; yet you can never purchase the blessings of the family altar for a thousand thousand times five dollars. Make time for prayer, before time and its sorrows make prayer your last resort!

Don't feel that you have to make special gestures, use particular postures, when you make your requests of God! None is recorded in our text. True, our land would do well to learn again the humility of kneeling before God. Too many of us have become so stiff-kneed, stiff-necked, and stiff-minded that we refuse to fall down to worship the holy, sinless, perfect God before whom even cherubim and seraphim shield their faces. Churches have sustained a heavy loss by making prayer easy and comfortable as congregations no longer prostrate themselves before Him whose name is above all other names. Particularly during the perils of peace, should America be on its knees in real repentance, honest humility, and firm faith! As we fold our hands to signify that we stop all activities, concentrating our attention and devotion on God, we should realize that mere posture and position, gesture and ceremonial, mean nothing to the Lord. A few days ago I entered a Confucianist temple in New York's Chinatown. There, amidst censers with smoking incense, sacred drums, and other objects of idolatry, was an immense statue of a laughing Buddha. "Rub his belly for good luck!" an attendant urged me. Of course, I refused; and I hope you will refuse anyone who tells you to accept and use any particular paraphernalia for prayer. The Savior promises that by faith in His atoning love you can come to the Father just as you are. Eight years ago a Pittsburgh girl wrote me that in all her life she had never been inside a church. Especially at Christmas, when she saw other young girls eagerly hurrying to worship, she grew indescribably sad. The reason she kept her distance from church was this: she felt her clothes were not good enough. We wrote her that if one could say, "Jesus, Thy blood and righteousness my beauty are, my glorious dress," earthly garments meant nothing in His sight. We asked one of our Pittsburgh pastors to call on her — and I thank you faithful co-workers in the clergy who generously labor with us in this mission of the air! For the first time in her life she entered a church. She received careful instruction in the Christian truth, was baptized, and learned to pray in victorious faith. By a special blessing from the Lord the girl who had never before been inside God's house there met a splendid Christian young man who later became her devoted husband. Now, close to Christ, she knows that through her Savior she can come directly to the Throne of Mercy without payment or price, without anyone to introduce her or intercede for her, without any requirement of expensive clothing.

Again, sincerity alone does not make a prayer acceptable to God. The priests of Baal on Mount Carmel were sincere enough when at the top of their voices they shrieked to their false god, frantically mutilated themselves to secure his answer. But their efforts were in vain. The Japanese were sincere enough when they worshiped their emperor and implored the help of their ancestral idols, but our second invasion army landed on Luzon against them without losing a man. Millions in America are sincere when they pray to a false god, but they are headed for spiritual defeat.

The Sweet Power of Prayer

While we should beseech the Lord for ourselves and our country, our entreaties must plead also for others. Moses did not raise his voice for himself, but for his people. Analyze your own petitions, and you may be surprised to find how completely your requests revolve around yourself. In effect, most daily entreaties simply say in one form or another: "God, give *me* this! God, give *me* that! God, help *me!* God, protect *me!* God, bless *me!* God, remember and reward *me!*" Is it any wonder that nations fight wars today when individuals can be so self-centered even in their communion with Heaven?

America should also learn that we cannot pray, *"Forgive us our trespasses,"* with the hope of receiving divine pardon, unless we are willing to add, *"as we forgive those who trespass against us."* Moses in the waterless wilderness was praying for people who had opposed him and would continue to assail him. In a hate-filled, war-mad world, Christians must learn to pray for their fellow men in Germany and Japan. I denounce the Nazi interference in matters of conscience and worship, the cruelty and atrocities practiced in their war; but at the same time I know that there are millions of Christians in Germany who had to be forced to fight. However the peace table decides the destiny of Germany and Japan, let the Christian world now pledge itself to bring the Gospel to these devastated areas, which will be won for Communism if not gained for Christ. American soldiers write that in occupied Germany they have found believers who eagerly look to the time when they can hear our broadcast. Instead of sending scrap iron to Nippon for the profits of junk dealers, but for the possible future loss of

American lives, let us now send ten missionaries for every one in the past and help win Japan for Jesus!

The most vital of all prayer lessons, however, and the most necessary for our age, is the climax truth, that penetrating, prevailing petition must always be made in the Savior's name; that is, not merely closing our requests with a quickly spoken "This we ask in Jesus' name," although politicians intentionally omit even this in their public petitions. I wonder what our Lord thinks when every real reference to Him as the Rescuer of the race is omitted from an article on prayer in one of America's leading church papers, written by a popular churchman.

Moses, fifteen hundred years before the Nativity at Bethlehem, knew the Savior and prayed with faith in His mercy. From Genesis, where he foresees Christ as *"the Seed of the woman"* who will destroy Satan, or where he pictures Jesus as Abraham's Descendant in whom *"all the nations of the earth"* shall *"be blessed,"* to his later books, where he predicts that the Messiah, as Ruler of the nations, shall come from Judah, a Prophet to whom all of Israel should hearken, Moses shows that he knows the Savior, believes in Him, and reveres Him. Unless you too know Him, your prayer, however piteously you cry, will not be answered; for our Lord states clearly and directly, *"Whatsoever ye shall ask the Father* IN MY NAME, *He will give it you."* Christ wants the repentant, reliant, reassuring faith which accepts Him as the Son of God, the Savior of mankind, the Redeemer of the race, the Reconciler of God and man, the Rebuilder of ruined lives, the Restorer of peace between Heaven and earth. As your first, last, and most important prayer lesson learn that before your petitions can be answered, you must make Jesus yours and approach the Father in His name who is *"the Way, the Truth, and the Life,"* without whom *"no man cometh unto the Father"!*

As Moses was heard in the wilderness when the bitter waters of Marah were sweetened, so the Almighty will hear your pleas spoken in the faith that looks to Calvary's cross. Our requests for earthly advantages, money gains, health improvement, even the preservation of life, He grants according to His will. He can always save, heal, restore, if that be His purpose. The late Dr. Howard A. Kelly, internationally known surgeon and widely honored medical authority, told Toronto newspaper men shortly before his death: "Prayer is the greatest instrument any surgeon can possess. Every true doctor, especially a surgeon, should call in the aid of prayer. . . . Patient and physician are both in our Father's hands. . . . All healing is of God." Sometimes, of course, the Lord loves us too dearly to grant our selfish, shortsighted, destructive wishes; then He answers our prayers in a far different, much higher and altogether better way. We ask for pebbles, and He gives us diamonds. Sometimes, too, He cherishes His children too deeply to permit them to linger longer in a world of wickedness and woe. He wants them to experience the joy of heaven early; so He calls them home despite the earnest, but sometimes self-willed entreaty of their loved ones. If only we knew what glories await us in that homeland, we would welcome death as the high blessing it truly is through Christ!

Nor will the Almighty always hear our prayers when, where, and how we wish. His divine delay is often for the fortifying of our faith, the strengthening of our trust.

But you can be sure, as the Apostle emphasizes: *"This is the confidence that we have in Him, that if we ask anything according to His will, He heareth us."* Build your faith on that truth! You who love the Lord Jesus know positively that He answers prayer. You have repeatedly experienced this blessing in your lives; and we have had His guarantee fulfilled in our radio mission. A few days ago one of the most encouraging of the many fortifying letters I have received in these twelve years of broadcasting was laid on my desk. It came — of all places — from Nigeria in dark Africa. Interesting pictures accompanying it showed large gatherings of black-skinned men and women, including public officials, listening to our broadcast. The letter explained that our transcriptions are being used throughout the stations of the Sudan Interior Mission and that in Nigerian villages often a thousand people gather to hear our messages. The officials have invited me to take the Clipper to Africa and visit their fields. I mention our work now to lay before you a startling proof of answered prayer. Years ago, when we could use only two stations, it was repeatedly predicted that because we had no other message than that of Christ, and Him crucified, our mission of the air could not succeed. Today, with almost six hundred stations in twenty-six countries and territories, our network growing week after week, we have an electrifying report — humbly and before God I call it one of the modern mission-miracles! — the response to our broadcast is greater, wider, more generous, and more blessed than ever before. How can we explain this miracle? Give me personally no credit whatever! No one knows better than I how every single blessing we have enjoyed comes directly

The Sweet Power of Prayer

from the almighty, all-powerful, all-loving God. Yet just as clearly remember: believers all over the country have earnestly and eagerly prayed that our Bringing Christ to the Nations radio mission would be kept on the air and increased despite our recent difficulties. How marvelously the Almighty has answered! The Lutheran Hour today is larger, stronger, more widely and generously supported than ever before. We plead for your continued prayer so that in the mightiest missionary movement of modern history we can broadcast Christ to war-stricken Europe and Asia in dozens of different languages.

My beloved, if you want real blessing for yourself, your family, your country, pray as you have never prayed before! Pray penitently and persistently! Pray confidently and courageously! Pray humbly and wholeheartedly! Pray in Jesus' name! Then God will hear you from heaven, and will sweeten any bitterness in your life! As you kneel in petition, you will be exalted in power. Therefore: On your knees, America! Pray, America, pray! Be blessed, America! Be blessed — in Jesus Christ! Amen!

CHRIST IS MY LIGHT

"I am come a Light into the world that whosoever believeth on Me should not abide in darkness." SAINT JOHN 12:46.

CHRIST, OUR SIN-BEARING, SIN-ATONING SAVIOR: Oh, that beholding Thee, agonized on the cross of shame and shuddering sorrow, every one of us could tell the world: This Jesus, the Son of God, is my Savior, who has atoned for all my transgressions! Oh, that every day we would take time to recall the mercy of Thy redemption and, kneeling in spirit before Thee, cry out: Thou must increase, but we must decrease! With the approach of the Lenten season, give us that trust and humility which, while fully realizing the damnable guilt of our abounding iniquity, victoriously clings to Thy greater grace! Sin-removing Lamb of God, may Thy Spirit lead our country and its godless millions to Thee in genuine repentance and real faith! Put the triumphant assurance of Thy salvation into the hearts and lives of our young men and women, far distant as many of them are from their homes! If it be Thy will — and we pray that it is — bless our country and all people with the benefits of peace that please Thee! Enrich each of us in this mission of the air with firmly founded reliance on Thine all-sufficient, all-comforting, all-sustaining grace! We plead with assurance, according to Thy promise. Amen!

Christ Is My Light

UNNOTICED, probably, by many of you, in newspapers crowded with accounts of crime and killing, divorce and desertion, was the recent sensational story of a scientific paper read before the American Physics Society in New York City. This told of experiments which have proved that light is able to spin or move solid matter. "So what?" some of you ask. Merely this, that these findings will very likely change some so-called scientific but really atheist accounts of the earth's creation. When unbelievers sneer at Scripture, they not only reject the rock-grounded foundation of faith and slip into the quicksands of spiritual quackery, but they also lose themselves in wide, deep, and repeated error. Thus, because proud, self-important men refuse to believe that God made this world and instead insist that the universe, all creatures, especially man, sprang into existence by mere chance (the mathematical possibility that your thirty-two teeth, if you still have your full set, came into their present order — only one factor — by accident, is so infinitesimally small that it is one chance in a number so great that it must be written by 332 followed by thirty-three zeros); because agnostic teachers have sworn, at all costs, to dethrone the Almighty as Creator, they have invented theories for the origin of the earth, which, one after the other, have been proved absolutely false. When I was a boy in a Boston grammar school, I was deliberately taught that the Bible creation record was wrong, in the same way that many of your children are misled today, as though there were no Constitution of the United States to prohibit tax-paid teachers from attacking religion; as though it were not a bully's crime for an adult instructor to take advantage of a child and try to destroy its faith. We were asked to believe the nebular hypothesis, the claim that in the beginning there was not God, but a cloudlike, gaseous substance, into which somehow a whirling motion came, with the result that the gases solidified (by the sheerest accident, of course), formed the world, and gave the globe its rotating motion. That error held sway for a generation, until discarded by all, except uninformed high school teachers and backwoods college professors, in favor of the tidal hypothesis. This asserted that a wandering star happened to pass too near the sun, drew out an immense, cigar-shaped section, which later, again by the purest chance, entirely without God, was subdivided to form the planets, including our world, and to give them motion. We predict that this opposition to Scripture, too, will soon be on the way out, since scientists have learned that light can move matter, just as this new claim, in turn, as far as it seeks to banish the Almighty, will take the same exit as every other outworn, outmoded, anti-Biblical teaching.

If only through the labor of their minds and the brilliant achievements of their brains, as the Almighty blesses them, men would know, confess, and proclaim that there is one Light which can move even human souls from death to life, a healing Light in the sickness of our sin, a warm, comforting Light in our cold, sorrow-filled world, a divine Beacon Light which can guide our souls to safety and salvation, a heavenly, re-creating Light to rebuild and renew our lives! This unfailing Brightness, which suffers no blackout, dimout, brownout, is promised us by Christ's unfailing pledge in our text for this Sunday, found in Saint John's Gospel (chapter twelve, verse forty-six): *"I am come a Light into the world that whosoever believeth on Me should not abide in darkness."* As we ask the Holy Spirit to apply this comfort to our souls, may every one of us be blessed by the faith which exults:

CHRIST IS MY LIGHT!

I

HE IS AN ALL-MARVELOUS LIGHT

Even to begin to understand the assurance of this truth, *"I am come a Light into the world,"* we should ask ourselves, Who speaks these words? Not a self-appointed, misguided human leader, of whom we have many today, who megaphones to the mob, "I am light; follow me," and who then leads into the darkness of destruction! Millions have been decoyed into disaster by staggering after the lure of such treacherous lights. No; this is the utterance of Jesus Himself; and the Christ who revealed Himself to men, whose life and love are predicted in the Old Testament and recorded in the New; whose atonement is the center of our creed, whose Cross forms the climax of every message on this international broadcast, is not mere man, perfect, holy, sinless, stainless as He was; He is also — hear it! believe it! cherish it! defend it! — your God, together with the Father and the Spirit, your very God, your true God, your only God. The Christ we preach, the Christ our world needs, the Christ you must have if you are to be saved, is incomparably greater than the counterfeit, only human Jesus, mentioned in ten thousand modernist pulpits today. You need not be a preacher or a theologian to know that a mortal Christ cannot save you from your sins, or to realize that only a heavenly Christ has the almighty power required to meet your needs, keep His word, fulfill His promises. Therefore when our Lord declares, *"I am come a Light into the world,"* you may not know how He is a Light; you may not understand how He can be a Light; you infidels may question, and you atheists deny, that He is a Light; yet all this cannot change the truth: Jesus, your God, is *"the Light of the world."*

We will also profit by learning *when* our Lord spoke these words. It was shortly before His betrayal and desertion by His disciples, and the soul-throbbing agony of His last Thursday night and His crucifixion on Friday morning. Together with the four succeeding chapters of Saint John's Gospel, this twelfth chapter may be regarded as part of our Savior's last will and testament. Surely, if the courts of our land uphold the wills of criminals in Sing Sing, the legacies in which the dying leave their fortunes to establish burial grounds for dogs, maintain lavish lifetime support for cats, then a million times more should men carefully hear and gratefully accept the heavenly riches in the Savior's legacy of divine love. Every word our Lord spoke, as truth and life itself, asks for your full, personal acceptance; but somehow, it seems, the utterances He made, as it were, in the shadow of the cross, carry a redoubled appeal for your faith and trust.

Particularly let us ask *why* Jesus declared, *"I am come a Light into the world."* Clearly, Scripture shows, because the earth, as men's souls, was covered in sin's darkness so deep that within a few days His hate-blinded countrymen would nail Christ, the Son of God, the Redeemer of the race, to the accursed cross! Today too the world is steeped in dark evil, because men are born in sin, grow in sin, live in sin, love sin, practice sin, multiply sin, glorify sin, justify sin, die in sin, and go to hell in sin. The heavy blackness of unbelief, immorality, rebellion against God, rejection of Christ, love of lust, have settled over vast areas. At a time when the light of human achievement was the brightest, our intellectual brilliance was blacked out by the tragedy of the widest bloodshed history has ever known. We pat our own shoulders to compliment ourselves on our advance in learning; yet the world's energies are concentrated on killing. We have destroyed, devastated, bombed, blasted, sown the seeds for further hatred, shoved nations over the brink of bankruptcy, brought militarism closer to peace-time United States because we fear further wars. A chilling gloom envelops much of American business, as deceit and defrauding of the Government in wartime contracts run into hundreds of millions, blood profit. Dense darkness has descended on many of our schools and colleges, where, the Word of God rejected, men grope falteringly for the truth, the decency, the honesty, the purity and moral strength our country needs. The blackness of midnight enshrouds our international relations.

The heaviest darkness, however, engulfs those places which ought to be bright beacon lights in the Lord — many churches. We feel deep-rooted resentment arise within us when we read the record of cruelty practiced by the Japanese in their prison camps on the Philippines. Like the indignant disciples, we want to call down fire from heaven to destroy the Japanese major, in charge of the American prisoners at Cabanatua on Luzon, who took a truck full of medicine that would have saved American lives and smashed it all, bottle by bottle. But what can we say of those preachers who take the Word of God, the healing of souls in our sick, sore age, and seek to destroy it, verse by verse? The light of the Gospel is often blacked out because churches refuse to go all out for Christ, but compromise with the world. We can hardly believe our eyes when we read that in England the House of Lords will appoint a committee to investigate the claim that the national Church there receives about $280,000 a year from London property rented for commercial vice. How can British youth have any respect for a Church which permits its real estate to be used by agents of prostitution? God keep American churches poor if wealth means surrender of His principles of purity! Even more, God keep our churches free from the darkness of denial by which the leader of one of the modern creeds here in Florida declares: "If my future state depends upon putting my whole trust in the death of Jesus Christ on the cross nineteen hundred years ago — well, you can put my future address as: Hell"! — He certainly knows where he is going; but why give his address? He will not get any mail there.

Now, Christ says not, "*I am come a Light into the world*' to bring light, provide light, reveal light," but He states clearly that He *is* "*a Light*," or, as other passages of Scripture declare — and this is the repeated teaching of the New Testament — He is "*the Light of the world*." Now, what does light do? First, of course, it drives away darkness, and similarly, our blessed Savior banishes all blackness of sin. But, some of you object, sin is not dark; it is light, bright, dazzling. That is the way it starts, but it ends with the night of despair. It promises gleam but produces gloom. It lures us with lust, illicit love, and brimful life; but instead it yields disgust, delusion, death. David can testify to that. It offers us the enticement of money and applause, but it leaves us poor, deceived, forsaken. Judas learned that. It holds before us glamor and popularity, but it substitutes tears and terror. Peter knew that. Today every one of you, if you would only be open and honest with yourselves, could prove in your own experience that the breaking of God's Law, the refusal to worship Him, the denial of Christ, the rejection of the Bible, the abuse of His holy name in blasphemy and profanity, your plans and programs of hate and envy, selfishness and strife, carnal desires, the vices of impurity, jealousy, slander, and covetousness have brought you your darkest moments. I have seen people bear the loss of fortunes first with grief, but then with trust; fathers and mothers, stunned by the death of their only son, can regain their balance in life. But I know others who have lost neither wealth nor child, yet have cringed in terror before the black specters of their sins and the gloom of their punishment. You object, "Well, I for one do not feel that way. I'm going to live my life as I want to, regardless of consequences." Are you? It is easy to speak bravely and boldly when you are making twice as much money as ever before, having twice as much pleasure, buying twice as many luxuries, wearing clothes that cost twice as much, paying cocktail bills twice as high. Be sure, however, whatever politicians promise, that the time can come for you, when waste will be turned into want, when $200 solid-gold pen-and-pencil sets will find their last use as people sign pawnshop receipts! To every one of you unbelievers, without exception, no matter how healthy, wealthy, or wise you may be, will come the deep, dread darkness of death, which makes you shudder even now whenever you think of your end and the Judgment you must face.

Jesus — praised be His name above all other names! — was born to banish that blackness from your life. He loved you, as these Lenten weeks, starting Wednesday, reassure you, with a divine devotion that earth could never fathom and only God could show. It meant bitter, brutal blackness for Him, the Son of the Almighty, to call you *"out of darkness into His marvelous light."* It meant the bloody sweat of Gethsemane; the cruel smiting before the Sanhedrin, the council of His countrymen; the jeering, cutting ridicule before Caiaphas, the high priest; the mockery before Herod; the crown of thorns and the bloody scourging before Pilate, the Roman governor; the collapse on the dusty road outside Jerusalem; the crushing nails of death crashing through His quivering flesh at Calvary. To become your Light meant that Jesus had to be condemned and crucified by those whom He had come to save and, hung on Golgotha's gory cross, to be forsaken by His heavenly Father as He suffered the punishment of your transgressions. God's eternal Law decreed, *"The soul that sinneth, it shall die,"* and His Law could not be broken. So Christ, transferring all your transgressions to Himself, bearing their guilt, their curse, paying the penalty, died as the world's Sinbearer. What endless mercy, depthless compassion, heightless love! How differently we deal with our fellow men! Out in Camp Roberts, California, an American soldier who refused to drill but expressed his willingness to do anything in the war effort except to kill was given a death sentence, which was commuted to life imprisonment only after public attention was focused on this brutality. Of the compassionate Christ, however, it is written, *"God sent not His Son into the world to condemn the world, but that the world through Him might be saved."* He does not merely commute our eternal death sentence; rather we are assured, *"He hath made Him to be sin for us, who knew no sin, that we might be made the righteousness of God in Him."* He took all your iniquities away, especially those which you think too vile to be forgotten, too filthy to be forgiven; and where there is no sin, there should be no darkness of despair, no doom of destruction. My beloved, in the Christ who loved you unto the end and who is able to save you unto the uttermost, is your Light and your Life.

The gloom of your transgressions dispelled, all other darkness is banished by Christ, the Light, particularly the heavy clouds of personal pain and affliction. Claiming the Psalmist's comfort and strength for yourself, you can declare, *"In Thy light shall we see light"* for the heaped sorrows of our war-racked world. Once the Savior brightens your soul and you believe with your whole heart that He loved you and gave Himself for you, you may experience rebuff and reverse, perhaps more frequently than ever before, since it is still true, *"we must through much tribulation enter into the kingdom of God."* Yet, no matter how hard the sorrows of your life may be — and your letters reveal that many of you are tortured by pain, riveted on sickbeds for years, burdened by heavy losses, misunderstandings, and mistakes, weighted by family trouble, money trouble, mental trouble — here, in the Lord Jesus, is Heaven's bright guidance for the midnight of your misery. Let me sum up for you in short, quick sentences, the truth of truths taken from God's errorless Word: First, with Christ as your Redeemer, no agony you suffer is a punishment from God, since the Father no longer punishes those whose iniquities have been removed. Second, each anguish is the sign of Heaven's love. Third, every visitation is for your good, since it is remedial, a reassurance of your Father's love, designed to fortify your faith and reinforce your reliance on Jesus. Fourth, God knows the way He leads you, and you will never be tried above your power to endure. Fifth, Christ Himself will share your sorrows. Sixth, every affliction will help widen your sympathetic love for the needs of fellow sufferers. Seventh, throughout every unrelieved sorrow you can triumph over your trials and join the Apostle in exulting, I know *"that the sufferings of this present time are not worthy to be compared with the glory which shall be revealed in us"* who love the Lord. My beloved, here is light for all the gloom with which this peace-robbed world may have surrounded you.

Jesus is also the Light of hope in the shadowy fears which sweep over your lives during these uncertain times. God's Word predicts that in the last days we shall see *"men's hearts failing them for fear,"* but this does not include Christ's own. True, if we had to brave the future alone, without the sustaining Savior, we would be hapless, helpless, hopeless; for we face a combination of selfish forces, which, if not restrained, can produce seething unrest throughout the nations, persecution of God's children, and the dictatorship of overbearing unbelief. Thank the Lord with me today that we have a better defense than our military might, the plans of our political strategists, the forecasts of international fortune-tellers; we have God's Son, whose Word pledges, *"Fear not; for I have redeemed thee, I have called thee by thy name; thou are Mine"!* In His blessed name I promise you, burdened by fears and phobias that are ruining your bodies, twisting your minds, terrorizing your souls: Here, at the Savior's cross is faith instead of fear, triumph instead of terror. Here, *"being justified by faith, we have peace with God through our Lord Jesus Christ."*

Our blessed Redeemer also shines as the Light of happiness into a world of misery. Many of you have failed in life because you do not know what to do with yourselves. Despite all outward show you go on from day to day in narrow, cramped, selfish existence, robbed of all real joy. Some of you are spiritually dead, because you have tried to live without Christ and have failed. Sir James Young Simpson, the celebrated Scottish physician and discoverer of chloroform, told some of his unbelieving friends: "You are spiritually dead on account of being cut off by your sins from communion with the living God. As a corpse cannot be aroused, so are you dead to all love of God and to everything pertaining to His Gospel . . . but in the infinitude of His love for our fallen race God offers to each of us, individually, a free, full pardon and life, now and forever, if only we believe on His Son, whom He sent to suffer in our stead." When you have that faith, you have heaven's joy in bringing the Gospel of grace to your fellow men. How sorely a world, ravaged and wrecked by war, needs your help in spreading the Gospel! Letters smuggled out of Holland reveal that the brave people there were often forced to eat rats during the hunger caused by the Nazi occupation, but no letters can describe the soul starvation which reigns over extended areas of this war-ravaged world, and even this country. Thousands of you, by the Spirit's help, could have the joy of bringing Christ to someone in your own relationship, your family, your home. "It's worth a million dollars to know that he is safe," a Chicago father told a *Tribune* reporter who brought the news that his son had been saved from a Japanese prison on the Philippines. How much is it worth to you to know that your dear ones are safe for eternity with Jesus? The Savior says not only, *"I am the Light of the world,"* but also, *"Ye are the light of the world."* We are to radiate our Lord's brightness by helping win others for His glorious grace — and that, I tell you from my personal experience, is one of the highest of earthly joys. If your life is empty, useless, disappointing, follow Christ in the spirit of humble service, and new joy, new interest, new purpose, in your existence will be granted you.

Light has many other uses than dispelling darkness. It makes creatures grow; and how you will develop in understanding, love, spiritual stature with God and man, in self-denial, in purity, in power, if Christ and His Spirit control your soul! Light helps restore health. The various infra and ultra rays have a definite part in modern medicine. The healing light of the sun is the Almighty's free and marvelous medicine, especially in consumption, rickets, certain forms of arthritis. Jesus, as *"the Sun of righteousness . . . with healing in His wings,"* can, should it be His purpose, cure the most treacherous diseases, restore the victims of nervous or mental breakdowns and rescue those for whom even a corps of medical experts has left no hope whatever. Yet our Savior can do far more; while He heals our bodies according to His will, He will heal our souls from the sickness of sin according to His unbreakable promise. And now, scientists tell us, light can move matter; yet long before this believers knew that the Lord, their Light, could move even mountains, move hearts of stone to repentance, move armies to victory, remove dangers from our pathway, and, as He moved the stone from His rock-hewn grave, so, blessed Son of God that He is, remove all terror of death.

Jesus can do much more for our souls than earthly light can do for our bodies; but only Christ is *"the Light of the world."* Don't tell me that I am narrow and bigoted when I emphasize that in Him alone you can find the eternal, unfailing Light you need! Don't listen to these *"blind leaders of the blind"* who tell you that any kind of creed leads to heaven, that any kind of worship saves, if only it is sincere! One of the latest to repeat this error is Hendrik Willem Van Loon, author of *The Story of Mankind*. If you have ever read that book, you know that the first pages, which attempt to account for the origin of the world and the beginning of man, abound with "perhaps," "if," "maybe." Now, I submit to you, if that writer cannot definitely state the physical facts of this earth, how can he know the spiritual facts of heaven? Yet, repeating the same mistake which certain scientists, politicians, soap manufacturers, have made, he steps out of role to write a pamphlet on Christianity. On its first page he attacks my Church, and on the last he repeats the age-old delusion which classifies all religions, Christian, Jewish, pagan, as one, and those who worship any supreme being, the God of the Bible, the Allah of the Koran, the Great Unknown of the agnostics, as "fellow travelers along the same road." Yet in Heaven's truth, *"there is none other name under heaven given among men whereby we must be saved,"* but the holy, precious name of Christ. He is not one of many lights. He is the one Light. Four nights ago we came in from sea to the Florida coast. Three dozen and more lights gleamed off the Fort Lauderdale shore. Now, did the captain say: "Look at all those lights! I can bring this ship in by steering toward any one of them"? No, he showed me two lights, one above the other, and said: "I steer straight for them. That brings me into the channel and right into the middle of the city." — If your soul is guided toward any other light than Christ, you are lost.

II

HE IS AN ALL-MERCIFUL LIGHT

I hear some of you saying, "Oh, that I could have Jesus for my Light!" Thank God, you can. No matter how completely you may have been deprived of earthly blessings, how unfairly men may have dealt with you, you can still have the brilliancy of His radiance. However strongly others may hate you, God's Son loves you. In our text the Lord declares that He came *"a Light into the world,"* that is, for the whole world, including you. A Chicago hospital bars a sick Japanese-American woman, who gave her blood to help save our soldiers' lives. But Jesus bars no one. He is not a partial Savior, the Redeemer of a select few, the Atonement for the better classes. He is the Savior of mankind, the Redeemer of the race, the Atonement of all ages, past, present, and future.

Therefore He can say, *"I am come a Light into the world,"* and add, *"that* WHOSOEVER *believeth on Me should not abide in darkness."* Blessed "WHOSOEVER"! You can put your name in place of that all-inclusive word in any Gospel promise. Here, then, is hope and happiness, promise and pardon, light and life for every one of you.

Yet even this does not begin to exhaust our Savior's mercy. The light Christ gives is free. Think of that when you pay your gas and electric bill each month! The radiance of His redemption, which the total treasuries in the world cannot purchase, the atonement that cost His life, cost you nothing. If our Lord had offered us even a little flickering candle of hope and said, "You can have this tiny flame if you are ready to earn it, pay for it with a lifetime of penance, with a thousand years in hell, or ten thousand years in some place of purging, and then heaven; in short, if Jesus had told us that we must buy or barter, earn or exchange, our salvation, giving the best we have, doing the best we can, suffering the most we can endure to secure our pardon, peace, and paradise, that would have been grace far beyond everything we have deserved. But listen! The Son of God Himself tells you today that you can have Him, the leading, living, loving Light — by faith. That, and nothing less, is His guarantee today, when He declares, *"Whosoever believeth on Me should not abide in darkness."* For this light, your rescue and redemption, believe Him, welcome Him into your heart, trust Him! Here, again, we have ascended the summit of salvation truth, the pinnacle of all promises, the highest pledge for your eternal happiness: *"Believe on the Lord Jesus Christ, and thou shalt be saved!"*

What, then, will you do with this heavenly Light? Every one of you will either follow the faith-illumined path to salvation or turn from the Savior and be lost. There is no third choice, no middle ground. Each of you is either for the Savior or against him. A Kansas City man placed this paid advertisement in a local newspaper: "Will exchange my interest in the hereafter for a productive lead on a clean, furnished apartment." Ready to exchange the prepared place in the many mansions of our Father's heavenly realm for an apartment in Kansas City! What blindness! Yet many of you are losing heaven without gaining even that much on earth, because you reject your Redeemer. Oh, today, when He promises that through Him you need *"not abide in darkness"*; when He offers Himself, the Light to remove the clouds of sin, sorrow, and suffering from your soul, may you repel all evil which would keep you from His grace, hasten to His cross, penitently bow to worship Him, and, as the Holy Spirit fills your heart, declare in firm, saving faith: "Thou, O Christ, art my Light. I shall not abide in darkness." Amen!

WAKE UP, AMERICA!

"He came and found them asleep again, for their eyes were heavy. And He left them and went away again and prayed the third time, saying the same words."
                                                   SAINT MATTHEW 26:43, 44

SUSTAINING SPIRIT OF TRUTH AND MERCY: Contritely we confess our repeated sins of drowsy indifference toward the suffering of our Savior Jesus Christ. Humbly we beseech Thee for His sake, who on the cross shed His lifeblood for us, to forgive, cancel and remove the transgressions committed during those hours in which we have slept in carnal slumber, instead of waking and watching with our Redeemer. Oh, that in these days of wide distress, when all men need Christ more than ever and, despite the best human plans, without Him can do nothing, we were fully aroused to the seriousness of our sin and its punishment, eternal death! Hear us and help us, we plead. Without Thee no sinner can call Jesus his Savior. Therefore lead men the world over to repentance and reliance on the Crucified! Bring many this day to faith and to the new birth in Jesus! Protect with Thy special love Thy children in military or civilian activities here in this nation and in every country! Keep them in Thy constant care! Strengthen them to resist evil! Fortify their faith! Make America penitent, and enrich us with the assurance not of a man-made but of a God-blessed peace! We pray hopefully, because we plead with the Savior's promise and in His name. Amen!

Do you know the most crushing sorrow and the torture of the heaviest agony war can produce? It is not dying itself, but the lonely, forsaken, deserted death many of our men suffer. With the casualty lists in this conflict far higher than the heaviest previous losses in America, those of the Civil War, it has happened in multiplied thousands of instances that soldiers have died on the battlefield or in the isolation of prison camps, without a friend, or even a fellow man, at their side to comfort and sustain them. Unnumbered sailors in the Navy and the Merchant Marine have drowned on the high seas with an anguish of loneliness that no words can describe. Airmen have been hurled to quick and horrifying destruction, in which not even an enemy could give them a last glance of compassion.

In his intimate account of the war, the book *Brave Men*, the late Ernie Pyle, acclaimed war reporter, gave a gripping account of lonely death as it often overtook our soldiers. He wrote that repeatedly during the Sicilian campaign dying men were brought to his tent, and that their death rattle kept silencing conversation. When a wounded fighter was breathing his last, the surgeon would place a piece of gauze over his face. This enabled him to breathe, but covered the horror in which his features writhed. Pyle referred particularly to one dying soldier, beside whom a chaplain knelt with the words, "John, I am going to say a prayer for you." "Somehow," the author related, "this stark announcement hit me like a hammer. . . . It was as though he had said, 'Brother, you may not know it, but your goose is cooked.' Anyhow, he voiced the prayer, and the weak, gasping man tried vainly to repeat the words after him. When he had finished, the chaplain added, 'John, you are doing fine.' Then he rose and dashed off on some other call. . . . The dying man was left utterly alone, just lying there on his litter on the ground, lying in an aisle, because the tent was full. Of course, it couldn't be otherwise, but the aloneness of that man as he went through the last minutes of his life was what tormented me. I felt like going over and at least holding his hand while he died; but it would have been out of order, and I didn't do it. I wish now I had."

Can you, even those who have profited from bloodshed, cry, "Hurrah for war!" if you picture the heartbreaking loneliness of that lad, who may have been the son of gold-star parents in this mission of the air? When we stop to realize that thousands of others suffer his agony, dying on battlefields before help can reach them, breathing their last in overcrowded rooms, where a newspaperman finds it "out of order," even to take the hand of a soldier gasping in his last breath, we wonder why Congress could clap in loud applause when war was declared more than three years ago; why, when American casualties reached more than three thousand a day, newspaper reporters could comment on the "humor" — they used that very word — which marked the meeting of the Big Three at Yalta. How can people find anything about which to laugh, with men dying every moment? How can night clubs be jammed, theaters featuring the vilest performances sold out months in advance, cocktail bars and dance halls overcrowded? Millions in this nation have yet to learn that war, even the most justified and necessary, is always a visitation from the Almighty which calls for contrite sorrow, not for sensual celebration.

If all Americans could know in a personal, intimate way the horror that marks just one of these solitary ends when fighting men, forsaken and deserted, enduring agony in their bodies, torment in their minds, and often torture in their soul, are pushed into eternity, they would indeed begin to recognize war's shocking terror.

Today, however, I call your attention to a death far more desolate than any solitary anguish in battle, and tell you that if all Americans would believe the New Testament record picturing the loneliness of the Lord Jesus in the Garden of Gethsemane and understand the reason for the solitude of His suffering, they would first be aroused from the stupor of sin, into which many have fallen, and then be brought close to Christ. With a prayer that God's Holy Spirit will lead masses to learn the vital Lenten lessons, I call out across the country:

WAKE UP, AMERICA!

This is the plea we should find in the record of our text, Saint Matthew, chapter twenty-six, verses forty-three and forty-four: *"He came and found them asleep again, for their eyes were heavy. And He left them and went away again and prayed the third time, saying the same words."*

I

MASSES SLEEP ON, UNCONCERNED ABOUT CHRIST'S SUFFERING

Soon after the Savior had instituted the Lord's Supper, the gift of His very body and blood, He led His disciples, on the last night of His life, the short distance from that upper chamber to the Garden of Gethsemane. Here, during the dark hours of night, He had frequently knelt and prayed penetrating petitions to His heavenly Father. When we contrast the deep devotion to which the Lord Jesus dedicated night after night with the godlessness and lust by which many in our country waste the hours before and after midnight, crowding places of sensual amusement, drinking themselves drunk, gambling their money away (easy come, easy go!), plotting ruin for themselves and their families, we ought to see clearly that we need to follow Christ's prayer life far more zealously. With the exception of the gold-star homes and the families with wounded and missing members, America did not feel any real hardship in the war. Millions have more money than they ever previously possessed and, consequently, less love for God, less consideration for Christ, less desire for fervent prayer. This has indeed been a comfortable, convenient, convivial conflict for great multitudes, even in churches; therefore we find so little yearning for the powerful, personal outpouring of sin-convicted, grace-seeking souls in fervent intercession. Many people pray, of course, but often it is the smooth, short, almost effortless reading of someone else's words, without any toil of the soul, without any pulsating power of victorious faith, and, therefore, without any personal joy and spiritual uplift. Our petitions to God, compared with the intensity of our Lord's prayers in Gethsemane, as He knelt, wept, groaned, cried with a loud voice, are as the pleasant murmuring of silvery brooks beside the roar of Niagara.

Note that from these first scenes of the Lenten story here in the Garden, when Jesus could have side-stepped danger and defeated His enemies, until the last moments at Calvary, when He, the almighty God, could have accepted the scoffers' challenge, *"Come down from the cross,"* our Lord's suffering was entirely voluntary. No one forced Him into Gethsemane; no draft board compelled Him to battle for us; no one could tell Him, "You must be crucified." Jesus had explained to His disciples that He Himself would willingly lay down His life; for He, the sinless Son of God, was guided in every step He took, every word He spoke from Gethsemane to Golgotha, by a depthless devotion to your soul. He entered the garden, with the never-to-be measured grief of its agony, moved only by the compassionate desire to save you for eternity.

There, in the shadows of Gethsemane, began an agony such as the world, with all its cruelties, has never witnessed. Don't think for a moment that the Savior's suffering was restricted to the anguish endured before His countrymen, the Roman governor, the coarse soldiers, and to the excruciating pain at Calvary. Right here, beneath the gnarled olive trees, Christ, the Son of God, is almost crushed into death. Hear Him cry, *"My soul is exceeding sorrowful, even unto death!"* and realize that these words mean everything they say, namely, that the torment He there endured almost took His life before His crucifiers had a chance to nail Him to the cross. See Jesus, gripped by tearing agony, throw Himself headlong on the damp garden ground! Study the record that *"His sweat was as it were great drops of blood falling down to the ground"!* Don't look for any medical explanation! I doubt that there is any, for no man has ever felt the crushing assault which struck Christ that night. Hear Scripture report that in His agony *"there appeared an angel unto Him from heaven, strengthening*

Him," and understand that the Savior's sorrows so nearly killed Him that a messenger had to come from heaven miraculously to sustain Him. A creature called to support the Creator! I have found in Foxe's *Book of Martyrs* the hideous account of Christians tortured under Nero. I have read how in the eighth persecution in the year 257 A. D., Emperor Valerian, the heathen hell-bound, sentenced Lawrence, a faithful minister of our Lord, to a horrifying death with these words: "Kindle the fire! Spare no wood! . . . Away with him, away with him! Whip him with scourges! Jerk him with rods! Buffet him with fists! Brain him with clubs! . . . Pinch him with fiery tongs! Gird him with burning plates! Bring out the strongest chains and the fire forks and the grated bed of iron! On the fire with it! Bind the rebel hand and foot; and when the bed is fire hot, on with him! Roast him! Broil him! Toss him! Turn him!" I have gone through the accounts of wholesale massacre led by Red tyrants, who twenty-five years ago lined Lutheran preachers up against the wall and sprayed them with machine-gun lead. I have clipped the stories of Nazi and Japanese atrocities in the war; but all this cannot begin to balance our Lord's ordeal in the Garden.

Why? Because there He, the Redeemer of the race, began to suffer in His own body, mind, and soul the punishment you and I deserved to endure in hell. There He began to pay the appalling penalty of torment, rejection by God, conflict with Satan and death, which you and I should have paid for our transgressions. Think of the horror of a single sin, as you read of a sixteen-year-old bobby-sox girl telling policemen: "Sure, I tried to kill my mother. Why not? . . . I wanted her to die. I'm not sorry!" Think of an Army lieutenant accused of murdering his own wife, burying her body in a foxhole, and then attempting suicide! Think of a callous youth sentenced to 207 years in prison for murdering his five-year-old niece with a hammer and a knife! Think of the evil promoters of this war, with the sins and misery that burden their conscience! Think of yourself, with the wrong and error that crowd into your life, and then try to realize — although you never can understand it — how horrifying beyond words was the total weight of humanity's woe which there pressed Christ to the ground when He began to suffer in atonement for all mankind's transgressions! No wonder that He cried out: *"O My Father* (this is the only time Jesus says, *"My Father"*), *"if it be possible, let this cup pass from Me"!* No wonder He sought the comforting companionship of His disciples! No wonder, as He faced death, not for Himself, but for each of us, He pleaded that His most trusted disciples, Peter, James, and John, watch with Him!

Yet great wonder that these men, privileged even above the other disciples, fell into heartless slumber and let Jesus meet this agony of agonies alone! Twice before our text the Savior had asked them to watch and pray, but their eyes had closed, and now for the third time we read, *"And He came and found them asleep again, for their eyes were heavy."* Those of whom the most could be expected actually gave the least, just as in our days the most distinguished may become the most dishonored. Not long ago, at Springfield, Massachusetts, a junior high school student was chosen the "all-American boy." Last week he was sentenced to life imprisonment for slaying a fourteen-year-old girl.

Note, however, that the disciples failed in a very small and easy matter! Jesus had asked of them only to keep awake with Him during the crushing conflict He had to endure; yet this little was far too much for them. While the Savior wrestled with the powers of darkness, they slept.

Before we center our rebuke on them, however, we should realize that today, nineteen hundred years after Gethsemane, with nineteen centuries' powerful proof of Christ as God and Lord, we, who should know far more of Jesus than those disciples did before the crucifixion, are often guilty of the same indifferent, careless, carnal slumber! Our country, which above other nations should be awake to the Savior's love, alert to the defense of His Gospel, alive to the power of His precious promises, is too often lost in self-satisfied slumber. Whether we realize it or not, a new philosophy of American life is in the making, which sidetracks God into a second place. Did you read the joint statement of the "Big Three" at the Crimean conference? It promises "all the men in all the lands . . . freedom from fear and want," which I again call the greatest and most tragic delusion modern history knows, because it is against the Bible's description of these last times and therefore impossible. This lengthy declaration of several thousand words does not once refer to God. It names forty-one individuals, but this document, which is to outline the plans for the postwar world and create a new age of peace, has not enough room to mention the Lord once, since some of the participants do not believe in Him. Because that is not the real American way, since we have God in the Declaration of Independence, God in by far the most of our

State constitutions, the cry which re-echoes throughout the land appeals: "Wake up, America! Don't sleep while sinister forces are trying to take the Almighty away from you! With repentant faith come back to Him who made you great and who alone can preserve you from disaster! Don't listen to those who cry, *'Peace, peace; when there is no peace'!*" Unforgiven sin must be punished in America as well as in Japan. Roger Babson, front-line statistician, pointedly warns his clients: "Only one thing will stop this coming chaos — a sweeping spiritual revival. Unless we have such an awakening of religious forces, we shall have a depression that will make the last one look like a Christmas Eve program." If you want that real revival (I prefer a thoroughgoing "reformation"), then cry out with all your might: "Wake up, America! Get right with God! *'Repent . . . and believe the Gospel!'* Come close to Jesus! Don't let atheists rob you of your greatest glory!"

Christ comes to us in the internal affairs of our country, and here, too, He often finds many Americans asleep amid the increasing menaces to our blessings and liberties. Those who have eyes to see and ears to hear should recognize the subtle and sinister attack on our Christian creed led by godless, Christless, Bibleless materialism. Anti-religious radicalism is steadily creeping farther into many sectors of our American life. Yet when I warn you against atheistic Communism, letters of protest come from university professors, ministers, people prominent in public affairs, claiming that the charge of infidel infiltration is just another "Wolf, wolf" cry without any support in fact. They will not say this ten or twenty years after peace is signed, when, unless God intervenes, we can witness a huge wave of unemployment, with disillusioned masses, unconcerned about God's Son, ready to try any radical program that seems to offer temporary relief. To prevent this uprising against God and His Anointed, American Christians must stop sleeping and hear the Apostle cry out to them, *"It is high time to awake out of sleep."*

The merciful Savior comes to the scientists and the teachers of America, those who should explain and emphasize Heaven's truth; but in far too many cases they slumber on, utterly indifferent to God's Word. "Science no longer teaches that man has descended from the ape," a university anthropologist declares; but before you Bible-loving Christians rejoice in the fact that Darwin and others, who actually taught that the human race has come from apelike ancestors, have been discredited; before you express your happiness that science itself has discredited these fictitious museum displays showing monkeys, orangoutangs, and chimpanzees, followed by low-browed, long-armed, primitive man, in alleged ascent, let me tell you that this same university anthropologist voices the claim, "Mankind and apes are descended from a common ancestor," making monkeys not the parents and grandparents of our race, so to speak, but the uncles, cousins, brothers, and sisters. While millions of dollars are annually spent thus to contradict God's Word and millions of people are being led from the comforting truth of the Gospel to the cruel delusion which teaches that we are only high-grade animals, created and evolved by chance, without a loving Father, the call to arms which should resound from coast to coast cries: "Wake up, America! Keep the Almighty as your Creator! Learn that no nation, even as wealthy as you, the richest of all people, can prosper without God and against Him!"

Our Lord comes to our entire educational and cultural life, only to find forces which should be alert and awake slumbering in unbelief. Ask American intellectuals who Jesus is, and how many can you name who bow before the Savior to declare with Thomas, *"My Lord and my God"*? A professor in Smith College wonders whether Jesus ever really existed. An American novelist classifies Christ with Nietzsche, the archinfidel. As this damnable denial increases, the Holy Spirit cries out to the believers of our land: "Christian America, wake up to the ugly truth that evil men are trying to tear the Savior from the hearts of our university youth, our high-school boys and girls, and, in some cases, our grade-school children! Support and promote education and culture that is *'not ashamed of the Gospel of Christ'!*"

Jesus comes repeatedly to American churches; yet again and again He finds them submerged in slumber. Many of you worship in groups that still set the Gospel aside to preach work-righteousness, urging you to buy your entrance into heaven. Some among you belong to the comfortable congregations in which the minister would never dream of hurting anyone's feelings, except, of course, to denounce our enemies across the seas and the public criminals, who never attend services to hear themselves assailed. Others support churches which cater to wealth, neglect the poor, feverishly feature card parties, gambling, theatricals, but leave the members little time and less interest for Bible study, fervent prayer, personal missionary work and spiritual life. With deep regret we recognized that the war has not visibly led all American churches closer to Christ. Before the handwriting of doom appears on the walls of many pretentious temples of unbelief, the Lord's eleventh-hour mercy cries out, "American churches, wake up! Repent! Return to God in His Son!"

Christ comes to each of you who bear His name, and often He finds even you sleeping, when you ought to be awake for Him and with Him. Making money, increasing money, investing money, saving money, spending money for luxury, sin, and selfishness, have become an obsession for many nominal Christians. Today, more than ever, the Savior's followers should be a separate people. Yet the love of sin, the devotion to evil, the pursuit of fleshly desires, the lure of lust, the selfishness of personal ambition, the mania of envy, hatred, strife, are tearing many from their Redeemer. How much real, active loyalty do you show Him — I mean the personal, pointed testimony to Him who is the sinner's last and only Hope? Multiplied millions are dying in this sin-cursed world without any knowledge of Jesus. Do you know that while we are being promised freedom from want, the recent famine in India took six million lives in the province of Bengal alone? But how many are dying spiritually all over the world from soul starvation? If you who say that you love the Son of God were ever forced to witness the death of an unbeliever, you certainly would be ready to rise from your sleep. Years ago, when Adoniram Judson, destined to become Burma's greatest missionary, was a college student without Christ, he spent a night at a country inn, next to the room in which a young man lay dying. As midnight crept slowly to dawn, Judson was forced to hear his shrieks of despair.

In the morning he learned that the young man who had screamed and moaned in horror until death took him had been his infidel chum at Brown University. The echo of his shrieking, dying cries of "death," "lost," "hell," gave Judson no rest, and finally led him to study for the ministry and devote his life to help the heathen world. What are you doing to awaken souls slumbering in sin? I do not know; but I am sure of this, that Christ is calling out to many of you, who with the Spirit's help could be mighty workers in the Kingdom: "Wake up! Watch, and work with Me for the salvation of souls!"

Again, the Savior comes to you who have willfully and repeatedly rejected Him, with His loudest warning and His strongest appeal. "Wake up, American unbelievers," He cries, "from the sleep of death!" No matter how you may pride yourselves on your achievements, your alertness, your success in business affairs, your zest of life, in God's sight you are spiritually dead. You are like the engineer on the Southern Pacific mail express which a few weeks ago in Utah crashed into a passenger train, killing fifty of our soldiers. Before the accident, while at the throttle, he died of a heart attack. He did not see the red signal and could not stop his train to avert disaster. You, too, may seem to ride on smoothly through life, but without Christ you are headed for death. Sometimes God in His mercy sends heavy, shocking blows to awaken you from your slumber. A patient in an Arizona sanatorium, experiencing this, wrote me: "If I never get cured, I will still thank God for sending me tuberculosis, because out here, alone, I found Jesus Christ as my Savior through your broadcast." Praise the Lord if He strikes you to the ground, makes you scream in agony, suffer crushing loss, until you are aroused from the sleep of death! Thank your heavenly Father if now, as the Savior appeals, "American unbelievers, stop your sinful slumber!" the Spirit prompts you to answer, "O Christ, send me sorrow and suffering, but awaken me to Thine all-compassionate, all-forgiving love!"

II

THE MASSES SHOULD AWAKEN TO CHRIST'S REDEEMING LOVE

Above all, every one of us should wake up to learn the blessed lessons of comfort and love which Christ would teach us in the Garden. We read that when Jesus found His disciples asleep the second time, *"He left them, and went away again."* Today, too, the Savior does not remain with those who repeatedly waste the time of repentance and return to Him. Jesus will not force you to accept His compassion. Some of you are sleeping away the last hours in your day of grace. Wake up to the marvel of your Lord's mercy before it is too late!

Jesus left the disciples, as our text records, *"and prayed the third time."* In every heavy hour of sorrow follow Christ and take your burdens to the Lord in repeated prayer! The newspapers reported that a B-29 bomber struggled back to its Saipan base with only two and a half engines, 147 holes in the fuselage and an unexploded Japanese shell over its fuel tank; yet not a single man of the crew was hurt. Why? Lieutenant Robert Sollok answers: "It must have been because every one of us was praying. I can assure you there were no atheists aboard. We had a good, spirited prayer meeting most of the way home." Similarly, pleading in Jesus' name can rescue you from ruin when all else fails. Therefore, America, wake up and pray!

Keep clearly in mind that the Savior *"prayed the third time, saying the same words"!* You see, God did not reply immediately, even to His Son; and in comparison with the sinless Christ, who are we to demand immediate response to our request? The Almighty's delays, as difficult as they seem, are not due to His inability to answer, but to some higher purpose in His program for your blessing. Therefore trust God, as His Son did, and know that His time, place, manner, and degree of granting your plea are always for your best! Wake up and, beholding Christ, *"pray without ceasing"* until your Father in His own best time answers you!

Note this especially: the ordeal of suffering for the sins of the world was so crushing that Jesus begged to have His cup of bitter anguish removed. Don't claim that Christ was a coward, afraid to face the cross now that it confronted Him! On the contrary, His courage has never been equaled by the bravest men. Yet the overwhelming, crushing, killing agony of body, mind, and soul, caused by our accumulated evils, was so horrifying that it made the sin-bearing Son of God gasp, *"O My Father, . . . let this cup pass from Me."* The Holy Spirit forbid that when you see your Redeemer wrestling in Gethsemane with the fearful forces of evil, you turn away cold and indifferent, to live on in further lust!

Yet in this last recorded prayer of our Savior before He was nailed to the cross He also pleaded, *"Nevertheless not My will, but Thine be done."* The Father's good and gracious will, the redemption of a sin-ruined world, was to be accomplished even if it cost Christ the pain which all the damned should have suffered, the God-forsakenness of the cross, the death-darkness of Calvary. What a marvelous Mediator He is — who *"having loved His own . . ., He loved them unto the end"!* Should our grateful faith not lead us to follow Him in submitting and surrendering to God's will? Beloved, especially in these evil days we may not be able to understand His leading, but more than ever, we, knowing that the God who *"spared not His own Son but delivered Him up for us all"* will *"freely give us all things"* necessary for our souls' salvation, should daily repeat His submissive *"Thy will be done!"* It takes heroic trust to repeat that prayer; yet born-again, faith-strengthened believers can rely on God even though He permits the slaying of their dear ones. A Minneapolis mother, deeply grounded in the faith, writes me: "My son Arthur was killed in action when a bomb exploded on his ship and took his and thirty-four other lives. You, no doubt, wonder how this is affecting me. I can say with a grateful heart that the Lord has been good. My boy was nineteen years old, and how he loved life! Yet he stood for the right, and he died the way he lived. Through Christ he was justified. How much better that it was my boy, who was ready, than some other boy who was not. . . . I have learned not to question God's ways, as they are always much more merciful than our ways. My husband went with us to church, and that he hasn't done in twenty years. Perhaps through our son's death his own father may find life." Is not that trustful reliance on Jesus the faith many of you need, now when sorrow and wickedness try to blast away the foundation of your lives?

Some of you, particularly those who do not know the Lord Jesus, are tempted to cast His direction aside and to say, "Not Thy will, but mine be done." The Holy

Spirit keep you from that fatal folly! A few weeks ago I pleaded with you men and women who are planning to ruin your own families by sinful divorce, and among the many important letters which came in answer were these lines from a Chicago woman: "I have listened to your Sunday broadcast only to turn you off several times, but this time I couldn't turn you off, even when every word you said was aimed directly at me. I am one of those women you mentioned . . . on the verge of a divorce. Until now I always thought my life was my own, and if I didn't like it, I could change it. We have three children. I never thought of their happiness but always preached hatred for their father. Your broadcast did something for me. Pray for me . . . to humble myself and get my family together again! You have something I wish I had. It must be wonderful to be a Christian. I wish I could be, but I am weak and have too many faults." I want to tell this woman, and all those who face similar sorrow, that as they thus wake up to the guilt of their sin, long for the Savior's greater grace, and submit to their heavenly Father's will, they can find the real joy of life and the one assurance of blessedness hereafter. Don't say, as the Chicago woman did, "I wish I could be a Christian, but I am weak and have too many faults"! Jesus wants you just as you are; and the weaker you are in your own sight, the more fully you lean on Him, the more completely you believe and declare:

> Just as I am, Thou wilt receive,
> Wilt welcome, pardon, cleanse, relieve;
> Because Thy promise I believe,
> O Lamb of God, I come, I come,

the more marvelous and magnificent His mercy will become to you, the more sure and certain your eternal salvation. Therefore throw away the sleeping pills of sin, the narcotics of vice, the anesthetics of unbelief, the drugs and opiates of iniquity, which seek to close your eyes to the salvation the Son of God offers everyone of you, by grace, through faith!

When you know that His solitary suffering in the Garden was for your deliverance, you may have to face many deep sorrows by yourself, without human help; but in Christ you can exult: "I am *'alone; and yet I am not alone,'* because the Father, the Son, and the Spirit are with me." *"Believe on the Lord Jesus,"* and God is always at your side! Last week I made an unforgettable visit to Dr. Carlsen's Home for Spastic Children at Pompano, on the Florida east coast. I saw children injured at birth triumphing over heavy handicaps; and I realized, as I saw twisted but happy faces, that the Savior offers constant companionship, especially to such little ones, and also your own underprivileged children. There I also heard of a father and mother, parents of a spastic boy, who, despairing of hope, planned to destroy themselves and their misshapen son. But God intervened and showed them that they were not alone nor without help. They discarded their suicide schedule, gave their child special training, and established a school for those similarly afflicted, in which many crippled and disfigured children have learned to become useful members of society. In a much higher sense I tell all of you weighted down by grim, dark loneliness, you gold-star parents, you isolated men and women in the armed forces, you deserted husbands and wives, you widows, orphans, and bereaved, you sick in sanatoria, homes for the incurable, and isolation hospitals, you men and women who have never married and who, as the years go on, find yourselves without relatives, you civil and military prisoners, you who have run away from your home and dear ones: Look to the agonized Sufferer in the Garden, and as He was delivered from death by His glorious resurrection, so, trusting Him in every lonely hour of trial, you will hear Him say, *"Lo, I am with you alway, even unto the end of the world"!* God grant that every one of you will wake up to the living grace of your Lord and to the assurance of His constant companionship! Amen!

A NEW TRIAL FOR CHRIST!

"There arose certain and bare false witness against Him, saying, We heard Him say, I will destroy this temple that is made with hands, and within three days I will build another made without hands. But neither so did their witness agree together. And the high priest stood up in the midst and asked Jesus, saying, Answerest Thou nothing? What is it which these witness against Thee? But He held His peace and answered nothing. Again the high priest asked Him and said unto Him, Art Thou the Christ, the Son of the Blessed? And Jesus said, I am; and ye shall see the Son of Man sitting on the right hand of Power and coming in the clouds of heaven." SAINT MARK 14:57-62.

PRECIOUS SAVIOR: Although we have often betrayed and denied Thee, who didst die on the cross for the full and free atonement of our many sins, we humbly beseech Thee, cast us not away! Rather restore and renew us through the Holy Spirit, that we repent of our evil and return to God by faith in Thy blood-bought mercies! May Thine enlightening, purifying Spirit lead unbelievers and scoffers to behold Thee on the cross, suffering the punishment of all human transgression, and acclaim Thee their Savior, Lord, and God! Humbly we ask Thee that Thou wouldst curb our inborn selfish desires and give us the willingness to sacrifice so that we may live to serve our fellow men! Endow the President and the Congress with the will and wisdom required to follow Thy revealed truth! Bless our people with obedience to Thy Word and the love of Thy salvation! Make us reverent and contrite, ready to receive the benediction of true peace by Thy power and for Thy glory! Hear us, precious Savior, who didst promise, "Him that cometh to Me I will in no wise cast out"! Help us, our mighty and merciful God! Amen!

A MEMBER of the Massachusetts legislature has introduced a bill which, if passed, will declare innocent all those who 253 years ago were falsely found guilty of witchcraft in Salem. The year 1692 brought a reign of terror to that town. Nineteen men and women, wickedly accused of entering into alliance with the devil and then practicing the black arts, were publicly hanged. One was crushed to death. Two died in prison, awaiting trial, and fifty-five were terribly tortured. So vicious and hysterical was this legalized murder that nineteen years later, in 1711, the Massachusetts colonial legislature declared the witch trials null and void. The jurors who had placed their signatures on the death warrants now signed a confession of their sins. Money awards were voted to bereaved relatives, and a whole day was set aside for public repentance. At that time, however, certain names were omitted from the list of those exonerated, and now the Massachusetts courts will again be asked to reverse the sentence of all those condemned in those terrifying trials.

Nineteen hundred years ago Jesus Christ was blasphemously accused of being allied with the devil. After facing a series of trials, which were wrong legally, wrong judicially, wrong morally, wrong politically (Jerusalem was fearfully destroyed because of this screaming injustice), He, the Son of God, was nailed to the cross between two crucified criminals. He had helped hundreds in their deepest sorrow and sickness, thousands in their hunger, tens of thousands in their soul needs — yet His enemies could not sentence Him to death quickly enough. He was condemned to the cross, contrary to Jewish law and Roman law, against human law and God's Law. Yet no one in official position has ever instituted a new trial for Christ or demanded that He be declared innocent.

Recently two men were sentenced to be hanged as Nazi spies. Their trial lasted more than a week, the jury sitting almost four hours before it gave its verdict; but the Son of God had no real trial, no fair jury, and the so-called hearing before His own people was over in a few hours. The Government gave those Nazis an attorney; yet Jesus had no one to plead for Him; even His friends deserted Him. The sentences imposed on those two enemy spies will be examined by a United States general; after he finishes, a board of review in Washington will further study the case; when they complete their work, the whole matter goes before the President. All this will take weeks, and the spies, who were captured last December, will probably have at least four months of life between their arrest and execution. How different the trial of Jesus! No one reviewed His sentence; no one except the hate-inflamed mobs who screamed: *"Crucify Him! Crucify Him!" "His blood be on us, and on our children!" "Away with Him!"* The entire time consumed by His betrayal, the arrest, the various hearings, the pronouncement of the death sentence, the torturous journey from Jerusalem to Calvary, the crucifixion itself, and His death was less than eighteen hours.

Although the Salem witches will twice be exonerated before Massachusetts tribunals, no one with official power has ever sought to declare Jesus innocent. There has been talk of a retrial for the Redeemer which would reverse His death sentence and reaffirm His innocence; yet, no formal step has ever been taken. One of the Savior's countrymen could immortalize his name by starting legal procedure which would declare the Savior's trial a monstrous mistrial and publicly reveal it as the hideous, hate-filled atrocity it was, all history's lowest, vilest, cruelest miscarriage of justice. However, instead of waiting for such action, let us today, in the midst of a world which still condemns Jesus, ask

A NEW TRIAL FOR CHRIST

in our country, our churches, our homes, and our hearts! May God's Holy Spirit lead especially you unbelievers, scoffers, infidels, who have already condemned the Savior, to grant Him a new hearing and then to render the revised verdict: "Jesus, falsely accused and wantonly crucified, is indeed the Son of God, the sinless, stainless Savior of my soul!" God help us to find this conviction in the truth of our text, Saint Mark, chapter fourteen, verses fifty-seven to sixty-two: *"There arose certain and bare false witness against Him, saying, We heard Him say, I will destroy this temple that is made with hands, and within three days I will build another made without hands. But neither so did their witness agree together. And the high priest stood up in the midst and asked Jesus, saying, Answerest Thou nothing? What is it which these witness against Thee? But He held His peace and answered nothing. Again the high priest asked Him and said unto Him, Art Thou the Christ, the Son of the Blessed? And Jesus said, I am; and ye shall see the Son of Man sitting on the right hand of Power and coming in the clouds of heaven."*

I

REJECT ALL FALSE WITNESSES!

From beginning to end the Good Friday trial was marked with wicked untruth and willful perjury. Today, lying under oath is regarded by many as a fine art, and the courts of our country are filled with this falsehood. Divorce hits high figures when, even in districts far removed from the usual centers of domestic debauch, the number of divorce decrees last year exceeded the number of marriage licenses. In many of the divorce trials husbands and wives commit studied perjury — and then foolishly think they can find happiness through falsehood.

The war, of course, has also produced an army of false witnesses. A few days ago the Comptroller General of the United States told a committee of the House of Representatives that in his opinion waste and crookedness in war contracts have cost the people of the United States fifty billion dollars. If you have six members in your household you will pay $2,400 for this dishonesty, and every step in this graft, bribery, corruption, has been marked by false oaths, untrue sworn testimony. All this, however, shocking as it is, may be only the beginning. Do you remember the scandalous revelations which followed World War I? They may be dwarfed in comparison when the story of World War II can be told, with the sordid record of grand-scale thefts in the cost-plus system — committed under sworn contracts. Be careful that you do not commit perjury! If unforgiven, it will consign your soul to hell. Never forget, it sent Christ to the cross!

Note that many false witnesses testified against Jesus, men, doubtless from Jerusalem's gutter and its gold coast, united in meanness and malice. How could anyone hate our Lord and testify against Him? we ask. Why should anyone hate Him today, when His divine love and power are directly responsible for everything good we enjoy? There is only one true answer: Black sin in the human heart, poisoned perversity in the soul, utter depravity in the mind without Christ. It is the same hellish hostility which makes atheists on this side of the Atlantic publish attacks on our Lord so vile and vicious that the Post Office Department ought to bar them forever from the mails, and which leads atheists across the ocean to print caricatures of Jesus so dirty and degrading that we wonder why the earth does not swallow them alive. How damnable the chatter about the inborn goodness of man and his gleaming virtues in an age which witnessed the widest war in human annals and then, not satisfied, waited only twenty-five years until it started a second global struggle, in which American losses already are more than twice as great as in the first conflict! How long before this impenitent, godless, ruthless race hurls itself into another total war only God knows. Yet everyone of us should know that when the next struggle breaks, because of the blackness of the human heart — and men without the Almighty are the same over the whole world, whether they are German or Japanese, British or American — it will be indescribably more destructive even than the present bloodshed and will massacre many more millions of civilians. I thank God publicly that over in England church leaders, Episcopal, Catholic, Baptist, Methodist, Congregational, Presbyterian, Quaker, and of other denominations, have issued an appeal asking Christians everywhere to protest against the shocking ruthlessness of war. I join them and ask you to protest against all brutality. If the Prophet Amos had to indict Old Testament nations for slaughtering a few hundred women and children, what must God say of us today when blockbusters kill thousands of babies, in-

A New Trial for Christ! 65

valids, and innocent civilians? The crying need of this bleeding hour is the recognition of the ruinous depravity in the human heart, that boastful bestiality which today, too, would sentence Jesus to the cross.

The men in Jerusalem behind the perjury and perversion were of the clergy, not those of the lower ranks, but of the upper classes, including the high priest himself. Envy, jealousy, unbelief, poisoned the minds of these officials, who should have been closest to the Son of God and realized how exactly He fulfilled the promises foretelling the coming of the Messiah. Men who were to save souls became murderers; clergymen, killers; priests, satanic schemers. That is the tragic trouble with too many churches today: their leaders deny our Savior's Word instead of declaring it, reject His grace instead of receiving it, ridicule the Gospel instead of revering it. Frequently officers, editors, theological professors, the very men who should be firm in the faith, promote this disloyalty. Not long ago a large official church paper printed without rebuke a statement asserting that Paul's "doctrine of the atonement and his Christology may not be the best for the twentieth century. . . . Salvation means character, and that involves the highest exercise of our minds, wills, and emotions. Any other salvation would be immoral. . . . All doctrine must change if it is to work at all." That rejection of Christ's divine redemption and atonement has eaten its cancerous way into many large denominations. Frequently the most important positions, leadership on mission boards, teaching positions in divinity schools, calls to the fashionable and best-paid pulpits in the land, are given men who put a question mark behind every fundamental fact of the Christian faith as it has been summarized in Scripture. Under their destructive direction many churches have become creedless, cold, and worldly-minded. A dispatch from London tells us that a new congregation there is to have "a hall for movies and stage plays, dressing rooms, club rooms, rest rooms, clinics . . . a restaurant, and buffet," where, the minister explains, "we can give people a cup of tea." — All the paraphernalia required for entertainment, food, health, and rest, but not a word about Christ! The same spirit prevails in our country, where religious groups have rejected the divine, atoning Redeemer just as completely as did Caiaphas, the haughty high priest in Jerusalem. We have modernist churches, social churches, worldly churches, money-minded churches, power-crazed churches, fashion-blinded churches, entertaining churches, slumbering churches, paralyzed churches, salvation-by-works churches, spiritually dead churches — all these without the red-blooded courage required to preach the crucified Christ as the redemption of sin-ruined men and women, unwilling to testify courageously and defiantly to the cleansing power of His blood. Therefore many churches have failed dismally, just as Caiaphas and the Jerusalem clergy failed. Much of the agony under which our age groans could be removed if believers would conscientiously stand up for Jesus, and boycott evil, as He has instructed us. If every Christian in America would vow not to enter places of gambling, even those with pinball machines and slot machines, this evil could be checked. If church attendants would refuse to vote a political ticket listing candidates with shadowy practices, crooks, grafters, promoters of immorality, and, instead, put consecrated Christian men into office, America would be a far better nation. If every believer in the country would keep his distance from dirty motion pictures and work to have others boycott filmed vice, it would not be necessary for an Ohio friend to write me, "My Protestant church cannot stop even one filthy movie, and that cries to high heaven." If those who love the Lord Jesus, yet somehow have preachers who silence the message of the cleansing blood, reject the atoning cross, ridicule the open grave, poke fun at the new birth and the work of the Holy Spirit, would cry out in unmistakable protest against this clerical betrayal of the Savior, many churches otherwise doomed to spiritual destruction could be saved. If American Christians would see to it that their pulpits preach the full, free Gospel of grace in the God-man Jesus; if they themselves would testify to the assured hope of heaven they have in their Redeemer, a spiritual force of tremendous blessing would be set to work. Until our churches come back to Christ, back to the Bible, back to the cross, back to the blood, back to the atonement; until preachers go all out for God, and not for personal glory; until they become *"all things to all men,"* by self-denial and self-sacrifice following in the Savior's footsteps; until denominations forget the delusions of grandeur, wealth, power, and increase a hundredfold the energies with which they direct people to Jesus — the churches in our country cannot hope for the top and bottom, inward and outward reformation of religious life that America sorely needs.

Finally priestly scheming and bribery produced two men, who, as we read, *"bare false witness against Him, saying, We heard Him say, I will destroy this temple that is made with hands, and within three days I will build another made without hands."* Jesus never said this. His enemies, under oath, put words into His mouth that He never uttered. What He did say was, *"Destroy this temple,"* meaning His body, *"and in three days I will raise it up,"* referring to His Easter victory. And that was true. They nailed Him to the cross; He died; but on the third day He was resurrected. A million liars cannot change that basic truth. Another million modernist preachers, were they to scream at the top of their voices, could not remove the Easter miracle. You can build your eternal hope on that. Because Christ arose from the grave, you too can challenge, *"O Death, where is thy sting? O Grave, where is thy victory?"* Because He lives, you too shall live. Your body may be disfigured, as war produces shocking mutilation, as many thousands of our men suffer the loss of one or more of their limbs. Yet, however badly bruised and broken you may be, believe that Jesus, the heavenly Architect, will rebuild the temple of your body without physical defects, without mar or blemish. What a radiant reunion in that reawakening! O God, bring us all to Christ for heavenly glory!

The mistake of those false witnesses was repeated during the Savior's entire life. Christ could hardly speak a truth pertaining to the soul without having it erroneously explained of the body. He promised Nicodemus the new birth, that is, the new existence which the believers enter by faith through the Holy Spirit; yet Nicodemus, that master in Israel, wondered how he, an old man, could become a child and enter the world again as at his first birth. Our Lord offered the woman at Jacob's Well in Samaria the living water, that is, the lifegiving, life-sustaining faith in His mercies, which can satisfy all thirst of the soul; but that woman, misinterpreting, immediately begged Him for the water which would never leave her thirsty. Jesus told His disciples that He had spiritual food, heavenly strength, and immediately they thought that some unseen friend had privately brought Him a meal. Our Savior, speaking of His crucifixion and death, told His hearers, *"Whither I go, ye cannot come,"* and at once they whispered, *"Will He kill Himself?"* He promised His countrymen, *"The truth shall make you free,"* meaning the freedom from the dominion of sin, death, and hell, but His hearers thought of earthly, political liberty and protested that they had never been slaves. Even on the cross, when He cried, *"My God, My God, why hast Thou forsaken Me?"* the cruel, curious mob speculated that He might be calling on Elijah.

This misunderstanding has continued and increased in our day. By one of the deepest tragedies in modern life too many teachers, forgetting that *"the letter killeth, but the spirit giveth life,"* have misinterpreted and misapplied the Savior's truth, mistakenly turning spiritual promises into bodily pledges. By twisting and tearing our Lord's words, by reading new thoughts into them, by ripping His statements out of their context, teachers of error today have likewise advanced the wildest anti-Scriptural doctrines. This soul blindness has helped divide Christianity into scores of schisms and sects, while Jesus on the very night of His betrayal repeatedly prayed that all believers may be one before the world. This substitution of man's mind for God's has produced untold hardships in the churches. Our Lord has clearly declared that no one on earth can foretell the time when the world will end and He will return to hold judgment; yet men who claim to know more than the Son of God have repeatedly set the time for the last moment, only to deceive themselves and others. Misguided teachers have proclaimed that Christ will establish peace among the nations, although He Himself has declared, *"Think not that I am come to send peace on earth";* and when war curses a generation, as it has ours, they are rebuked and discredited. Often, likewise, our Savior's words are misinterpreted and used against Him by His enemies. Look at the literature published by the American Association for the Advancement of Atheism, and you will see how men have worked overtime in the attempt to put false meaning or fictitious sense into the statements of the Gospel, just as many people claim that Jesus has failed to keep His promise, since He has not answered their selfish, destructive prayers.

Yet, even as the testimony of those perjured witnesses did not agree, so in our own day the accusations of infidels contradict each other. We have glaring proof in the many volumes written to discredit the Bible. Critics have torn the five books bearing Moses' name from him; yet when they are asked to mention the author of these portions of Scripture, they disagree violently. No two outstanding enemies of the divine truth are entirely agreed as to who, exactly, wrote each part of the Old and New Testaments, just as the critics of Christ are not united in every point of their opposition. Their whole testimony is contradictory and mutually exclusive. It must be so, because every one (and I include the big-name, headline infidels of our day) who raises any charge against our Lord is a liar and on the losing side. Jesus challenged His enemies, *"Which of you convinceth Me*

A New Trial for Christ! 71

of sin?" and all those blasphemous wretches could do was to lie, call Christ a Samaritan and charge that He had a devil. But His challenge, *"Which of you convinceth Me of sin?"* still remains unaccepted. Scoffers have raised millions of dollars to show what they call the mistakes of Christianity, but they have all failed. Hundreds of books have been written to expose the so-called errors of the Gospel, but they are full of mistakes. Every action of Christ, every word He spoke, every doctrine He taught, has been examined under the microscope of the closest investigation by His bitterest enemies. But where — I challenge any of you atheists and infidels in this audience to produce a single instance — has He, the Son of God, ever spoken an untrue word, ever given a dishonest promise, ever done a harmful deed, ever issued an evil command, ever endorsed a wicked plan, ever encouraged an impure desire? When the shouting and the tumult of treacherous slander subsides, God's Son and Mary's is still the stainless Savior, whom all critics and atheists cannot successfully attack. He remains perfect in His purity, complete in His holiness, flawless in His deity, untouched by evil in His love for sinful, suffering mankind.

If you have any other opinion of your Redeemer; if somehow you have found fault with Him and therefore reject His mercy; if you are one of those overbearing, insolent individuals who abuse His holy name in profanity; if you have been one of those self-satisfied know-it-alls who has been content to classify Christ with human reformers, marked by all their weakness and woe, then give Him a new trial before your conscience! Review the story of His suffering! See if you can honestly lay a single charge against Him! Many who have hated Jesus, but who, led by the Spirit, have studied His life have been turned from denial to deep faith. History is filled with startling examples of infidels who, re-examining the Gospel of grace, changed the verdict given by the council of the Savior's countrymen, *"He is guilty of death,"* into, "He is absolutely innocent."

The deep-rooted trouble, of course, is that some of you are not interested enough in the truth to read the Scriptures. In November of last year a young army flier stopped in the Detroit Statler Hotel for a few days and placed $500 in a Gideon Bible in his room for safe-keeping. He had left the hotel and was on his way to Alaska, when he missed the money. Mentally retracing his many stops, he remembered that Detroit incident and telegraphed the Statler manager to examine the Bible in the room he had occupied. Since his departure several others had lived in the same room. If they had opened the Gideon Bible, they would have discovered the money; but the manager found it still within the covers of Scripture and returned it. With treasures of far greater value than $500 close to them in their Bibles, millions of Americans leave these spiritual riches untouched. If only they would delve deeply into the wealth of Holy Writ, they could find that, while Christ is not guilty of any charge which sinful men have raised against Him, they themselves are guilty before God and their own conscience of damning, soul-destroying sin. A Pomona, California, listener recently wrote me that two soldiers, AWOL, armed with a machine gun, held up the filling station in which he worked. They opened the cash register, filled with bills and coins, but suddenly closed it, left the money, and drove away. Why? Before the cash register lay a New Testament open at Hebrews 4:12 and the words, *"The Word of God is quick and powerful and sharper than any two-edged sword . . . a discerner of the thoughts and intents of the heart."* My beloved, may the Holy Spirit send that quick, powerful, and sharp Word into your heart, to convince you, in a new trial, that Jesus is the sinless, spotless Lamb of God, while you, on the contrary, are false, full of shame and sin!

II

ACCLAIM HIM YOUR SAVIOR AND YOUR GOD!

When the testimony of the conflicting false witnesses collapsed, the chief priest, as a last resort, tried to force Jesus to talk, hoping He could be made to say something which would convict Him. We read: *"The high priest stood up in the midst and asked Jesus, saying, Answerest Thou nothing? What is it which these witness against Thee?"* Yet the startling record testifies, *"He held His peace and answered nothing."* In fulfillment of Isaiah's 700-year-old prophecy, *"As a sheep before her shearers is dumb, so He openeth not His mouth,"* our Lord refused to reply to Caiaphas, the arch criminal in priestly robes. Why? Not because He was afraid of consequences, but because He, the All-knowing, understood that nothing He might say would restrain His enemies from their bloody course. He could have delivered a defense which would completely outrank the most brilliant oratorical plea ever made in any court; He could have sent the whole smirking Sanhedrin sprawling helplessly on the ground as He had hurled the armed mob prostrate in Gethsemane. He could have wiped out Jerusalem in an instant, but He did not; He kept His silence. Here is Heaven's highest mercy: He wanted to suffer for you; He wanted to go to the cross there to atone for your transgressions; He wanted to die that death of agony and shame to give you everlasting life. Though He had a hundred opportunities to escape and utterly destroy His accusers, yet, spurning them altogether, He permitted Himself to be beaten and blasphemed so that you could be freed from the fear of hell. What marvelous mercy!

A few days ago I was privileged to read a touching letter from a young lieutenant who several times sang in the chorus on this program. Explaining that probably he would soon be rushed to the front lines, he wrote his young wife: "Next to God, you are everything to me, my darling. It's because I love you so very much, and you're so very sweet. In my prayers every day and night I ask: 'Father in heaven, I commit to Thy protecting care the dear one from whom I am for the time separated. All that I would gladly do for her, if I could, do Thou for her, if it be for her good and according to Thy Fatherly will! If she is in danger, protect her! If she is in sorrow, comfort her! If she is happy, make her happier still! If she is sick, grant her Thy healing!' And then, darling, I add this: 'Father in heaven, if it be Thy will that I shall not again see my darling wife, Velma, whom I love next to Thee, I beseech Thee, heavenly Father, through Thy grace and mercy and unfathomable omnipotence, and for the sake of Thy Son, Jesus, who died for us and all sinners, to let me see my darling Velma in heaven. This I pray in Jesus' name! Amen.'" If only every husband could share the devotion of this young Christian who wrote, "Sweetheart, I'll be fighting for your and my stake in this better world of freedom, democracy, right to worship, and all the other good things we're fighting for, but especially for your share, my darling"; who added this postscript, "Honey, the One Hundred and Twenty-first Psalm is my daily reading for you"; and who, by God's mysterious, unfathomable ways, was killed in action soon afterward in Belgium! Even such love, however unusual and unselfish as it is, cannot stand beside Christ's devotion to you and me. He loved not only those who loved Him but those who hated Him; He faced danger and death not because He had to, but because He wanted to.

Has His love won your heart? Has His marvelous, merciful compassion so stirred your soul that you love Him above yourself and others? It is not enough that you are religious; that you are sincere; that you have been confirmed; that you belong to a church; that you attend services; that you support your congregation, sing in the choir, serve as officer of a youth program, a ladies' aid, or an entire congregation; that you are the Sunday school superintendent, or even the pastor of a church. These privileges are glorious aids to a Christian life, but the first and most essential requirement, without which you can never see God, is: you must love Jesus as your Savior and Substitute, your Guide and God.

This becomes clear from our text. The high priest, enraged by the silent Sufferer's refusal to speak, directed one more question to Him, the last and all-decisive: *"Art Thou the Christ, the Son of the Blessed?"* Here, then, was the climax issue, which would make or break the Savior's conviction. If that poor, haggard, harassed, peace-robbed Prisoner — so Caiaphas reasoned — now completely overpowered by His enemies, would dare to repeat what He had previously declared and insist that

He was Christ, the Son of God, His own words would convict Him. This, then, was one of history's great crisis moments, when the two high priests faced each other — Caiaphas, arrogant, sensual, scheming, murder-minded, and Christ, calm, sinless, stainless, majestic even in His sorrow; and because further silence would have been misunderstood, Jesus answered decisively, "*I am.*"

Only two words, but what an eternity of meaning! "*I am!*" He cries out to a world of unbelief. "*'I am'* the Christ, the long-promised Anointed of God, the Redeemer from ruin, predicted on that ancient day of tragedy when sin entered the world, the suffering Servant of the Lord, of whom Old Testament prophecy foretold, '*He was wounded for our transgressions, He was bruised for our iniquities; the chastisement of our peace was upon Him, and with His stripes we are healed. . . . The Lord hath laid on Him the iniquity of us all*'; '*I am*' the Christ whom Zechariah, long before Judas' day, saw betrayed for thirty pieces of silver, whom Isaiah previsioned as counted with the criminals, whom David beheld with hands and feet nailed to the cross.

"'*I am*' your Christ, Caiaphas," Jesus implied, just as He could tell you who are living and dying in sin, priding yourself in your unbelief, boasting of your brazenness in transgressing God's Law and man's: "'*I am*' your Christ. Therefore, compute the awful curse on your evil ways! Then come, penitent and believing, to My mercy, for, '*Him that cometh to Me I will in no wise cast out!*'"

Now, if a mere man should speak these words, we should be obliged to classify them with the exaggerated promises and the cunning falsehoods through which dictators, selfish politicians, and international schemers have decoyed millions into disaster and death. But, praise God! Jesus is more than the greatest man, the strongest man, the wisest man, the kindest man, more than all men in their total strength, wisdom, greatness, and goodness. He is more than patriarchs, prophets, and priests, more than kings, emperors, and presidents, more than cherubim, seraphim, and archangels; He is, as He told Caiaphas, *"the Son of the Blessed,"* yes, God Himself, coequal with the Father and Spirit. Listen, then, as His triumphant *"I am the Son of God!"* rings throughout a world in which a large part, even of the churches, denies His deity and craftily seeks to palm off a counterfeit Christ, who is only a leader, a teacher, a model, a reformer, a revolutionist, even a Communist, as they like to claim today — anything except the true, triumphant God! Believe with your whole soul that Jesus is God almighty, with the help you need in every difficulty; God all-knowing, with the guidance you require in dark days like these; God all-comforting, with the love and consolation you must have if you are not to be crushed by your increasing burden; God all-merciful, whose blood, shed on the cross for you, cleanses you *"from all sin";* God all-faithful, who stands by you when friends, even family, fail you; God all-embracing, who yearns for you, no matter how men may despise your skin, your nationality, your low social rank, your modest means, and your unpretentious home! Fellow sinners and fellow redeemed, hear it again, for it cannot be told you too often: this Christ, on trial before Caiaphas a few hours before He goes to be crucified on Calvary, is nothing less than your God and your Savior, who loved you and gave Himself for you, and who is yours — without price or payment, merit or worthiness, contribution or character, good resolutions, good intentions, good works — simply by faith and through His divine grace! Prophets predicted it, Evangelists recorded it, Apostles reaffirmed it, converted sinners testified to it, glorified saints exalted it, devils conceded it, angels asserted it, the Father publicly proclaimed it, the Son repeatedly taught it, the Spirit constantly certified it: Jesus is the everlasting Son of God!

If until this moment you have denied these basic, blessed truths; if you have never thought much of our Lord and have been satisfied to dismiss Him with the impression that He was, perhaps, an ideally minded Friend of the human race and nothing more, I beg of you, give Him a new trial! Get down on your knees today, now, and ask the Spirit's help in believing and accepting the real Redeemer! I pray that this day many of you will turn from sin to the Savior. What joy you could have in Him!

Give Christ a new trial in your heart and soul as you take time to read His Word and every week to hear it in a true Gospel church! The *Wall Street Journal* reports that during the tobacco shortage thirty-two million American smokers spent an average of fifteen minutes daily searching for cigarets. This means a full day's working time for one million persons, or eight million man-hours a day. If that were devoted to prayer, Bible-searching, and the works of faith — is it asking too much to give God at least the time devoted to cigarets which help burden large numbers of American young people with consumption and other serious diseases? — masses in our country could be shown the way of their salvation. In Jesus' name I plead with you: Give Christ a new trial, a real trial, a fair trial, an open trial — and the happiness of heaven will be yours!

Unless you grant Jesus that trial and receive Him as your Redeemer, a truly terrifying trial awaits you. Listen to the last words our Lord spoke there before His countrymen: *"Ye shall see the Son of Man sitting on the right hand of Power and coming in the clouds of heaven"!* He would come again, He declared, not as the judged, but as the Judge, both of the living and of the dead. My countrymen, the hour of His return is at hand. All the signs foretelling His second advent are being fulfilled as never before. Captain Eddie Rickenbacker, World War I ace, holds that we may be headed — and these are his very words — "toward a third world war, in which robot planes and bombs will destroy not only man and his works but the very soil itself." He believes that the bomb may soon be developed which will literally wipe out all life on our planet. Now, if mere men, as Rickenbacker specifically predicts, "will be able to sit at home, press buttons, and destroy at will Paris, London, Rome, Berlin, New York, Washington, Chicago, Miami, or San Francisco" — cannot the Almighty, before whom mankind is as dust, keep His word and annihilate the world, when our royal Redeemer, now enthroned at His right hand, returns as Judge?

Oh, while there is still time, before the midnight of man's madness closes the day of grace, give Christ a new trial! For the salvation of your souls, for real peace with God and your fellow men, for hope and happiness, for the blessings of the Father, the love of the Son, and the guidance of the Comforter, change His sentence of guilt to this verdict: O Christ, in all truth and triumph, Thou art the Son of God, the Savior of the world, the Redeemer of my soul! The Holy Spirit strengthen you in this assurance for Jesus' sake! Amen!

HOW DO YOU BEHOLD THE MAN?

"Then came Jesus forth, wearing the crown of thorns and the purple robe. And Pilate saith unto them, Behold the Man! When the chief priests, therefore, and officers saw Him, they cried out, saying, Crucify Him, crucify Him! Pilate saith unto them, Take ye Him, and crucify Him; for I find no fault in Him. The Jews answered him, We have a law, and by our law He ought to die, because He made Himself the Son of God." SAINT JOHN 19:5-7.

CHRIST, OUR KING, OUR SAVIOR, OUR GOD: Help us behold Thee with the eyes of faith that find in Thy suffering, crucifixion, and death the gleam of heavenly brightness for our dark day and the unfailing light for all gloom in our own lives! Show us, as we study Thine agony anew, that because of our transgressions we are lost and condemned without Thee, but that since Thou didst take the sins of the entire world upon Thyself, heaven, hope, and happiness are ours always through trusting Thy saving truth! Make us a humbled, hallowed people, reliant on Thy mercy and guidance! Comfort all in distress and danger, particularly Thy children in the Army, Navy, Merchant Marine, whose souls are exposed to constant peril! We thank Thee for the victories Thou Thyself hast granted us, for we know that Thou art the God who alone dost make war cease until the end of the earth. Send Thy Holy Spirit into many hearts throughout the land, to give the oppressed Thy soul peace, the spiritually hungered the bread of life, the destitute and forsaken the promise of Thine unfailing companionship! Enrich us with the assurance of Thy sin-destroying, sorrow-conquering love! Hear us, precious Savior, as Thou hast promised! Amen!

How Do You Behold the Man?

THE most urgent question to be answered by everyone of you, soldiers and civilians, men and women, young and old, rich and ragged, scientists and simple folk, capitalists and laborers, politicians and plain citizens, believers and blasphemers — the vital question for war and peace, Church and State, soul and body, heart and mind, the question of questions for the United States and Canada, for this continent and the rest of the world, for the Big Four and the less-than-the-dust seventy million outcastes in India, is — God help every one of you answer it aright today! — "Who is Jesus Christ?" Other penetrating personal inquiries stir multitudes in our country today; yet incomparably more important is this issue, involving life or death, heaven or hell, for each one of you: Who is Jesus, and what is He to you?

Recently an interesting book appeared which gives the opinion of four hundred men and women, past and present, concerning Christ. Some of these statements, repeating the testimony of the Old Testament and the New, of psalmists and sages, disciples and apostles, acclaim Him Lord and Savior and say, *"To Him be glory both now and forever!"* For the most part, however, His Godhead and grace are rejected. Jesus is called "the author of the Golden Rule," "a hero," "a genius," "a reformer," "a martyr," "a romanticist," "a mystic," "a humanitarian," "a prophet," "a poet," "an example," "a pattern," "a teacher," "a peasant," "a carpenter," "a rabbi," "a leader," "a friend," "a guide," "a good guide," "a lonely figure," "an inspired Galilean," "a man of great power," "a virtuous, amiable man," "a wise man," "a man among men," "a man of balanced character," "a remarkable personality," "a symbolic figure," "a crystal figure," "a psychologist," "a son of his time," "an advocate of eugenics," "a revolutionary," "an interpreter," "a pillar of democracy," "an opponent of capitalism," "a father of socialism," "a promoter of the social gospel," "a Communist opposed to private property," "a pious person," "a ragged, unlearned young Jew" — and, besides these forty-two, a score of similar names. Not a few of the distinguished authors cited in this book use the superlative and call our Lord "the greatest moral reformer," "the greatest wit our world has ever known," "the greatest rebel of history," "one of the greatest of the gay philosophers," even "the one superman of history"; yet all these titles fall far short of expressing devotion to a divine and delivering Christ. Some of these writers, whom the world greets as great, dare to question whether Jesus ever lived, while others do not hesitate to put Him on the same level with Buddha, Baruch Spinoza, Walt Whitman, Shelley, Sophocles, and even the madman Nietzsche.

The book which presents all these opinions is called *Behold the Man!* — the very words spoken by Pontius Pilate during the Savior's trial. Because many of you are in danger of continuing to *"behold the Man"* with the mistaken, jaundiced, poisoned, blurry vision that finds in Him only a man, although the highest, only an example, even though the best; and because every one of you, under the inevitable necessity of giving your reply when asked, "Who is Jesus?" should this day learn the triumphant truth, I ask you to stand in spirit with Jesus, bound and beaten, as He was led into Pilate's court, and in the conviction which, I pray, will help turn you to your salvation, answer this all-important question,

HOW DO YOU BEHOLD THE MAN?

May the Spirit give each of you the faith and fortitude required to declare, "I behold Him as my King, my suffering Savior, my God of glory" — the very answer we can find in our text, Saint John, chapter nineteen, verses five to seven: *"Then came Jesus forth, wearing the crown of thorns and the purple robe. And Pilate said unto them, Behold the Man! When the chief priests, therefore, and officers saw Him, they cried out, saying, Crucify Him, crucify Him! Pilate saith unto them, Take ye Him, and crucify Him; for I find no fault in Him. The Jews answered him, We have a law, and by our law He ought to die, because He made Himself the Son of God."*

I

BEHOLD IN HIM YOUR KING!

Pontius Pilate, the Roman governor before whom Christ was brought in His life-and-death trial, was an ambitious, power-craving politician, the like of whom we today have far too many. Convinced that Jesus was absolutely innocent, the Victim of priestly envy and hatred, Pilate took these steps in our Lord's behalf: First, he tried to make his silent, majestic Prisoner speak in His own defense. Second, He sought to have Him released instead of Barabbas. Third, Pilate received the warning by his wife against issuing the death sentence. Fourth, he demanded of the Savior's accusers, *"What evil hath He done?"* Fifth, he reported that Herod found no guilt in Christ. Sixth, he repeatedly stated, *"I find in Him"* not only *"no cause of death"* but also *"no fault at all."* Seventh, he called Jesus *"a just Person."* Eighth, he steadfastly *"sought to release Him."* Ninth, even when he scourged Him, he hoped that this terrifying cruelty would satisfy the bloodthirsty persecutors and thus save His life. Tenth, he repeatedly placed the bruised and beaten Nazarene on exhibition before His enemies to soften their hard hearts. You see, Pilate did about everything but accept Christ, defend Him to the end, and release Him. He even tried to cleanse his conscience and relieve himself of personal guilt by washing his hands of the whole trial.

If men cannot purify their hands even by the use of the most powerful antiseptics, how much less can they hope to rid their souls of responsibility in rejecting the Redeemer? Nations can hardly be neutral in war, and no man can ever be neutral toward Christ. Jesus Himself clearly warned us, *"He that is not with Me is against Me."* World leaders should learn this truth. I have been savagely attacked in certain newspapers because I have dared to say that the Crimean conference will fail in keeping its promise of no more war and want for everyone of humanity's two billions, now and here ever after. With the support of the Bible, I still maintain that this entire Yalta program of world reorganization will fail, not because it does not mention God, but because some of the participants directly oppose Him. Think of it, in America I am assailed for asking that the Almighty be accorded His place in a new world order! The mention of God might offend atheists! Only last week a national news magazine printed a revealing story about one of the highest of the high, the mention of whose name would cause a University of Chicago instructor to raise some stupid, vicious charge against me. That world leader, habitually pictured with a cigar in his mouth, was recently admonished by a friend: "You very seldom go to church. Do you give any support to the Church?" He answered, "I do, like a buttress, *from the outside.*" We need far more who will support the church as pillars from the inside; who will not grudgingly and distantly endorse its work, as a man sends alimony to a divorced wife, but instead go all out for the Lord; world figures who will speak not only of God, the Supreme Potentate, but also of Jesus; who will not only pray but plead in that Redeemer's name; who will never permit or sanction any program opposed to the clear Word. Can you imagine what would happen if all those in charge of human affairs would go inside the Church? By the Holy Spirit's blessing we could have the happiest and best age men have ever known. A Christian professor in China's Nanking University maintains that America's annual bill for chewing gum and cosmetics is large enough to provide a hundred times as many missionaries as were ever sent to Japan at one time. With Jesus, international leaders could rebuild the world for mutual co-operation instead of suicidal competition; without Him, though infidels may promote powerful alliances, though statesmen may call men the masters of their own souls, though power politics may blueprint an entirely new era, in which science and military might are to guarantee the peace, all this is only a dream and a delusion.

Pilate refused to take the decisive step and acquit Christ, just as many of you, not in high places, have never received and have therefore rejected Jesus. You say that you hold nothing against the Church; yet you keep your distance from it. This is the more serious for those of you who once knew the truth, but who today have broken your vows of loyalty and are actually numbered with the Savior's enemies. Little by little, some of you have permitted yourselves to be coaxed from your Lord. Psychologists tell us that if one pours boiling water into a pail with a frog, it will immediately jump to safety; but if you place a frog into a pail with cold water, it will not leap out even if you gradually add enough hot water finally to scald it to death. Similarly some of you would have resisted any sudden, bold, blasphemous rejection of Christ; yet you have permitted unbelievers, who started with apparently insignificant denials of Holy Writ, to feed you constantly increasing doses of spiritual poison, until today you are without the Church, without Jesus, without pardon, peace, and the promise of heaven. God have mercy on your souls! Now, while there is still time, before the doors of grace are closed on you, repent, return to your merciful Redeemer! Revere Him, instead of rejecting Him! Pilate, we have reason to believe, ended with a suicide's despair and damnation. The Holy Spirit keep all of you who write me that you have come to the end of your help and hope from that terrifying eternal curse, by showing you your Savior's limitless love!

To win popular approval, Pilate permitted the soldiers to robe Christ in mock royalty, and to press upon His whitened brow that sarcastic wreath of cutting thorns. We read: *"Then came Jesus forth, wearing the crown of thorns and the purple robe. And Pilate saith unto them, Behold the Man!"* The cold, calloused Roman governor wanted to excite public sympathy, just as many a shrewd defense attorney places his client before the jury, emphasizes his suffering, seeks to have him acquitted, at least less severely sentenced, since he has already endured much or because he is harmless, helpless, misunderstood. The Roman governor never dreamt that his three words, *"Behold the Man,"* would live forever. However unknowingly he may have spoken, today I ask everyone of you to look unto the captive Christ. Set aside anything else which now claims your thoughts and seeks to divert your attention: world events, comic pages, your breakfast dishes on the West Coast, your dinner dishes on the East, and for these few moments which, by the Spirit's grace, can give you eternity, *"Behold the Man!"* Once when I similarly appealed, "Drop everything you are doing, and hear Christ's promise of salvation!" three listeners in Pennsylvania did drop everything and concentrate their thoughts on Jesus. That led them to their Savior and to a happiness which even their glowing letters cannot fully describe. Perhaps this is your day of decision for the Lord. Forget everything else, then, and *"behold the Man!"*

Look carefully at that thorny ring of ridicule crushed into His sacred head, which drips with crimson blood. He had called Himself a King, and now the hatred of His enemies has crowned Him with a cutting coronet of anguish. Examine His robe of princely purple, a garment of cruel mockery, and then ask yourselves how men, even in their total depravity, could stoop to such hellish depths that they hurled infernal jibes at Jesus, who had never raised His voice, except to instruct, warn, help, and heal, never lifted His hand, if not to support and sustain some wavering, faltering soul, never moved His foot except on errands of mercy and compassion. O God, how gracious Thou art, still to deal mercifully with men, when the mania and the madness of unbelief so savagely mocked the Messiah!

Look at the thorny crown and purple robe again to realize, by contrast, how worldly many churches have become and how widely they are separated from the Lord's poverty! The crown of a mighty ecclesiastical leader contains 11 sapphires, 19 emeralds, 32 rubies, 229 diamonds, and 252 pearls — all costly flawless gems, studded in purest gold; yet the *"Son of Man"* not only had not *"where to lay His head,"* but in His agony had nothing to lay on His head as protection against the tearing thorns. The churches of Christ could be unspeakably more effective and helpful if they would disavow the driving desire for accumulating wealth. It is strange to the human mind, but true in God's omnipotence, that the Church was spiritually richest when it was materially poorest. The only costly robe Jesus ever wore was the garment His murderous enemies forced on Him! May the foes of the full, free, final Gospel never succeed in coaxing believers to lay so much stress on the cut and cloth of clerical gowns that the spiritual robe of the Savior's righteousness, without which we can never see the Father, is neglected or forgotten! May our sanctuaries always be adorned with the beauty, reverence, and joy befitting our faith! The best we can give to enhance our worship is not enough. But more inestimably glorious than all outward adornment are the *"beauties of holiness,"* the radiance of a reborn life, the splendor of a soul redeemed and remade for heaven's unspeakable majesty.

Study the crown of thorns and the purple robe once more, for they are truly the marks of real royalty! Jesus —

let the earth and the heavens hear it! — the captive Christ of bruised and bleeding body, is in all truth a King, not a sovereign like Italy's Victor Emmanuel, who resigned under the pressure of war, for the harder the conflict, the more striking our Lord's triumph; not like Belgium's Albert, who was taken captive by the Nazis, for our risen Redeemer now controls men and sways the universe; not a ruler like Marshall Petain, who habitually consulted a clairvoyant in Vichy, yet was tried for treason to France, for our Savior sees all, knows all, and forever keeps His word; not as England's Edward who abdicated his throne, for of Christ it is written, *"Thy throne, O God, is forever and ever"*; not as Britain's George, on whose realm, it is said, the sun never sets, for our Lord truly rules unto the ends of the earth; not as anyone in the thin line of sovereigns which the war is steadily decreasing, for Jesus rules into eternity. He is — how humble in spirit you hear this! — the Ruler in a threefold realm. First, He is the King of Might, who upholds all things visible and invisible, this universe with everything in it, the Lord of unlimited power, who created you and who sustains you. Then, He is the King of Mercy, the Monarch of His Church, which He victoriously defends against the very gates of hell, and in which He appeals for your faith, your loyalty, your love. In celestial climax, He is the King of Glory, who, with the Father and the Spirit, rules the heavenly domain, prepares the priceless places in the many mansions and welcomes each believing soul after the trials and turmoils of life. He is — cherish it, defend it, proclaim it, believe it! — the King of kings, the Lord of lords, the Ruler of rulers — even more, He is the Sovereign of your soul.

Have you acclaimed Him, the Christ of the thorny crown and the robe of ridicule, *your* King? Have you pledged Him your allegiance for time and eternity? Unless you bow humbly before Him here, you can never reign victoriously with Him hereafter. For joy, peace, and power, for triumph over trials, trouble, and temptation, for citizenship in the realms of grace and glory, crown Christ your King!

II

BEHOLD IN HIM YOUR SAVIOR!

To be your eternal Sovereign — and again we approach Scripture's Holiest of Holies, the crucifixion at Calvary — Jesus had to be your Savior. As you *"behold the Man,"* you ask yourself why He who sways the universe and upholds *"all things by the word of His power"* is a prisoner in a Roman court, persecuted by His countrymen. The answer is the most magnificent message of mercy the Lord Himself could plan, produce, and publish. Jesus — praise His glorious grace! — "suffered under Pontius Pilate," as we declare in the Apostles' Creed, so that we need not suffer under Pontius Pilate's and our Judge. He was scourged and slain so that through Him we could escape the doom our violations of the divine Law have brought upon us. He suffered as our Substitute and Atonement, our Ransom and Redemption, because He transferred our transgressions to Himself, permitted the weight of our iniquities to crush Him, fulfilled God's Law, satisfied divine justice in our stead, bore in His own body, mind, and soul the guilt, the curse, the penalty of our sins, even God-forsakenness, so that in Heaven's sight those who believe in Him are saved from the dominion of death, damnation, and the devil.

How Do You Behold the Man?

The proud human heart rebels at humbling itself before the scourged, suffering Savior; yet how sorely a war-weary world needs the redeeming Christ today! We like to emphasize our goodness, but in God's sight *"all our righteousnesses,"* our trumped-up achievements, and our veneered virtue *"are as filthy rags."* Remove the disguises from our human nature, take away restraints and inhibitions, and you will uncover the human heart as the source of all vile, smelly, perverted evil. Ask any dentist to describe the reactions of patients when, fully under the influence of anesthesia, their subconscious mind begins to express itself, and you will be told that often they reveal deep depravity, speak and do shameful things. Take away the restraints of good society; let men live to kill, as they do in combat — and you will see that lust knows no bounds. In the First World War, for example, the casualties from venereal diseases were 40 per cent greater than all other casualties combined; and in World War II Army medical corps experts are beginning to predict that despite previous rosy promises, these horrid diseases may keep proportionate pace with their frequency in the last conflict. Let the dictators dethrone God, and as they crush their fellow men, you behold shocking cruelty. Let the war reduce the standards of decency, and married couples clamor for divorce in reckless abandon and unparalleled frequency. Let the bars of morality drop during global strife, and within six months Chicago opens more than five hundred new drinking places, but probably fewer than five new churches. You can see how foul human nature is, when you realize how depraved even the Temple priests became. Look at these Jerusalem churchmen! Pilate told them, *"Behold the Man!"* Yet we read, *"When the chief priests, therefore, and officers saw Him, they cried out, saying, Crucify Him, crucify Him!"* The mob, under their direction, screaming, *"His blood be on us and on our children!"* asked for the terrifying destruction which overtook the capital, killed and enslaved hundreds of thousands, among them doubtless many who on Good Friday cursed themselves with unbelief. Today, likewise, American scribes, university teachers, are invoking divine wrath. A Smith College professor calls the Bible "part history, part legend, part fact, part fiction." Fifteen hundred clergymen answer a questionnaire and 86 per cent of them join Caiaphas in rejecting the necessity of Christ's blood for salvation. Eighty-nine per cent deny the Virgin Birth and make Jesus only human, even as you and I are.

Indeed, you need not go beyond the limits of your own life to recognize that you yourself are lost without the Savior, that by the impulses of your heart, the desires of your soul, the plans of your mind, the words of your lips, the deeds of your hands, you have broken the divine Law into countless fragments and that therefore, above anything else in life, you yourself need a Redeemer.

Thank God with me, here He is in Christ! As we *"behold the Man,"* may we find in Him the complete Savior, with pardon for the deepest perversion; the merciful Savior, who gives His redemption freely, without payment or price; the unchanging Savior, who, come war, come peace, never loses His love for us, though we deny and desert Him; the unfailing Savior, who will not refuse to receive and bless those who trust in Him; the strengthening Savior, who by His Spirit fortifies our faith to conquer evil, resist temptation and choose the good; the comforting Savior, who lightens our burdens, shares our sorrows, and builds our trust; the transforming Savior, who can turn bodily pain into spiritual pleasure, earthly loss into heavenly gain; the renewing Savior, through whom, born again by faith, we become new creatures; the all-sufficient Savior, the riches of whose grace are able to supply every need that may confront us; the eternal Savior, before whom we, His disciples, will stand in the resurrection with bodies resembling His glorious body; the sure Savior, whose reconciling love is gloriously guaranteed us by God and His unbreakable Word; the universal Savior, the promise of peace through His blood being equally offered all men, without preference or discrimination of color, clime, or condition; the only Savior, therefore, the one real Deliverer; and finally, in supreme blessing, *your* Savior, through whom you are brought back to God!

As you *"behold the Man,"* do you join Pilate in our text, saying, *"I find no fault in Him,"* and then turn away from Jesus? If you value your soul, don't think that you can repeat the Roman governor's pronouncement *"Take ye Him and crucify Him!"* and thus pass on to others the responsibility for killing your Lord! In the midst of this Lenten season, stop! *"Behold the Man!"* and confess that your sins sent Him to the cross, that He there endured the agony you should have suffered, died the death you should have died, in punishment for your transgressions; and as you bow contritely before Him, knowing that *"where sin abounded, grace did much more abound,"* cry out, "O Christ, tormented and tortured in Pilate's court, Thou art, now and forever, my sin-removing, sin-atoning, sin-destroying Savior!"

III

BEHOLD IN HIM YOUR GOD!

Then you will be ready to receive, believe, and treasure this supremely sacred truth: Christ is King and Savior because He is God — not merely godly, Godlike, God-sent, God-directed, God-inspired, but the true God, the eternal God, God in the full, unlimited, undiminished sense of that revered term. No man, not even the wisest, kindest, truest, best, who ever lived or ever will live, could be sinless and perfect enough to fulfill the divine Law. No priest, patriarch, or prophet, not even the aggregate of the humblest and holiest of the heroic, could love their fellow men with the all-embracing devotion required for their redemption. No friends, parents, children, not even the entire company of your dearest ones, could die the death required to ransom your soul and reunite you with the Father. No student, scientist, scholar, not the combined faculties of the largest universities, could raise a single corpse from the grave and thus give you the pledge of your own resurrection with the promise of heavenly glory. No model saint or radiant angel in heaven, not even those closest to Christ, could overcome sin and death, its wages. Only God could do this; and, praise His pardoning love! only God as Christ, and Christ as God truly did all this for you. Therefore, when Pilate proclaims, *"Behold the Man!"* believingly behold in Him the Almighty, with the worlds of wisdom, wealth of love, wideness of power, wonders of grace, the Lord alone possesses.

How Do You Behold the Man?

Of course, this triumphant truth has been blasphemously and boastfully denied. Two women, who founded religious groups now claiming many thousands of followers, have openly opposed the revealed truth that Jesus is God. One of them, who taught reverence for India's fakirs, miscalled "holy men," claims that to assert Christ's deity is to degrade God and degrade Jesus. She blankly reports, "I rejected it" (our Savior's godhead) "from beginning to end." Our Lord has rejected her for time and eternity; He still warns every scoffer, *"If ye believe not that I am He, ye shall die in your sins."* Such denial is not new. Listen to Christ's own countrymen as they challenge Pilate, *"We have a law, and by our law He ought to die, because He made Himself the Son of God." "He* MADE *Himself the Son of God,"* they sneered, as though they were talking of an impostor, a pretender, a liar. He *is* the Son of God, we insist with Scripture, which gives Him God's names and God's honors. He is the Son of God, His startling miracles and wonders prove. He is the Son of God, the holy angels of heaven proclaim. He is the Son of God, masses of you, the redeemed, affirm in the Spirit-given assurance of a reborn life. He is the Son of God, the Father Himself recorded.

"What shall I do then with Jesus?" you ask, repeating Pilate's question. — What, indeed, if not to behold in Him your God, your all-powerful, all-knowing, all-changing, all-controlling, all-embracing Lord, with a billion times more than everything you will ever need for earth and heaven? What can this mission of the air do to help you receive, believe, trust, honor, and glorify Him, your Sovereign, Savior, and God? We, together with many thousands of Christ-exalting pastors and Christ-dedicated

laymen, offer you, wherever you are, whoever you are, and whatever you are, our prayerful help in leading you to peace and promise in Jesus. Therefore *"come thou with us, and we will do thee good!"* Write us! With the Spirit's guidance and the co-operation of thousands of Christ-directed ministers and laymen we will help you rightly to *"behold the Man"* as your God, who loved you and gave Himself for you.

More, beholding Jesus daily, constantly living close to Him in His Word, the reflex of His redeeming love, will glorify your life. Leaning on Him who came *"not to be ministered unto but to minister,"* the Son of God, who laid down His life for us, you will be strengthened to spurn selfishness and also live for others, with the promise of divine blessing on yourself and your service. How richly the Holy Spirit has blessed those who have constantly kept the Lord before them!

This broadcast originates in Fort Wayne, a powerful center in the history of my Church and a strong American Christian community. A humble gravestone in one of the cemeteries of this city emphasizes the blessing and power Christ can give every one of you. It marks the last resting place of Sammy Morris, born in west Africa, a pure Negro of the Kru people. Early in life he was sold into slavery, cruelly beaten and oppressed. When he was twenty years old, he walked many miles to meet a missionary, and he was soon converted. His hunger for Christ could not be stilled, and when the missionary could give him no further instruction, she told him, "If you want to know any more, you must go to Stephen Merritt in New York." After many weary days he reached a harbor from which a small ship would sail for America. He rowed out to the boat and asked the captain to take

How Do You Behold the Man?

him to New York, but he was answered with curses and kicks. Three times he repeated that request, and finally, almost in desperation, the captain took him aboard as cabin boy. While crossing the Atlantic, that unlearned Negro lad was used by the Holy Spirit to convert the captain and half the crew. In New York the young believer found Stephen Merritt, who sent him to school here in Fort Wayne. A biographer records, "He turned the university upside down," through his Christian life and testimony. He was in this city only a few months, preparing himself to bring the Gospel back to his own people, when he took fatally sick. Without a word of murmur and complaint, but with praise to God and a plea for missionaries to Africa he died, declaring during the siege of his sickness, "Since I have found Jesus, death is my friend." Were all his efforts a failure? Never! On the night after his funeral three of his fellow-students volunteered to take his place and proclaim the Savior to the dark, sobbing continent.

God can give you, far more richly-blessed than that penniless, persecuted Negro boy, the same great benedictions. He can free you from the slavery of sin, grant you a consecrated life, show you the victory over death, and use you mightily in winning souls for His kingdom. Therefore may the Lord today enrich you with the faith that beholds the Man martyred for your salvation and then lead you to declare with all your soul, "Jesus, Son of God and Son of Man, my Prophet and my Priest, my Conqueror and my King, Thou art indeed, and ever wilt be, on earth and in heaven, my Savior and my God!" The Holy Spirit bless all of you with this courage and conviction of redeeming grace! Amen!

DON'T GAMBLE YOUR SOUL AWAY!

"They . . . parted His garments, casting lots, that it might be fulfilled which was spoken by the Prophet, They parted My garments among them, and upon My vesture did they cast lots. And sitting down they watched Him there."
SAINT MATTHEW 27:35-36

JESUS, WOUNDED FOR OUR TRANSGRESSIONS, BRUISED FOR OUR INIQUITIES: Banish all doubt from our wavering hearts that Thou, O Son of God, on Calvary didst remove our sins, redeem our souls, and restore us to our heavenly Father! Fill our hearts with Thy Spirit's immovable conviction that Thou alone art our certain Redeemer from ruin and eternal destruction! Take away all ifs, perhapses, maybes, and help us now bow before Thee on Thy cross, declaring: We in this radio mission believe and are sure that Thou art our Deliverer from death! So enlighten us by the indwelling of Thy holy Comforter that we refuse to risk gambling our soul's eternal salvation by heeding even for a moment any man-made creed which questions Thy gracious Gospel pledge of a blessed eternity! In Thine endless mercy look down compassionately on those who suffer from loss, loneliness, lingering pain, or lasting sorrow of any kind! Reveal Thyself to them as the divine Friend who never forsakes those who truly trust Him, the unfailing Helper of the afflicted and bereaved who cling to Him! In war, as in peace, Thou canst do all things, for Thou art our God. Therefore save us and strengthen us, as Thou hast promised! Amen!

Don't Gamble Your Soul Away!

Not long ago a Los Angeles court found Samuel Whitaker guilty of murdering his wife. When the judge pronounced life sentence, the prisoner jumped to his feet, threw up his arms, and cried, "If I am guilty of this horrible crime, may God strike me down before I get to my cell!" Before Samuel Whitaker entered death row in San Quentin, he suffered a heart attack and fell over dead.

The pages of history are filled with similar startling, shocking evidences of the Bible truth, *"Be not deceived; God is not mocked!"* After the Revolution, Newburg, New York, became a notorious center of scoffers. Thirty-six atheists organized a club, called the Society of the Druids, which met regularly to ridicule Christ's religion. Once, as part of their blasphemous orgies, they burned the Bible, baptized a cat, and gave Communion to a dog. What happened to these men? Careful investigation, sworn to before New York State public officials, revealed that two died that very night, a third perished suddenly three days later, and within five years all the remaining thirty-three had been destroyed. Two of them starved to death, seven were drowned, eight were shot, five committed suicide, seven ended on the gallows, one froze to death, three perished "by accident." These and many other instances show how utterly destructive it is to take the slightest chance of challenging the Almighty, of gambling with God's grace.

Many of you are guilty of this fatal folly. You do not arise on a public platform and challenge the Lord to strike you dead; you do not step out in a thunderstorm and clench your fists against the Almighty, as a Casco Bay, Maine, fisherman did, who was almost instantly killed by lightning. You may be church members, or even officials; you may come from a long line of Christian forefathers; you may spurn every thought of risking your money on the throw of dice; yet you are gambling with higher stakes than those ever paid at Monte Carlo; you are toying with the salvation of your soul.

God's Holy Spirit therefore warn every one of us, but also comfort us in Christ, as we consider the most tragic of all gambling scenes, that under the cross of Calvary, recorded in our text, Saint Matthew, chapter twenty-seven, verses thirty-five and thirty-six: *"They . . . parted His garments, casting lots, that it might be fulfilled which was spoken by the Prophet, They parted My garments among them, and upon My vesture did they cast lots. And sitting down they watched Him there."* May each one of us, across the country, personally heed the appeal these words stress:

DON'T GAMBLE YOUR SOUL AWAY!

I

DON'T TAKE THE FATAL CHANCE OF REJECTING CHRIST!

After our Savior had been nailed to the cross, the Roman legionaries sent to Calvary began to do the usual thing at public executions — take the dying victim's last possessions, his clothing. What a vicious and repulsive role military men played during the entire crucifixion story! And how close the danger that our soldiers forget their God and blaspheme their Savior! When I recently warned of the perils in compulsory peacetime conscription for our high school students, some of you protested and insisted that military service makes men. I say: Only

Don't Gamble Your Soul Away!

one power can make real men, the Gospel of our crucified Savior, through which we are reborn with the promise, *"If any man be in Christ, he is a new creature."* Because war is not our Lord's way; because He never blesses mass destruction, murder of women and children, the brutality and the degeneracy which often accompany bloodshed, military men are constantly confronted by sin and sordid temptation. A Christian soldier convalescing in a California Army hospital writes me: "What burns me up is that foul-minded, immoral fellows start bragging about their filthy deeds. I tell them" [and I hope everyone of you Christian men and women in the service has the same courage]: " 'Fellows, if you must talk that way, don't do so in front of me, as I don't want to hear it. Even if you guys don't believe in religion, don't you have enough decency and self-respect to keep yourselves clean and pure for your own sake and, if you are married, also for your wife's sake?' " A Christian corporal in France writes me, denouncing camp "movies" for "all the charm and lust that modern photographers can develop." He adds: "I have come up against the viciousness of indecency and vulgarity I had not known to exist prior to my induction. And what disturbs me most is that such environment has slowly but surely brought me to a state where I no longer feel the sting and hurt which at first was the case." He concludes, "I sometimes wonder how God can possibly find that this world will ever again deserve peace in any form."

The Roman soldiers at Calvary began to cast lots, or gamble, as we know from Saint John's Gospel, for the Savior's one valuable garment, the robe without seam. Gambling is nothing new. — Military authorities sent our troops 175,000 pairs of dice as morale builders, and you can be sure that they were not used for parchesi. Playing for money is not restricted to soldiers, however. The Gallup Poll has shown that last year practically every other American risked money in bets or some form of gambling. Do you know that the amount annually spent in horse-racing wagers totals ten dollars a head for every person in the United States? Do you know that not long ago some of these tracks had million-dollar betting days, while our fighting men were risking their lives in mud and filth for less than two dollars a day?

As you see the soldiers roll the dice beneath the cross at Calvary, to us the spot with the most sacred association on earth, remember this evil is not only beginning to creep into many American churches — it is there, definitely, brazenly! How shocking to read in the newspapers that a church will raffle a house! How distressing to see signs like these: "Prize Bingo at Saint Luke's"; "Banko and Screeno at Holy Trinity"! What an insult to Christ when churches buy and sell tickets reading: "One chance at Saint Elizabeth's Carnival. First prize, one case of whisky. Second prize, twenty-five-dollar war bond." What offense to God and man when a newspaper must report that twenty-one of fifty pastors in a Protestant denomination at Chicago admit favoring "a bit of gambling for the sake of zest and income at church affairs"! How shocking beyond all words to have professional cardplayers, managers of gambling establishments, declare that church games of chance offer even less chance of winning than a roulette wheel!

"What is the matter with gambling?" some of you ask. "Why, the word 'gambling' is not even mentioned in our Bible!" True, neither do the words "rape," "manslaughter," "larceny," "suicide," "embezzling," "bootlegging," "white slavery," "racketeering," occur in Scripture, but the evils involved in all these, as in gambling, are clearly and repeatedly condemned. "What objection can you have if the proceeds go to hospitals, to the state, to religious purposes?" others demand. Simply this, that the end never justifies the means. Sin can never pay for its own ruin. For instance, the State of Massachusetts received $13,000,000 a year as income from liquor licenses and revenue; yet drunkenness, with its resultant crimes, mental and physical illness, and the public support of its victims, cost Massachusetts $61,000,000.

"Say a few words against gambling in one of your Sunday sermons," an Edwardsville, Illinois, woman asks. "I can't convince my husband that it is sin. He spends an awful lot of his earnings on poker, punchboards, and buys all kinds of tickets, but he never wins anything." To her husband and all overcome by this weakness I say, gambling is wrong — and I mean every kind: dice, bingo, beano, tango, screeno, roulette, lotto, lottery, raffles, card prizes, betting, punchboards, the number racket, which, I am told, has invaded the Government offices at Washington. First, it is based on the desire to get something for nothing, while Christ's followers should *work and eat their own bread.* Gambling is wrong, in the second place, because it violates the Christian's stewardship of his time, money, and effort. Gambling is wrong, in the third place, because it is allied with dishonesty. Someone has well said, "There never will be an honest horse race until there is an honest human race." Gambling is wrong, in the fourth place, because it encourages serious crime. Chauncey Depew, New York lawyer and politician, ascribed 90 per cent of the ruin among young people employed in places of trust to this evil. Gambling is wrong, in the fifth place, because it produces public bribery and graft paid to politicians. Gambling is wrong, in the sixth place, because it takes millions of dollars from families and legitimate business. Gambling is wrong, in the seventh place, because it weakens character, particularly of women and children, by showing an easy, effortless way to obtain money. Gambling is wrong, in the eighth place, because it is too often associated with notorious underworld characters, prostitutes, and public enemies. Gambling is wrong, in the ninth place, because it can become an obsession which hinders wholesome, useful living. Did you read of Horace King in Walthamstow, England, who won $84,000 in the Irish sweepstakes? His ticket cost him only $2.50, but the prize cost him his friends, his happiness, and his life. With this easy money he became a drunkard, and killed himself.

Therefore, stamp out this evil! Banish it from your churches! Don't make any concessions whatever! Think of these soldiers gambling under the cross, and resolve that, in the Holy Spirit's strength, you, especially you Christian pastors, will lead in helping crush this destructive menace!

While the soldiers gambled, we are told, the crowd *"stood beholding."* Today we try to remove the shame and pain from public executions. We seek the quickest and easiest way of taking a murderer's life, so that his agony will be reduced to a minimum. Yet the fiends who killed Christ sat jeering, gibing, cursing, watching, waiting, without a shred of sympathy. There on that bleak, skull-shaped hill, His arms, never otherwise raised than in benediction, now stretched wide on the cross beam; His feet, never otherwise lifted than on errands of mercy, now pinned by big square, crushing nails to the gory post; there, naked before those whom He had come to clothe with heavenly righteousness, cursed by His own countrymen, whom He blessed, deserted by friends who had pledged Him their loyalty; there, on the cross of agony and disgrace, suffering torture of soul and spirit, mind and body, beyond everything that all men together have ever yet endured — there hangs the Son of God, crucified for all mankind's transgressions, paying the price of the entire race's redemption, giving Himself as the atoning Redeemer for your sins and mine; and only a few feet away the mob gathers to watch Him, to ridicule Him, to curse Him.

Don't speak to me of the goodness of humankind when its hatred and perversion helped send to the cross One whom its own leaders declared innocent, just, and righteous! Don't tell me that we can expect help and hope for the higher things in life from humanity itself! No matter how rich, how educated, how powerful, how cultured, how scientific, men may be, they are fundamentally foul and filthy; and if Christ were with us today to repeat His scathing rebuke of godlessness, lust, covetousness, greed, the mob would still find some way to send Him to a death of agony and shame. We say of a person that he is a born musician, a born poet, a born leader; but we cannot say that he is born sinless, stainless, perfect; for all people, the wisest, richest, best, are born in sin, live in sin, and grow in sin. Therefore all need Christ, the only Savior from evil. Yet, when He came to redeem men, they crucified Him, and until He died, many sat by idly, cruelly, bestially. Why? They wanted to see what would happen.

Christ did not come down from the cross. Blessed be His boundless love; He wanted to stay on that accursed tree to complete our redemption. He did not save Himself from the horror of death because He wanted to spare us the anguish of enduring the penalty of our transgressions. Neither Elijah nor God came to help Him, and He, the loneliest, most deserted Figure in all history, had to cry out, *"My God, My God, why hast Thou forsaken Me?"* The mob saw only a bleeding, death-marked Sufferer, who, gathering His waning strength together, commended Himself into His Father's hand and then, after He had cried, *"It is finished!"* collapsed in death. They wagered and wasted away those precious hours in unbelief at the cross — and they lost their souls.

Many of you are likewise gambling precious opportunities away. You think that you may accept Jesus sometime, but not now. What a fearful chance you are taking! Not a week passes in which the mail does not bring repeated notices of men and women in this audience suddenly struck down by unforeseen disaster. How do you know that the Christ, whom you have repeatedly rejected, will always await your pleasure twenty, thirty, forty years away? Can you not see how every day you live without Him brings you closer to the inevitable, inescapable Judgment? It is bad enough when people bet and lose thousands of dollars; but how terrifying beyond words when they risk and ruin their own opportunity for enjoying heaven's happiness by delay, postponement, excuses? Today, while the Spirit touches your heart, get right with God, the only way you can, through repentant reliance on the Redeemer!

Others among you are risking your salvation by continuing in sin, taking a chance that your evil will not be discovered, hoping that you can escape divine punishment. What folly! *"Be sure your sin will find you out!"* Don't you understand that the Almighty, who sees all and knows all, can penetrate into any secret affair or hidden desire and uncover its damnable guilt? Even if you proudly boast that you are beyond the reach of God's Law, the time is approaching when its vengeance will overtake you and you will tremble in terror. What if the Lord demands your soul before this day closes? Will you, this moment living in sin, rejection of Christ, rebellion against God, be prepared to face your Maker? Receive Him now!

Again many of you are gambling your souls away by attending and supporting churches which dethrone the Savior, deny His deity, decline to accept His sin-removing love, desire to set aside His cross, determine to remove the cleansing power of His blood. Do you say: "Well, what difference does it make which creed you follow? All have the same end in view. All hope to lead to heaven." When you are sick, do you say: "Get me a doctor, any kind of doctor! They all have the same end in view; they all hope to cure me"? No; you want the best possible physician or surgeon. With your eternal soul at stake, should you be less cautious? If God should come suddenly to summon you into eternity, what hope would you have as a member of a church that believes in salvation by good works, human attainment instead of the Savior's atonement, redemption by your sacrifices rather than by Jesus' bloody self-sacrifice at Calvary? A few minutes' delay has often proved disastrous in war, but your perpetual postponing, your all-out desertion of the Lord, will prove eternally disastrous for you. Don't deceive yourself into believing that you can enjoy the lusts of the flesh while you are young and then repent in old age! Many of you will not live to be forty or fifty. Don't think that you can find a more *"convenient time"* for coming to Christ, when you will not be as busy, not as worried, as now; that time may never come. One thing is sure, however, the day of grace is here for you on this second Sunday of March. *"Now is the accepted time." Now* the Savior pleads with you to receive Him. *Now* the gates of heaven are open to you. With your immortal soul at stake, the soul which Jesus said is worth more than the world with its vast accumulation of treasures, can you go on, toying with eternity, gambling your soul away in unbelief, denial, doubt, refusal to repent and return to God in His Son?

II

BE SURE THAT YOU HAVE ACCEPTED CHRIST!

How blessed that you can have absolute assurance concerning Christ, your blessed Redeemer! The milling mob at Calvary could have known definitely that He was the Redeemer had they only turned to the Bible. They did not have to gamble away the afternoon in order to learn who Jesus was and what He could do; for it was clearly foretold long centuries before just what would happen on grim Golgotha's brow that Friday. Our text testifies to this, for it shows us that even that casting of lots over the Savior's clothing was predicted ten centuries before by David, the Psalmist. We are told that the soldiers divided the apparel, *"that it might be fulfilled which was spoken by the Prophet, They parted My garments among them, and upon My vesture did they cast lots."* One of the most positive and easily understood proofs for the truth that, according to God's plan, Jesus, the Son of God, died for everyone is the astonishing fact that each major part of our Lord's suffering was foreseen and foretold long before it happened.

Think of it, within less than twenty-four hours all these prophecies were fulfilled! First, the Savior was to be betrayed. Second, the traitor was to receive thirty pieces of silver. Third, this money was to be thrown down in the Lord's house. Fourth, it was to be used in purchasing a potter's field. Fifth, Christ was to be forsaken by His disciples. Sixth, He was to be accused by false witnesses. Seventh, He was to be beaten. Eighth, He was to be spat upon. Ninth, He was to keep silent before His oppressors. Tenth, He was to be wounded, bruised, beaten with stripes. Eleventh, He was to have His hands and feet pierced. Twelfth, He, the Son of God, was to be numbered with the transgressors, crucified with thieves. Thirteenth, He was to plead for those who persecuted Him. Fourteenth, the jeering mob would wag their heads. Fifteenth, they would ridicule Him with taunting sarcasm. Sixteenth, they would stand and gaze at Him. Seventeenth, they would divide various articles of His clothing among them. Eighteenth, they would cast lots for one piece of His apparel. Nineteenth, He would be naked on the cross. Twentieth, He would be tortured by thirst. Twenty-first, He would cry, *"My*

God, My God, why hast Thou forsaken Me?" Twenty-second, His murderers would give Him gall and vinegar. Twenty-third, the mob would tauntingly ask, *"Let God deliver Him!"* Twenty-fourth, He would cry with a loud voice. Twenty-fifth, He would be pierced, but, twenty-sixth, not one of His bones would be broken. Twenty-seventh, He would be laid, not into a criminal's grave, but into the tomb of a rich man. — Now, if these clear, precise prophecies were fulfilled in less than one day and night, how can anyone doubt that the Bible, with the whole record of your salvation, is entirely right, absolutely unbreakable, positively sure? You don't need to gamble about Scripture's truth.

Now draw this definite, personal conclusion from these twenty-seven prophecies fulfilled in less than twenty-four hours: God never fails. *"Heaven and earth,"* He says, *"shall pass away, but My words shall not pass away."* How different the pledges men make! Goebbels assured the German people that their cities would never be bombed, but many have been wiped out by aerial destruction. Prime Minister Churchill declared that this would not be a peace of vindictive hatred, but he has clearly changed that position. The Polish people were solemnly guaranteed that their territory would be fully restored; that likewise has been cast away. Happy couples pledge themselves to lifelong loyalty; yet last year more than 300,000 marriages were broken by divorce. I challenge every skeptic, I include especially the loud-mouthed atheists, to prove that even one of Christ's personal prophecies concerning His life, death, and resurrection has not been truly, blessedly fulfilled.

When you believe this sure, certain, solid Word, all

risk of ruin is removed from your life; the gambling with your soul stops. There is no mere luck, good or bad, no chance happening in your life. When you have Christ, you know that you did not come into this world as a "biological accident"; that you did not haphazardly descend from some long-armed, low-browed, hairy-bodied, apelike animal ancestor. In absolute certainty you have the inner conviction: "God made me. He knew me before I was born. Through Jesus I am my heavenly Father's, and He is mine. Therefore I am more than a beast, more than a helpless atom in the universe, more than a human molecule quickly crushed out of existence." You are assured that the God who loved you enough to create you will guard you as the apple of His eye and protect you, if necessary, with a miracle of His almighty power.

At Calvary you understand, too, that life is not a series of good fortune and bad, of boosts and blows, charities and cruelties. Clinging to the cross, you can exult: *"I know whom I have believed, and am persuaded that He is able to keep that which I have committed unto Him against that day. . . . For I am persuaded that neither death nor life nor angels nor principalities nor powers nor things present nor things to come nor height nor depth nor any other creature shall be able to separate us from the love of God which is in Christ Jesus, our Lord."* You have the divine pledge, even though you may not be able to analyze and explain it, that because you are the Savior's, because your sins have been removed by His atoning death, because you have been restored to your Father and reborn a new creature, you are under God's grace, not under His wrath; that the sorrow He permits to come upon you in reality is the disguised evidence of His love, the gracious help by which He can tear your desires from the world, bring you closer to His compassion. Great numbers of you, as your letters reveal, have suffered heavily during the past years because of family trouble, marital trouble, money trouble, business trouble, or the burden of sickness, loneliness, misunderstanding, personal loss. What a privilege for me to proclaim, and what a blessing for you to believe, that Christ, who loved you and gave Himself for you, knows every anguish you endure, feels the pain which racks your souls, understands the agony torturing you. A Nazi official in Cologne urged the people there to stay with him and fight until the last man; yet, when our troops drew closer, he fled to safety and had transcriptions of his speeches broadcast to make the citizens think that he was still in the city. Christ never stoops to deceit. He is truly with us, and He understands your grief, for He has suffered more than all the agony you can ever bear. Oh, bring to Him everything which keeps you bowed down and brokenhearted! Trust Him without question, and you will experience peace, joy, and strength greater than you have known. You will be able to thank God for your afflictions.

As Jesus gives sustaining, comforting answers to the questions: "Whence came we? How can we solve the difficulties of this life?" so He, our Savior, also offers us absolute assurance when we ask: "Whither do we go? How can we secure the blessings of the life to come?" You need never gamble nor speculate on the hereafter if you have Christ. Because He died for you, heaven is yours. Because He was robbed of His clothing, you shall be robed in eternal righteousness. Because He was resurrected on the third day, you who die in the Lord will be restored to life with new, glorified bodies, reunited in the celestial homeland with all departed believers.

I am not broadcasting theory, speculation, wishful thinking, pulpit phrases, pious patter. This is God's truth, sealed with Jesus' blood, endorsed by the Holy Spirit. It will remain unchanged and unshaken, long after so-called international agreements have been broken, long after a hundred new theories of psychology, psychiatry, psychoanalysis, have dropped into discard. Here they are, the great facts of our faith and in God's own Word. We ask, "What does God say of all men?" and divine Truth answers, *"All have sinned, and come short of the glory of God."* What, we continue, is the consequence of our sin? Scripture replies, *"The soul that sinneth, it shall die."* Can we ourselves redeem our souls from this penalty of eternal death? No, the Bible declares; for *"all our righteousnesses are as filthy rags."* Can anyone else, father, mother, pastor, priest, saint, or martyr, save our souls? No, the Bible asserts; for *"none of them can by any means redeem his brother, nor give to God a ransom for him."* Are we hopelessly lost, then? Oh, thank the Almighty for the mercy of this promise: *"God so loved the world that He gave His only-begotten Son, that whosoever believeth in Him should not perish but have everlasting life"!* How can God's Son save us? Holy Writ explains: *"He was wounded for our transgressions, He was bruised for our iniquities."* God *"made Him to be sin for us who knew no sin, that we might be made the righteousness of God in Him." "While we were yet sinners, Christ died for us."* What must we do to be saved? What must we give? What must we pay? Scripture states plainly, *"Believe on the Lord Jesus Christ, and thou shalt be saved"*; and it adds, *"a man is justified by faith without the deeds of the Law."* Is this positive and certain? Most assuredly; for the holy God in His own unbreakable Word guarantees, *"This is a faithful saying and worthy of all acceptation, that Christ Jesus came into the world to save sinners."* What blessing do we have from all this? The defeat of death and hell, the gift of heaven, for Jesus Himself declares, *"I am the Resurrection and the Life; he that believeth in Me, though he were dead, yet shall he live."*

That is the true Christian faith. It made our country great. It offers you peace in war, comfort in sorrow, strength in weakness, light in darkness. That faith our world needs today, when the temptation is close at hand to gamble with grandiose schemes, which not only omit God but rely on those who deny His very existence. Yet sinister forces, godless Communists, scoffing atheists, powerful infidels, are trying to drive this Gospel out of America. Twentieth-century Sadducees and Pharisees, Annases and Caiaphases, are seeking to remove this cross-crowned conviction from the churches. The devil is toiling overtime to tear this blessed assurance from your soul.

My beloved, before God I ask you: Can you who until now have spurned Jesus and pushed His outstretched arms aside afford any longer to gamble away the time of grace? Will you risk refusing another invitation to accept and acclaim Christ your Savior and your God? Dare you run the chance of living even one more uncertain day without clinging to Him who is Pardon

Don't Gamble Your Soul Away! 115

and Peace, Life and Blessing itself? Think of the awful alternatives at stake! In May, 1844, when Samuel F. B. Morse ticked out the first message over his telegraph, he wired, *"What hath God wrought!"* A century and a month later, in June, 1944, when the first American radio station in Normandy after D Day sent one of its initial messages across the sea, by some unexplainable perversion, it flashed the message, "What the ——— hath God wrought?" These two completely opposed exclamations express the inevitable destiny of all men. For you too it is either the wonder of heaven or the horror of hell. Which shall it be? This radio mission, Bringing Christ to the Nations, with its almost 600 stations, pleads with you to stand at Calvary, behold the Crucified, and cry out, "*'What hath God wrought'* for me!" Testify that Jesus has saved you from death and hell! Stop gambling away your soul, your salvation, your hope of heaven! Turn to assurance in Christ, the cross, the Bible, the blood! The Holy Spirit give every one of you sure, certain faith in the crucified Savior! Amen!

"I THIRST"

"Jesus, knowing that all things were now accomplished, that the Scripture might be fulfilled, saith, I thirst."
SAINT JOHN 19:28

BLESSED SAVIOR, WHO ON THE CROSS DIDST CRY, "I THIRST": Contritely we confess with shame that our sins helped nail Thee to Golgotha's gory tree, that our transgressions made Thee suffer and thirst. Yet gratefully we acknowledge that Thou didst stay on the cross to endure the appalling penalty of all our iniquities and by Thine atoning death to finish forever the plan of our salvation. Praised be Thine eternal love that Thou didst leave nothing undone for the redemption of our souls but didst pay the whole price and completely ransom us from ruin! Teach us that as long as we cling to Thee, we can be confident of our salvation and find strength for our trials in the fulfilled promises of Thy holy Word! In every moment of suffering, may we turn to Thee for comfort and courage! Help us spurn sin! Remember our military and civilian youth! Keep them from bodily harm and soul danger! Support the victims of war with Thy sustaining love! Give each of us today that inner peace — peace with God, our fellow men, and our conscience! Have Thy way with us, Lord, but bless us with faith and trust! We have no hope for our blood-soaked earth and our sin-stained lives outside the radiant assurance of Thy Gospel. Therefore send Thy Holy Spirit this day to bring back those who once knew Thee but have turned from Thy truth, and to strengthen us who love Thee as our God and Guide to endless blessing! Thou hast promised to hear us when we pray to Thee. Therefore we confidently await Thine unfailing answer. Amen!

"I Thirst"

Have you ever known what it means to suffer from deadly thirst, to be without even a drop of water, to have your throat parched, your lips cracked with heat, your tongue thick and heavy, your whole mouth dry as an oven? Captain Hershel Horton was tortured by that agony when, as he lay mortally wounded near the Japanese lines in New Guinea, he eagerly scooped up the water in holes filled with seepage from the bodies of dead enemies. One hundred American soldiers at Munda, in the South Pacific, felt the terror of burning dryness when they spent days, surrounded by the Japanese, in a small area without a single spring. They even licked the leaves of trees and bushes for dew. Ceaselessly they pleaded with God for water, water, water, some kind, any kind! And the Almighty heard them, for, as Private B. N. Covington tells the story, "suddenly one of our artillery shells, aimed at the enemy lines, fell in the jungle right on our trail. It blasted a hole. Water gushed out." The Lord who refreshed Israel in the desert and caused springs to flow from rocks, remembered His children there in the Solomons' wilderness and cooled their burning throats. The same all-powerful God can revive your drooping spirit, refresh your soul in any fiery, withering sorrow. Trust Him to the utmost! *"Prove Me!"* He invites.

When these hundred men at Munda were thus marvelously supplied with water, many of them, we are told, "took out their Bibles, thumbed to the One Hundred and Seventh Psalm and read, '*He turneth the wilderness into a standing water, and dry ground into watersprings.*'" They might have turned in their New Testament to the record of history's deepest Sufferer, tormented by the torture of burning fever, parching dryness and by inner agony beyond all measure, to find that His love can also relieve the soul's raging dryness. To Him we devote our attention in the midst of this Lenten season, as we ask the Spirit's blessing on our study of the fifth word from the cross,

"I THIRST"

This is recorded in Saint John's Gospel, chapter nineteen, verse twenty-eight, *"Jesus, knowing that all things were now accomplished, that the Scripture might be fulfilled, saith, I thirst."* In this passage may we find the soul-strengthening answer to three questions: By whom were these words spoken? When were they spoken? Why?

I

BY WHOM WERE THESE WORDS SPOKEN?

At the height of the war, in a New York City court a man convicted of vagrancy asked that he be sent back to his native Czechoslovakia. The judge replied that he would gladly grant his request but that the war prevented him. "What war?" the prisoner asked. The magistrate explained that Hitler had taken over the Czech state. "Who's Hitler?" the convicted man continued. If it seems incredible that some people are so ignorant regarding a subject featured on the front page of every newspaper, in radio reports and private discussion, then remember that the masses of our countrymen are far more woefully uninformed concerning Him whose parched lips pleaded, *"I thirst!"* To the venom and hatred of His countrymen, especially many priests, He was an enemy of God, a vile blasphemer; to crafty Pilate, He was a harmless enthusiast, a mistaken idealist; to some of His disciples, disappointed in His capture and crucifixion, He was a martyr; but to the centurion, the captain of the Roman troops — and I pray the Lord, to everyone of you, likewise — He was the Son of God.

You cannot understand this, but you can believe it: the Sufferer on the cross, forsaken by His heavenly Father, deserted by His friends, taunted by His crucifiers, the Captive here on the central cross between two vicious criminals, enduring pain of body, anguish of mind, and agony of soul, above our poor powers of penetration, is the Son of God!

What supercrime is committed here at Calvary, when sin-cursed men lay blood-stained hands on their Lord! No wonder, with the divine Christ nailed to the accursed tree, with the mobs shrieking, *"His blood be on us and on our children,"* God's wrath was hurled against Jerusalem, the center of sin which planned and plotted the crucifixion! Men have witnessed savage slaughter, yet seldom, if ever, anything more shocking than the carnage which followed the siege and capture of that city, less than forty years after Jesus was crucified. During the French Revolution hardened women sat knitting steadily before the Paris guillotines, not dropping a stitch even when a head fell from the blade to the ground. They saw horrible sights, but not so terrifying as some of those women beheld who rejected their Savior with the cry, *"Away with Him, crucify Him!"* and who lived to see their city gripped by such desperate starvation that some hunger-crazed people ate human flesh. Air raids on London and Coventry, Amsterdam and Rotterdam, Dresden and Berlin, as on many other cities, have taken their hundreds of thousands; yet in this one city, Jerusalem, death in its most violent forms, by crucifixion, until the wood supply ran out, then by sword and spear, took more than one million lives.

What a powerful present-day sermon the crucified Christ thus preaches to overconfident America! Reject Him, and we place bombs under our nation's structure which can destroy us more completely than any enemy devastation. Spurn Him, and all our stored treasures, our diplomacy, our military and naval might, our brain trusts, cannot save us. Yet despite 15,000 casualties in a single week; despite the tragedy that the Percy Jones General Hospital at Battle Creek, Michigan — just one institution of many — every week for a long period supplied artificial legs or arms for approximately 140 war amputations, this conflict, the worst struggle in which we have ever engaged, has not brought our country closer to Jesus. Masses in America, with more money than they ever had before (what a startling contradiction, richer in bloodshed than in peace!), are farther from Christ than ever. Millions who ought to feel the Almighty's punishing hand in this bloodshed, hear the call of repentance sounded from every ruined city, and find a chastening rebuke in the heaviest casualty list this country has ever known, are still not walking in God's ways, heeding His Word, accepting His promise in Jesus. Even churches, which should be our first and last lines of defense, have sometimes become worldly, grasping, lukewarm, selfish, unbelieving.

How all-important, then, that you who know the Lord Jesus and believe in Him, pledge your continued faithfulness and promise to stand up for your crucified

"I Thirst"

Savior, even in your own compromising churches! You, God's children, truly *"are the salt of the earth."* Keep your savor! Out in Hutchinson, Kansas, a former center of the salt industry, great hills of salt, exposed to sun and storm, cold and heat, became useless and had to be thrown away. City authorities, thinking it could be used for road making, covered a broad avenue with a foot of this savorless material. After a few months, however, it became clear that the tasteless salt was less than useless in road making, for the highway became one of Hutchinson's worst. It is claimed the salt so poisoned the soil that the tall shade trees along the sidewalks of this street soon dropped their foliage and died. A similar tragedy can overtake this country if you twice-born Christians, loyal followers of the Savior, lose your trust, compromise the truth, surrender to the Lord's enemies. God keep you in the faith, fortify you with the power of protest and the undefeated eagerness to testify to Christ's truth!

Jesus had been on the cross at Calvary about six hours when He spoke the first and only word of the seven sacred utterances expressing His own physical pain. That zealot, or whatever he may be, who a few days ago was partially crucified in Chicago, was removed from his smooth cross after only two hours. Remember, only his hands were nailed; his feet were supported by a rest. Yet, how he screamed and moaned until the police removed him! Now think of our blessed Redeemer! Since about nine o'clock on the preceding night He had been betrayed by His disciple, forsaken by His most intimate followers; He had wrestled in Gethsemane, when His sweat was as blood; and He might have died had not an angel from heaven strengthened Him. Through sleepless hours of the early morning He was bound and struck by the high priest's henchmen. He was dragged from one tribunal to the other, again to be beaten by the soldiers and spit upon. A crown of cutting thorns lacerated His head. He was scourged with a leaded lash, so that His whole back ran red with blood. He was forced to carry His own cross until He collapsed; and then, in hellish climax, came the crucifixion, a method of capital punishment so horrifying that Israel never employed it, that the Romans used it to create terror in the minds of their subjects. Yet, during these fifteen hours of incessant suffering, not once does the Savior speak of His bodily agony. Hats off in admiration to those courageous Americans who, imprisoned by the Japanese, endured inhuman torture without a whimper! But on our knees in adoration before the Christ who suffered a thousand thousand times more without a protest! Only after He had pleaded for His crucifiers, *"Father, forgive them; for they know not what they do!"* (the spirit of pardoning love, which is an uppermost necessity for our postwar world); only after the crucified Son of God had provided for His mother (may all you young folks follow His example and care for those who, under God, gave you life); only after He had assured the thief and murderer crucified at His right that immediately after his death he would be with Him in Paradise (cling to this promise of free grace, the pledge that heaven is ours without good works, without any period of purging, without any prayer for the dead, simply by the Savior's limitless love!); only when the long exposure to the sun and wind, the raging fever in His body, the inflammation of His wounds, and especially the agony of His soul tortured Him beyond endurance, did His parched lips gasp, *"I thirst."* A single word, as recorded in the Greek New Testament, but what a world of meaning it contains!

Few pains are comparable with the torment of thirst, which can drive men mad. Soldiers who escaped from Japanese prison camps on the Philippines report concerning the death marches: "The sun beat down, the dust choked us, the smell of the dead was everywhere. We didn't even think about the dead any more. All we thought about was water, water. We would see a glass of water in our mind . . . but in our mouth there was nothing but dust. . . . We were half crazy with thirst. We had to get water. We would stop and drink water out of a mudhole where dead carabaos were lying in the middle of it."

Beside that bodily thirst, however, Christ was tortured by a spiritual thirst for His Father's presence, which made Him cry out, *"My God, My God, why hast Thou forsaken Me?"* It was not just the death of a martyr, that crucifixion at Calvary; it was rather — and here is the cornerstone and the keystone, the foundation and arch, of our faith — the death of an atoning Savior. He suffered there for all humanity's endless disregard of divine Law. At Golgotha's high altar He sacrificed Himself as *"the Lamb of God, which taketh away the sin of the world."* He took the transgressors' place, suffering in His own body and soul what every sinner should suffer and will suffer without Him. Think of the punishment one fracture of the divine Law can bring into your life, and then measure, if you can, the unnumbered millions of myriads of iniquities in the lives of all men! Old Adam Clark estimated that a single thistle seed will produce more than a hundred flowers each with 300 or 400 seeds. The fourth generation of a single thistle seed could thus produce the unbelievable sum of 7,962,624,-000,000,000,000,000 seeds. The crimes of two billion human beings multiply even with far more shocking horror; yet Jesus bore them all, for it is recorded, *"The Lord hath laid on Him the iniquity of us all."* If a single evil thought or act can send our souls to hell; if the transgression in only one man's life can push nations into war, destroy thousands of soldiers, bring misery on masses, and lead multitudes to eternal ruin, how terrifying beyond human understanding must have been the weight of sorrow which helped make Jesus cry, *"I thirst,"* and almost crushed His soul into death!

A missionary in the South was telling the story of the crucifixion to mountaineers, when suddenly a little boy broke in to demand, "Did the Germans do that, too?" Yes, we answer, not only the Savior's countrymen and the Romans crucified Him, the Germans helped, too, especially through the cruel criticisms of the Bible which sprang up in their country a century ago, and which continue in the assaults of National Socialism against our faith. But the British helped crucify Him, too, with their increasing rebellion against the Redeemer. The customs office in New York City held up large quantities of atheistic, antireligious literature printed in England during the blitz when that nation should have been on its knees — destructive material which somehow high American officials later permitted to enter our country over the collector of customs' protest. We Americans also helped nail Jesus to the cross, with our false claims of superior righteousness despite increasing sins, with our ingratitude to God, who helped us escape the horrors of the war while people across the seas have suffered unspeakably. Even you and I — let every one of us say, "especially I" — helped crucify Christ at Calvary. The hymn which should constantly be on our lips sings:

> Chief of sinners though I be,
> Jesus shed His blood for me.

Unless you — and I do not care how important and widely publicized you may be — realize in a contrite, believing heart that your transgressions made God's Son moan, *"I thirst";* that your violations of the divine Law riveted Him to the cross and sent Him to death — you have forfeited heaven; you have sent yourself to hell.

America is not troubled by thirst today, when despite wartime restrictions, liquor flows in wide, treacherous streams — eight billion dollars' worth bought in our land last year. Eight billion dollars — and much of it consumed by young people who forgot God and purity; by grown-ups who used it to promote unfaithfulness, marital strife, crime, and murder; by oldsters who drank it to forget the Lord, continue in lust, and fill our poorhouses, hospitals, and asylums! The Germans lost a bridge over the Rhine because they were drunk; and many people in our nation have lost their decency, their opportunity in life, their immortal souls, because they were overcome by liquor. The newspapers used large headlines to tell us that the Russian delegation at Yalta brought 14,000 bottles of vodka and wine to the conference, but no successful international accord was ever written with that much liquor. America, I repeat, is not thirsty; but many of you will be spiritually parched if you continue to reject your Redeemer. I have seen wealthy people who gave up their church driven by restlessness and even mental disturbance. I have received, from some of you without Christ, letters which show that your soul, dry and bitter in sin, suffers from unrelieved sorrow. Look to the cross; hear Jesus plead, *"I thirst";* accept Him as your own Savior! Then on the deserts of sorrow through which you must travel you will have the soul-sustaining water of life which the Savior promised when He cried out in the city of Jerusalem, *"Whosoever drinketh of the water that I shall give Him shall never thirst."*

This blessed supply of the water of life can be yours, no matter how handicapped or burdened by sin you are. Fellow sinners and fellow redeemed, Jesus never bars any repentant sinner from His mercy. A Champaign, Illinois, baby dies because its parental blood types clashed; but the blood of Jesus Christ never kills — it always cleanses and saves. The Holy Spirit grant that today, as you hear your dying Savior gasp, *"I thirst,"* you will bow before Him, admit your guilt, and capture the heavenly guarantee of His grace!

II

WHEN WERE THESE WORDS SPOKEN?

This pardon comes to you with double certainty as you find the answer to the question: When were these words, *"I thirst,"* spoken? The text replies definitely: after Jesus knew *"that all things were now accomplished."* The thirst-tortured Christ first thought of others, then of Himself. He was concerned more about your deliverance than His own suffering. What a blessed, uplifting thought and example for you, the sick and afflicted! Your burden will be lightened if in your sorrow you try to help others. Hear the story of Elizabeth Johnson, who lived in Casey, Illinois, not far from St. Louis! As a young girl she was afflicted with an injury to her spinal column that made her spend the rest of her life in bed. Her head could not be moved even two or three inches without causing excruciating pain and bringing the danger of death. Before this heavy burden was laid on her she had pledged fifty dollars which, a missionary told her, would purchase freedom for an African slave girl. As she lay on her bed in constant, unrelieved pain, the thought kept running through her mind: "I must fulfill my pledge to redeem that African slave girl. I must earn fifty dollars." But how? Finally, her father made an elaborate arrangement whereby Elizabeth, without raising her head, could make a quilt. Daily she toiled, and, as she later wrote, "each stitch caused pain." When the quilt was finally finished, no one offered to buy it. For fourteen years it lay in her room, while daily she prayed that God would help her free an African slave girl. Then one day a clergyman, who heard of Elizabeth's sacrifice, took the quilt, showed it wherever he went, in "trains, hotels, private homes, or in church," and told its story. He finally sold it for six hundred dollars. But that was only part of Elizabeth's devotion. By making bookmarks with Scripture verses, the helpless sufferer, with the aid of her family, gathered twenty-five thousand dollars for Christ — and untold happiness for herself. What are you with good health and large incomes doing for the Savior? How are you on sickbeds, in hospitals, and asylums helping your fellow men? At least you can pray and follow the crucified Christ in turning your thoughts from yourself by helping others.

Note especially, however, that when Jesus cried, "*I thirst,*" He knew, as our text emphasizes, "*that all things were now accomplished.*" Through His death, which followed within a few moments, all things required for the deliverance of sinful man would be completed. God had a plan for your salvation, made long before you were born, ages before the world was created — a plan of marvelous mercy, foreknown in all its details, the most perfect, powerful program God Himself could decree. This eternal outline of redemption demanded that Christ lay down His life for sinners, pay the entire price required for their ransom and atonement, go the whole way in redeeming and restoring them to God, leave nothing undone which would help reunite us with our heavenly Father. It is not Bible truth that man must help in his redemption. Because of our transgressions we are spiritually dead; and just as little as a corpse can move its lips or raise its arms, so little can we bring ourselves a small quarter of an inch closer to heaven. Jesus did all, suffered all, paid all, fulfilled all, so that nothing remains for us to complete. Our salvation is not a half-and-half proposition. Our deliverance from ourselves, from sin, death, and the devil's dominion is not even 99.999999 per cent Christ's and 1 billionth or 1 trillionth of 1 per cent ours; it is all Christ's. When He died on the cross, "*all things were . . . accomplished.*"

Have you ever stopped to realize that our Lord's full salvation is one of the few finished tasks men know on earth? We are told, of course, that as a result of the war we will be able to say, "All things are now accomplished which serve to remove fear and fright, need and want, political sins and suffering — for all men throughout the world." Be sure of this, however; bloodshed on the world-wide scale of the second global conflict never finishes anything; rather does it create and intensify new international difficulties, new national problems. Jesus could say, *"It is finished,"* when He died; yet, when many millions of soldiers and civilians are killed in the brutality of history's heaviest struggle, we cannot say, "It is finished." Indeed, many of our difficulties are only begun. For instance, our hardest financial problems have just started. You cannot laugh a $300,000,000,000 debt away by saying that we owe it to ourselves. You cannot guarantee 60,000,000 workers steady employment through a paper program. A day of real reckoning awaits the United States, despite the glowing pictures painted by politicians, unless we truly repent and return to God. As citizen to citizen, I ask you: Have you seen any real, nation-wide evidence of that repentance? We had an impressive, Spirit-blessed service in Chicago last Sunday, where 25,000 Christians gathered in the Stadium to confess their own sins and their share of the nation's shortcomings. But where, outside certain church circles, do you hear anything of true repentance at a time when America needs it most?

Nor can we say, *"All things were now accomplished,"* when we think of the moral problems the war has created. The blood our men shed in New Guinea, Tarawa, Saipan, Luzon, Iwo, on the Aleutians, throughout North Africa, Sicily, Italy, in France, Belgium, Germany, has not made us a morally better nation. A Washington authority now discloses that about 8 per cent of American children are born illegitimate. Medical experts assert that about 20 per cent of American mothers practice prenatal murder.

Again, we cannot say, *"All things"* are *"now accomplished"* in our poltical life, or truthfully claim that the freedoms and liberties for which the lives of our youth have been sacrificed are now positively guaranteed for us; that the world is ready for the warless period repeatedly promised. The world is ready, unless God intervenes, for further upheaval. Does it look to you, as you see the startling flare-ups of red radicalism throughout continental Europe, that we are headed for a smooth and happy existence in our own country? Do you really believe our free government is automatically assured to us, entirely apart from God, when the forces of atheism have constantly increased throughout the earth, even in our own land? I know that these questions will produce another flock of unsigned letters. A member of the Communist Political Association in St. Louis warned me that he and his comrades were taking down every word I uttered and that the time was coming when they would use every syllable against me. But I offered, and this holds for any of you, to send them a full copy of each message, and thus save them considerable trouble and expense. At the same time I told them that no minister of the Lord Jesus Christ could ever be intimidated by the threats or the practices of atheists.

Everything else in life is incomplete, unfinished, uncertain; but, thank God with me today, your redemption is sure, because it is sealed in the blood of the Lord Jesus! He left not even the tiniest part of your salvation unpaid, undone, unfinished. Believe it with all your hearts and defend it, if necessary, with your lives, especially after the war, when schisms, sects, and heresies will be spawned over the face of the globe. Though these new creeds (some of them recently revealed as religious rackets) may claim distant connections with Tibet, India, China, or emphasize absurdities like "tuning the soul to cosmic rays," all of them agree in teaching that the Bible on which America was built is not sufficient revelation; that the self-sacrifice of Jesus at Calvary is not complete redemption; that the blood which flowed from Christ's thorn-crowned head, from His scourged back, from His nail-pierced hands and feet, from His riven side, is not adequate cleansing; that the death He died at gory Golgotha must be supplemented by human efforts, individual sacrifices, personal payments. Church councils have damned us for repeating the words of Scripture itself, *"By grace are ye saved, through faith,"* or with the ring of Luther's Reformation cry, *"Therefore we conclude that a man is justified by faith without the deeds of the Law."* Powerful religious bodies teach today: Souls have to be prayed or paid into heaven; every one of us must try to earn his way; saints and martyrs, angels and archangels, can help make way for us. Yet Jesus Himself plainly asserts, *"I am the Way . . . no man cometh unto the Father but by Me."* My beloved, your salvation is all grace, all mercy, all compassion, because it is all of Jesus and His limitless love. When He bowed His head into death at Calvary, it could truly be said, *"All things were now accomplished." "It is finished."* Therefore stop doubting whether you can be saved! Stop putting question marks behind the thousands of Scriptural promises, torturing yourself with the thought that you must be good, do good, live right, think right, speak right, before these pledges of Gospel grace hold for you! Rather remember with every glass of water you drink how the tortured Savior cried, *"I thirst"* — only when He knew that *"all things"* required for your salvation, your sanctification, your strengthening, your comfort, *"all things"* necessary to defeat your own evil nature, the supremacy of sin in your life, the darkness of death, and the hideousness of hell, were accomplished for you.

III

WHY WERE THESE WORDS SPOKEN?

Even this does not exhaust the rich comfort of the fifth and shortest cry from the cross, *"I thirst."* We gain further assurance when we ask, "Why were these words spoken?" Here, too, our text gives us an unmistakable answer, for we are told that Jesus raised His voice *"that the Scripture might be fulfilled."* In each of our Lenten messages this year I have been trying to show you with the Spirit's help what a sure and certain basis our faith has in Scripture; and here is evidence piled on evidence. Nothing was accidental at Calvary. The action of Christ's enemies, the greed of His crucifiers, the tactics of the soldiers, the ridicule of the rabble, were far more definite than the schedule of trains on your timetable even when they are on time. A thousand years before Golgotha, David had foretold this burning thirst; and thousands of years before that, God foreknew even the smallest happening on the Hill of the Skull. Now, to impress us with the truth that *"Scripture cannot be broken,"* to show us in our troubles how the wondrous Word must go into fulfillment, Jesus said, *"I thirst."* He was thinking of you also in His agony; and during the last moments of His anguish He placed a final seal on Holy Writ so that friends would be strengthened and foes startled into studying its truth.

May His words, by the Spirit's blessing, have a similar glorious effect today! Believers who bow before the

Lord Jesus as your only Redeemer, trust the Savior when He assures you, *"the Scriptures must be fulfilled"; "all the promises of God in Him are yea, and in Him Amen"!* When Christ offers guidance in your darkness, comfort in your affliction, love in your losses and bereavements, friendship when others desert you, hope when despair would destroy you, forgiveness when your sins alarm you, life eternal when you hover at death's edge, heaven when your eyes close the last time, then with all the strength of your soul, the might of your mind, the power of your spirit, believe — don't try to understand, just trust God! — that the earth below you will disappear and the skies above vanish before one syllable of His divine, cross-gained, blood-sealed promises proves false!

You to whom this broadcast is particularly dedicated, who have never known the joy, peace, blessing, that can be yours through Jesus — will you not for the sake of your immortal, preciously purchased soul stop resisting Christ and by His Spirit's leading be fair enough, wise enough, to study the Bible, to examine the record of His redeeming love? You can read the whole of Saint Matthew's story of our Savior's suffering in twelve minutes, and you may thank God in eternity for the Spirit's help in answering this invitation to devote the twelve minutes to the royal Redeemer.

In the last century William Hone, a London author and bookdealer, sacrilegiously devoted much of his energy and talent to writing satires on Scriptures, parodies on the sacred truth. One hot summer's day, while riding in the country, he too became thirsty and stopped at a cottage for water. A young girl there was so rapt in reading a book that at first she hardly heard his request. Filled with wonder that any story could so absorb her attention, he asked, "What book are you reading?" "It is the Bible, sir," she replied. "But why," the man of letters continued, "instead of playing on this beautiful day, do you read the Bible?" The answer was simple and direct, "Because I love it, sir." William Hone drank the water to still his thirst, but the Holy Spirit began to show him the Living Water for his parched soul. He rode home slowly with these thoughts continually flashing through his mind: "She loves the Bible. Perhaps there is something in it which I have never discovered." Before he went to bed he had resolved to read it through carefully and learn what made the child cherish it. That study of Scripture poured the Water of Life into his parched soul and led to a conversion which made William Hone, one-time infidel and scoffer, Christ's devoted follower. He burned all his own blasphemous books he could recall in an effort to undo the harm his sacrilegious writings had caused. To the end of his life he proclaimed the marvelous mercy Christ had shown him.

Perhaps some of you unbelievers have been placed before your radio this Sunday so that I could point you to Him who cried, *"I thirst,"* and tell you that He, your Savior, has eternal refreshment for your famished soul. Now that you have heard the truth, you must decide for Jesus or against Him. A courageous preacher in Washington well closed his sermon with the alternative: "Choose God" (I would say, "Choose Christ") — "or go to hell." But today, beholding all history's heaviest and deepest Sufferer, hearing Him plead, *"I thirst,"* I end my appeal to you with the invitation with which Scripture itself closes: *"Let him that is athirst come. And whosoever will, let him take the Water of Life freely."* God grant that *you* will all come! Amen!

STAY WITH THE CRUCIFIED CHRIST!

"There were also women looking on afar off. . . . Joseph of Arimathaea, an honorable counselor, which also waited for the kingdom of God, came and went in boldly unto Pilate and craved the body of Jesus. And Pilate marveled if He were already dead; and calling unto him the centurion, he asked him whether He had been any while dead. And when he knew it of the centurion, he gave the body to Joseph."

SAINT MARK 15:40, 43-45

O CHRIST, CRUCIFIED FOR US AT CALVARY: Draw our souls to Thy cross of shame and agony! Make our Spirit-filled hearts realize unmistakably that our sins helped betray Thee, condemn Thee, and finally nail Thee to the accursed tree! Above all else that Thou, our omnipotent God, canst give us this Holy Week, grant us a soul-deep sorrow over our many transgressions, together with a fervent, ever-deepening love for Thee, Thou Lamb of God, who through Calvary's torture takest away the sins of the world! What an all-loving, all-merciful, all-forgiving, all-comforting Savior Thou art, with pardon and peace for every one who trusts Thee! Yet how false and full of wrong we are! Since we have no hope but Thee, draw our country, our churches, our homes, our souls, ever closer to Thee! On this Palm Sunday, as we recall Thy triumphant entrance into Jerusalem, keep us from waving palm branches today only to brandish hammer and nails tomorrow, crucifying Thee anew through unbelief and carnal pleasures! Guard our loved ones, especially those in the armed forces, and help them walk always more closely with Thee! Hear us, forgive us, bless us, and strengthen us; for Thy truth's sake and for our eternal salvation! Amen!

ALFRED NOBEL, the Swedish dynamite and munitions manufacturer, who died fifty years ago, left a fund of many million dollars, from which five prizes of about $50,000 are awarded annually, one of them to the man who makes the most noteworthy contribution toward peace. With a hundred cities smoldering in war's ruins; with thousands of mass graves dug for women, children, invalids, and aged, cut down by the savagery of civilized nations; with tens of millions of our fellow men absolutely impoverished by this struggle, their possessions burned, blasted, or stolen, and their loved ones killed; with bloodshed and brutality wider than the world has ever before known, the Nobel Peace Prize Commission at its last session found not a single soul among humanity's two billions who has really advanced the cause of international harmony.

"But," you ask, "have those in charge of bestowing this prize not read and studied the remarkable plans now drafted to guarantee a warless world? Why have they not selected the author of one of several peace programs recently suggested?" Perhaps the Nobel Prize officials are becoming disheartened and disturbed. If you look over the list of Americans who have won the $50,000 award in the past, you will realize that the war has wiped out completely every proposal in their various outlines for peace.

There is One, however, who should receive the Nobel Prize for last year, this year, next year, and every year. Today, on Palm Sunday, I nominate — and I hope that you second this — Christ, the Son of God and the Redeemer of the race, as the mightiest Power for peace men have ever known. If Alfred Bernhard Nobel, who

Stay with the Crucified Christ! 137

made part of his millions by manufacturing explosives used to destroy human lives, had given his multiplied millions to bring Europe Christ's Gospel, he could have helped the world surely advance toward Him who *"is our Peace."*

At the beginning of the week commemorating the Savior's suffering, crucifixion, and death for the sins of mankind, I pray that you will find calm in Jesus. When on this Sunday He rode into Jerusalem over a carpet of clothes, amid waving palm branches and to the exulting cry, *"Hosanna! Blessed is He that cometh in the name of the Lord!"* even unbelievers recognized Him as the Peace Bringer. As they saw Him, not on a warrior's prancing steed, not brandishing a sword and carrying a shield, not at the head of armed legions, but riding on an ass and clothed in a workman's garb, and followed by psalm-singing civilians, they cried out, *"Who is this" "Prince of Peace"?* and welcomed Him with the same wide acclaim by which you fathers and mothers who have had sons overseas would cheer anyone who, you believe, could stop war's horrors. The tragic trouble with some of those Palm Sunday enthusiasts lining the streets of Jerusalem was this, that they shouted, "Hurrah for Jesus!" when the crowd was with Him but *"Crucify Him!"* when the mob turned against Him. They were for Christ at the beginning, but against Him at the end; and they lost Heaven's mightiest mercy.

Many of you likewise were once ardent followers of the Savior, but now you have turned your back on Him! Indeed, on Palm Sunday thousands of you recall the day when you knelt at the altar to promise before God and man that you would remain true to the Redeemer, even at the pain of death; yet today you are numbered among His enemies. Therefore, as I ask you to stand in spirit once more beneath the cross at grim Golgotha, I plead with all, in His name,

STAY WITH THE CRUCIFIED CHRIST

even unto the end, as the believing, sorrow-filled women, the centurion, and Joseph of Arimathaea did! Of them our text (Saint Mark, chapter fifteen, verses forty and forty-three to forty-five) testifies today when it says: *"There were also women looking on afar off.... Joseph of Arimathaea, an honorable counselor, which also waited for the kingdom of God, came and went in boldly unto Pilate and craved the body of Jesus. And Pilate marveled if He were already dead; and calling unto him the centurion, he asked him whether He had been any while dead. And when he knew it of the centurion, he gave the body to Joseph."*

I

DEVOUT WOMEN STAYED WITH HIM, AND AMERICAN WOMANHOOD SHOULD, TOO

It was about three o'clock on Friday afternoon when Jesus, commending Himself into His Father's hands, died, murdered by those He had come to save. Thank God, Good Friday is being observed in wider circles. This year especially America should be on its knees in complete repentance; yet massed millions of our fellow men will never know that the sixth day of this week marks the anniversary of Christ's self-sacrifice as their eternal sin-atonement. They will keep on playing, sinning, blaspheming, as though the Son of God had never shed His blood to redeem them. Friday afternoon and

Stay with the Crucified Christ! 139

evening cocktail bars, dance halls, night clubs, will be jammed, while many churches will not open their doors, and most of those that do will have plenty of seating space left. Because I want to meet you before the throne in eternity, I plead: think of your crucified Savior every day, but with double devotion on His death day, this Friday!

Never forget that the last word Jesus spoke from the cross, His farewell to a world that destroyed Him, was a Bible passage, *"Father, into Thy hands I commend My spirit,"* a quotation from Psalm Thirty-one! Will you have the solace of Scripture on your lips when you die, or will you end with moanings of pain, long-drawn shrieks of despair, even bloodcurdling curses? You cannot cite Scripture unless you know it; you cannot know it unless you read it or hear it. I join the Apostle in commending *"you to God and to the Word of His grace, which is able to build you up." "Search the Scriptures!"* Throw out the dirty sex magazines, the lust-laden books cluttering your shelves! I have visited exquisitely furnished apartments where not a speck of dust would be tolerated, and found the printed poison of degenerate minds openly exhibited on hand-carved bookshelves. — When Stanley began his trek into the heart of Africa to find Livingstone, he started with seventy-three volumes, weighing 180 pounds. After he had gone several hundred miles, he threw away some of these books because of their burden. As his journey lengthened, his library grew smaller and smaller until at last he had only one book left. You know what it was — the Bible, which he read through three times on that journey on which he found Livingstone — and Christ. Similarly, if you can read only one book, read

Scripture! Find time, take time, make time, for the Word of Truth with its winsome love of Jesus!

Had the world stopped when the Son of God stopped breathing, had fire from heaven destroyed the crowd at Calvary, who could charge the Almighty with cruelty? But though the sun darkened and the ground shook, the earth did not come to its end. No fire fell. The mob which had witnessed this most atrocious of all crimes, suddenly seized by fearful remorse, *"smote their breasts and returned"* to the city. Only a few stayed on the Hill of the Skull, among them chiefly a group of faithful women, who kept their watch a short distance from the cross. Thank God for their devotion! No one but Christ Himself knew how much comfort they gave Him. It took courage for them to admit devotion to One crucified as a criminal; still they remained with His dead body. It almost broke their hearts to behold the brutality with which sinful men murdered Him; but they remained on the spot.

Who were these loyal women, with the dying Savior until the end? Not the rich and influential, not the socially and politically prominent, but Mary Magdalene, who had been cleansed by Christ; Mary, the wife of Cleopas, and Salome. You can tell all that we know about these women in fewer than a hundred words, but in God's sight and by His grace they deserve our earnest gratitude. They had sacrificed the comfort of their home to serve the Master during His hard Galilean ministry; and now, when everything seems lost, when priestly hatred threatens to persecute those who followed Jesus, they still show their allegiance by staying at Calvary. Besides these two Marys and Salome we also see on

Stay with the Crucified Christ! 141

grim Golgotha's brow *"many other women which came up with Him unto Jerusalem,"* unnamed, unknown, unhonored, heroines of the faith, even as many of you women who quietly witness for your Lord.

The men, practically all of them, including even the disciples, had deserted their crucified Savior, but the women were found faithful. Is it not the same today? Who makes up the greater part of our church attendance? Who prays the harder, works the more earnestly, gives more liberally of themselves, their energy, their time, their money — the men or the women? Who suffers more for their faith, helps build the moral life in our country more effectively, influences the lives of the children, and therefore the nation of tomorrow, more directly — the men or the women? From Calvary on, the history of the Church answers: usually the women of God. The Lord bless them!

It is high time that many of you, who pride yourselves on being strong, virile, red-blooded he-men, but who truly are spiritually anemics, cripples, reject the damnable delusion that religion is a woman's concern; that the church is here for your wife and children; that religion is all right for those who like it, but you would rather bowl, play cards, go fishing, than attend services. You think you can have your faith in your wife's name and give your conscience a sop by sending your children to some kind of Sunday school; yet you have not enough courage to take what it costs to be a Christian. You big, six-foot two-hundred-pounds-plus men, who snicker at our creed as something weak and womanish, could not begin to show even a fraction of the fearlessness brave Christian girls have displayed. The very sight of a red-hot branding iron would make you turn pale and give up any principle you ever had; yet teen-age maidens, for the sake of their faith, have stood still and silent while fiery irons burned their flesh away. It is always proof of fatal religious decline when husbands, required by God to be priests of His Word in their own homes, fathers, directed to bring up their children *"in the nurture and admonition of the Lord,"* sons, instructed by Scripture to follow the pathway of divine truth, turn away from the Lord, find no time for church, never read the Bible. Those sinister signs of the time are evident in America now. Before we fall victim to the fatal folly which has helped ruin Germany and undermined other countries where religion is often regarded as the woman's concern, may the Holy Spirit awaken within the hearts of you men who have spurned your redemption the deep, personal realization that you are lost without Jesus; that the Savior you have denied will deny you before His Father! Men of America, turn to Christ!

Today, probably more than ever before, we need mothers and daughters who will stay with the suffering Savior until the end. Women have helped save America in the past; they must do it today. During the War of 1812 two British warships sailed into Massachusetts Bay, near Scituate, to capture American barges carrying precious flour. With no American battleships and no troops to resist the marauders, Rebekah and Abigail Baites gave the alarm throughout the village, and then, hiding behind the sand hills, out of sight of the British, these two girls marched, fifing and drumming with all their power. The enemy, hearing the military music, thought a large force was approaching against them and hurried back

Stay with the Crucified Christ! 143

to sea. These two courageous, resourceful sisters rescued not only the flour but also the barges and their crews. As Rebekah and Abigail Baites remained hidden from public view, so today women who love the crucified Christ can do even more. In the quiet of their homes American mothers, as they teach their children the first prayers, show them the Savior's love, help make their family circles dwellings of the Lord; as they work for their husband and his happiness, find time not only for the social side of the church but first of all for the direct service to Jesus; as they lead clean, chaste lives through every day's work and play, in schools, offices, factories, stores; in short, as Christian women follow the example of their sisters at Calvary, who remained with their crucified Redeemer until the end — they, under God, will be a mighty force in defeating America's most sinister internal enemies: atheist communism, materialism, sensualism.

We must admit, however, that the war, with all its clamor, high wages, false-front patriotism, has led masses of American women, young and old, away from the Christian ideals. One of the most shocking war casualties America has suffered, outside the fatalities on the fields of battle, has been a coarsening of its womanhood. Six brides successively marry a motion-picture comedian. Williamson County, Illinois, recorded more women divorced than married last year. A Chicago newspaper cries out, "Who'll take a baby?" and emphasizes that in this one city more than 5,000 infants, orphans from broken homes, need love and tender care. Many wives have learned to curse, drink heavily, waste their time in gambling; far worse, to spurn purity, marital faithfulness, and the devotion to their husbands overseas, as they neglect their homes, their families, and their God. One of the widest and most alarming spectacles in this decline is the fact that women who certainly ought to know better often take part in the present-day public ridicule of religion. We had a startling example of that here in Saint Louis a few days ago. A woman's club held an immense banquet at one of our leading hotels, and the entertainment actually featured a heaven — high up in the ballroom balcony, with fleecy clouds, golden harps, angels, and an archangel — for women who paid at least twenty-five dollars more than the rest. This hotel heaven, which followed cocktail parties, looked down on a skit presenting suggestive talk and action. Heaven is no joke; it is holy and hallowed. The Son of God had to lay down His life to give us its glory. It is bad enough, God knows, when men speak impurely and abuse the Lord's holy name; but when women sacrifice their finer, gentler qualities, even in public entertainment, it seems doubly dangerous. Again, it is tragic enough if women outside the Church listen with applause to the ridicule of decency; but what shall we say when among those present at this Saint Louis mock celestial banquet were matrons associated with the churches?

Mothers and daughters of America, spurn all the present-day wartime temptations to be bold and brazen, smart and sophisticated! Avoid double talk and double lives! Stay close to the crucified Christ, who redeemed you with His precious blood! Live for Him and by Him! With the Spirit's help lead modest, trusting, temperate, chaste, useful, honest, God-pleasing lives! Then you will find joy and comfort in every sorrow which may befall

Stay with the Crucified Christ! 145

you. Think of the agony in the hearts of those women watchers at Calvary, how they screamed, doubtless, when a Roman soldier plunged his spear into the Savior's side! Recall the numb pain and the anguish of torn souls which marked their homeward journey in the dark! But keep in mind that forty hours later some of these very women, the last at the cross, were the first to hear the cry of Easter victory, *"He is not here, He is risen!"* Similarly, if you stay with the crucified Christ until the end, His merciful help will brighten your darkest hours, lighten your heaviest burdens. An Arizona listener writes that her husband has left her because of relatives' interference; a Wisconsin wife finds letters from other women in the uniform of her husband, home on furlough; a Minnesota listener is married to a man who has not spoken to her for months and who is infatuated with a girl twenty-three years younger than he is. These records of sorrow are but a few of those which have come to my desk in the past week. Yet, to you crushed by the cruelty of such sins I say: Go to Golgotha! Behold the cross! Believe the Crucified's promises: *"I will give you rest"*; *"My peace I give unto you"*; *"Let not your heart be troubled"!* Then you will be mightily sustained! Women of America, stay close to the crucified Christ!

II

BELIEVING MEN STAYED WITH HIM, AND AMERICAN MANHOOD SHOULD, TOO

However, some men also, thank God! remained with their crucified Redeemer at Golgotha. Foremost among these was the centurion, the officer who had come to Calvary probably scoffing at the Savior, but who had left believing in Him. When Pilate heard rumors that Jesus had died, we read that he *"marveled if He were already dead; and calling unto him the centurion, he asked him whether He had been any while dead. And when he knew it of the centurion,"* he gave consent for our Lord's burial. That commander of the troops detailed to supervise the cruel business of the crucifixion knew Christ was dead because he saw Him die. But he saw far more. As he beheld the sun darken, felt the earth quake, heard Jesus pray for him and the other crucifiers, he cried out to the sobered mob, *"Certainly this was a righteous man,"* and again, *"Truly this was the Son of God."* Saint Luke tells us that *"he glorified God."*

This first convert beneath the cross was a Gentile, to show us that in Christ no classes or castes are preferred, but that all men, of every color and condition, stand before Him on the same level. The newspaper debate on how to punish the German war criminals continues. A British archbishop cries out: "Kill them"; but I always shudder when I hear ministers of God scream for blood. This is a decision for the State, not for the Church. A Negro high-school student in Columbus, Ohio, suggests that those responsible for the war be punished by having their faces blackened and being forced to live as many American Negroes must exist. That might be worse than quick death, for colored people are continually exploited, oppressed, and refused permission to occupy even a rear pew or a balcony seat in some churches. During the war, for the first time in the history of the United States, Negro and white troops fought side by side in the First and Seventh Armies, helped to capture enemy positions, and shortened the struggle. Now, if dark-skinned soldiers can battle shoulder to shoulder with white, can they not worship with them, particularly when they have no church of their own? The high priests at Jerusalem, revilers of the crucified Redeemer, would have kept that centurion out of the Kingdom had they been able, but — thank God! — in Christ's sight no color, class, or condition ever excludes a man from grace.

Keep in mind especially that this centurion, with Jesus until His death, was a soldier who did not hesitate to confess Christ! Men and women in the American armed forces, God wants you likewise to stay with the self-giving Savior. The danger to your soul is far greater after the victory than before. A director of the War Production Board, according to the Associated Press, declared that in Paris drinking and vice have been restricted because of transportation difficulties and high costs, "but," this Washington official added, "when France gets organized, I think you can confidently expect a little sin." How do you think American soldiers react when they see a Washington official wink at the wiles of the flesh? What do you Christian parents say when a man whose salary your taxes pay encourages defiance of divine truth among our armed forces? To counteract this, send us the names of your sons and daughters in the service, so that we can ship them Testaments, prayers, Scripture messages, and other helpful material!

We thank God especially for the centurion's faith. He recognized that Jesus was innocent, that the priests and the mobs were bloodthirsty liars. When our Lord died, this Roman officer cried out in deep conviction, *"Truly, this was the Son of God."* Have you military and naval men and women looked up to the cross and repeated the centurion's *"Truly, this was the Son of God"?* Don't be satisfied with any other creed! I hear it said almost every day, "It does not matter what religion you have as long as you are good, sincere, honest." That was not the centurion's faith; it is not Christ's teaching; it is not Bible truth. It is good Mohammedanism, for the Koran expressly maintains in twenty-eight places that all creeds are true in one respect or another and that no charge should be raised against any religion teaching the existence of God and the necessity of doing good. However, Scripture plainly declares that *"there is none other name under heaven given among men whereby we must be saved"* but the Savior's precious name. The infallible Word tells you that you can never earn heaven, because you were born in sin, because you live in sin, without Jesus die in sin, and go to hell in sin. You can be redeemed from eternal ruin only, but surely, by faith in the suffering Savior's death. Stay with the crucified Christ!

Praise God! some civilians also remained with the Redeemer to the bitter end, and even after He died! Our text tells us, *"Joseph of Arimathaea, an honorable counselor, which also waited for the kingdom of God, came and went in boldly unto Pilate and craved the body of Jesus,"* and that Pilate *"gave the body to Joseph."* What a remarkable man this Arimathaean aristocrat was — a well-known personage of wealth, probably of noble birth, and, what is more, *"a good man, and a just,"* who *"waited for the kingdom of God,"* namely, for the promised Messiah! He was a public official, a member of the Sanhedrin, the council which had condemned Christ to the cross; yet he had not agreed to this decision and had no part in sentencing the Savior. Indeed, Matthew calls him *"Jesus' disciple."*

We need twentieth-century Josephs in America's public life. Too often you Christian citizens have stood by idly while governmental offices were seized by unbelievers, atheists, and even felons. Right here in Saint Louis it was recently discovered that nearly half the regular employees in the office of State Motor Vehicle Registration had criminal careers. One had been arrested five times for holdups and robbery; two, seventeen times; others arraigned for grand larceny, drug act violations, automobile theft, gambling, and similar lawbreaking. Men with a criminal past have been found also in Federal offices at Washington. Only a few days ago officials uncovered the police records of several Commodity Credit employees. How many more ex-felons the Federal and State pay rolls contain is beyond our knowledge; and we all should be genuinely happy if these men would truly repent and reform. But we do know that there are far too many ex-convicts who continue in sin, and that far too few followers of our Lord are willing to enter political life.

This becomes the more serious when we realize that America needs Christian statesmen today if our blessed country is to repel the increasingly destructive assaults of godlessness. In Lutheran Finland, left-wingers, including members of the Communist Party, last week secured a majority in parliament, and crowds in Helsinki sang the International, the Red battle hymn! Remember what happened in Rumania a few days earlier and look forward to atheistic victories throughout war-weakened Europe and to the repercussions of this struggle throughout postwar America! Can you not see, then, that we must have in public office more men with Joseph of Arimathaea's spirit, disciples of the divine Christ, to resist the onrolling rebellion against God and His Anointed?

The crucified and lifeless Savior, according to the usual procedure, would have been removed from the cross and then quickly interred in potter's field. If a German prisoner dies in our country, that enemy soldier is buried with full military honors here in a foreign land; yet the body of Christ was to be thrown into a shallow hole beside the remains of murderers and blasphemers. However, it was predicted in Isaiah's fifty-third golden Gospel chapter that though they *"made His grave with the wicked,"* nevertheless He was *"with the rich in His death."* How marvelous that Joseph, as our text emphasizes, *"went in* BOLDLY *unto Pilate and craved the body of Jesus"* and gave Christ a costly rock-hewn tomb. Follow him, you men of wealth, not in honoring a dead Christ, but in acclaiming the living Savior! It is a shocking truth that today despite lavish incomes the cause of the Kingdom receives less financial support than it did during some of the depression years. Many of you moneyed friends are heading for the same disillusionment widely experienced after the last war. People lost the money they selfishly kept from the Church. Your swollen riches will not help you in your soul's crises. American soldiers on Bataan, a few hours before they surrendered to the Japanese, lit cigarets with $100 bills to prevent this money from falling into enemy hands. Ill-gotten gain never brings blessing. Some of you have grown rich through the sweat and tears and blood of your fellow men on the battle front, since this is a financially profitable war for millions in America. When victory approached, the New York stock market recorded a two-billion-dollar loss in one day!

Joseph resembles many of you in his one outstanding weakness. He had been only a secret follower of our Lord, because he feared the consequences of confessing Christ openly. He was like Nicodemus, who, out of fear of his countrymen, once came to Jesus at night, received the radiant promise of the new birth, heard the glorious assurance of John 3:16: *"God so loved the world that He gave His only begotten Son, that whosoever believeth in Him should not perish but have everlasting life,"* yet would not stand up for the Crucified publicly. Only when the Savior had died, did he come, probably with Joseph, who asked Pilate for the lifeless body. It took adversity to make these men speak for Him, and it has taken war's affliction similarly to bring many to God's Son. In a French internment camp two young men, harassed by long suffering, decided to answer the Holy Spirit's call and become missionaries. May God use whatever means is necessary to make some of you hidden, secret disciples open, bold, brave confessors of the Lord Jesus! Why are you afraid to go all out for Him? What can men, your business associates, your friends, your enemies, do to you if you are with the Lord? *"If God be for us, who can be against us?"* How the cause of the Redeemer could be strengthened if some of you big businessmen, doctors, lawyers, teachers, you members of Congress, city and state officials, would stand up boldly against the Savior's enemies, and, instead of speaking uncertainly of God, would proclaim Jesus' saving name! With the Spirit's help you could start a new day for America if, instead of hush-

hushing the Gospel, the promise of the atoning blood, the truth of Scripture, the saving power of faith, you would shout the glad tidings and publicly stay with Jesus until the end. God give many of you Joseph's joyful courage!

Four years ago the *Benares*, a large liner, headed for America, was sunk in mid-Atlantic by a German submarine. For several hours Jack Keely, an eight-year-old British refugee, kept himself afloat by clinging to pieces of wreckage. When he was picked up, half dead, the lad's first question to rescuers on the raft was, "Which way America?" At the beginning of this Holy Week we ask — in a different sense, but with the same love for this country as a land of liberty and realm of refuge, "Which way, America?" Are we to continue in the way of sin, pride, selfishness, lust, crimes, drunkenness, and especially idolatry, forgetfulness of our heavenly Father, rejection of His Son, and grieving of the Holy Ghost? Or are we to go the way of repentance, remorse for our transgressions, return to God, rededication to the Savior, rebirth and renewal? The Spirit give every one of you the humility, the faith, the loyalty, the love, which will enable you to stay with the Crucified to His end at Calvary and to your end in life's last moment, always with the faith and prayer of this ancient Lenten litany:

"O Christ, Thou Lamb of God, that takest away the sin of the world, have mercy upon us!

"O Christ, Thou Lamb of God, that takest away the sin of the world, have mercy upon us!

"O Christ, Thou Lamb of God, that takest away the sin of the world, grant us Thy peace!" Amen!

THE DAY DEATH DIED

"We also believe and therefore speak, knowing that He which raised up the Lord Jesus shall raise up us also by Jesus, and shall present us with you." II CORINTHIANS 4:13-14.

O CHRIST, THOU CONQUEROR OF DEATH: Eternity itself will not be long enough worthily to praise Thee, Thou Son of God, for having on the third day after Thy cruel crucifixion burst forth from the grave, resurrected in radiant glory. Give us Thy Spirit, so that we, being raised with and through Thee, may here on earth seek those things which are above and constantly praise Thee, our Savior, our God, our Life! Send an overflowing measure of Thine Easter joy into our war-scarred, sorrow-burdened world, and by this broadcast show masses throughout the country, that because Thou didst make full atonement for all our sins on the cross of shame and then didst rise from the dead to prove that Thy self-sacrifice was accepted by the Father, those who believe this truth of all truths have been fully freed from the curse of sin, hell, eternal death, and can look forward to seeing Thee face to face in the resurrection of the body, before Thine eternal throne! Bring this Easter gladness into many forlorn and bereaved lives, especially into hearts and homes overshadowed by war's death and destruction! As on the first Easter Day Thou didst greet Thy disciples with the promise of peace, so on this anniversary grant us the assured pledge of Thine unfailing peace of soul! Thou art risen indeed! Rise within us for our everlasting exaltation! Amen!

"THE Lord is risen." — May your hearts across the nation respond, "He is risen indeed," as you sweep doubt aside to believe the most blessed truth in human history—your Savior's resurrection from the dead! Do you recall the deception of victory rumors that swept our country? Radio stations broadcast the "electrifying news" that the President and his cabinet "were met, preparing for word of victory." Listeners were told, "The Germans quit." In Los Angeles the city council heard an announcement of surrender and rose to its feet, applauded, and repeated the oath of allegiance. Chicago courts in the criminal building were told "the war in Europe is over," and immediately a murder trial adjourned and other courtrooms were cleared. A New York newspaper reported almost 3,000 telephone inquiries. The prices of grain futures dropped two cents, showing again that trading may be more profitable in war than in peace. A few minutes later radio stations issued corrections and restatements, explaining that the reports were mistaken.

On Easter, however, we can announce, not in misleading rumors, but in assured truth, the final defeat of a far deadlier foe than any Axis alliance, not the conquest of an earthly enemy, but of a satanic foe, not a promise restricted to one group of nations, but unspeakable gladness for the whole world. That eternal, unchanging, positive victory is our Savior's destruction of death, His resurrection from the grave, the greatest event in world history, the mightiest miracle even the Lord wrought, the most striking of the Bible's proofs that Christ is our God and Savior, the strongest comfort in sorrow, the brightest light in darkness men can ever know. For heaven's answer to the disturbing question, "What lies beyond the grave?" for God's own promise to His children, bereaved by the death of their beloved; for the Holy Spirit's unfailing assurance that Christ crucified on Calvary is the complete, total, all-conquering Savior, who has made our departure from this earth a glorious entrance into heavenly life, stand with us today in spirit at the open grave, hear the angel proclaim, *"He is not here, for He is risen,"* and believe with all your heart: that first Easter is

THE DAY DEATH DIED!

Hear this marvelous promise in our text (Second Corinthians, chapter four, verses thirteen and fourteen), *"We also believe and therefore speak, knowing that He which raised up the Lord Jesus shall raise up us also by Jesus, and shall present us with you"*!

I
DEATH DIED FOR CHRIST ON EASTER

Note the assurance with which Saint Paul begins his praise of the resurrection and the promise of its blessing! Right at the outset he contradicts all atheists, infidels, scoffers, God haters, who claim that the Easter story is myth, fairy tale, folklore, oriental saga, the imagination of silly women, the wishful thinking of deluded fishermen. He begins, *"We also believe and therefore speak,* KNOWING" that God *"raised up the Lord Jesus."* No wisp of uncertainty lingers there. The Apostle says here, as he repeats elsewhere, "I know," not, "I guess," "I wish," "I hope," "I think," "I imagine." Read through this great man of God's other utterances in Acts as well as in his Epistles, and you will see that in twenty other passages his words ring with the same fact-not-fancy assurance, "I know," "We know." Our Christian creed is founded on God's truth, and the keystone in its arch of assurance is the sure and certain record of our Lord's resurrection.

Proud, blind men, of course, have contradicted the Bible. They hate to think that the Christ whom they have rejected may be resurrected and that they must face the living Jesus, who can send them to hell for their blasphemy. A few years ago, in one of the most carefully planned attacks on Bible truth, the claim was advanced that the remains of our Lord had actually been found by a world-famous archaeologist. But the whole thing was a fraud and was completely disavowed. The man who found the coffin never claimed that it was Christ's, nor do any traces show that a body ever reposed in it. No recognized scholar will dare to assert that the remains of Jesus have been found. Only amateur, irresponsible and unnamed enemies of Christ continue these discredited assaults. They revive the old, outworn lies that the crucified Savior's body was stolen from the tomb, that Jesus never really died on the cross; but both of these malicious lies condemn themselves. Even foes of the faith who slashed Scripture into a thousand fragments have been honest enough to admit that the resurrection is historically assured. The German Bible critic De Wette, a radical among radical enemies of the inspiration, declared on his deathbed, "The fact of the resurrection can be doubted just as little as the assassination of Julius Caesar." Even that is an understatement. Do we have the testimony of any eyewitnesses who saw the assassination of Caesar or attended his funeral? Not one! But we do possess the statements of

Matthew, John, Peter, Paul, truthful witnesses who actually saw the risen Christ and heard Him speak. Patriarchs foreknew it; Psalmists foretold it; Prophets foresaw it; Evangelists recorded it; witnesses reassured it; Apostles reaffirmed it; angels preached it; the empty tomb proclaimed it; our Lord's repeated post-Easter appearances proved it: the Christ who at gloomy Golgotha on Friday suffered agony beyond description, understanding, or measure as in His own holy body He bore the sins of all the world, their guilt, their curse, their punishment; the Savior, who with His own blood, body, and life paid the appalling price through which alone we could be ransomed from hell and death; the Redeemer who at Calvary Himself atoned fully and freely for the total transgression of all mankind; the Son of God, who, murdered by His fellow men, died amid unequaled agony and was laid into a sealed, guarded rock-hewn grave, on the first Easter burst the bonds of death as He emerged from the tomb — the Victor over death, the Conqueror of the grave, the Lord of life.

We who love the Savior can join St. Paul in our text, *"We also believe and therefore speak, knowing that"* God *"raised up the Lord Jesus."* Christ had to be resurrected, first of all, to fulfill the Old Testament promises, which are not, as Nazi agitators scream and American college professors echo, worthless, worn-out writings, but the sacred oracles of God. Second, Christ had to return to life to keep His own promises that though they might break the temple of His body, yet on the third day He would rebuild it. Third, Jesus had to break forth from the tomb to show Himself the almighty God with power even over death. He had to rise from the grave, fourth, to prove Himself the true Savior, since a dead Redeemer could be of no help; fifth, to give us daily the comfort and assurance of a living Christ; sixth, to guarantee our reliance on every one of His other pledges; seventh, to curb wickedness in a world of war and woe; eighth, to grant us the new life, by the rebirth in the Spirit; ninth, to come again in His second advent; tenth, to give every one who believes, eternal life. A Christ moldering in a Palestinian grave would fail in all this. Without His resurrection our hopes for time and eternity would be shattered.

Deep below Westminster Abbey is a burial vault for ancient kings. One morning, we are told, a visitor was accidentally locked in this ancient crypt behind its thick, solid door. All his shouting and knocking was of no avail. When the caretaker made his usual rounds, the imprisoned man heard him draw near but then walk away until finally his footsteps died in the distance. All day long the entombed man, hoarse and exhausted, had cried as loudly as he could and in terror dashed himself against the solid oak door, until at evening, when the abbey was hushed, he heard the creak of the entrance doors, and it dawned on him that he was buried alive. Just before leaving the building, however, the janitor stopped, for he seemed to hear a slight tapping. He listened more carefully, and there in the silenced abbey he heard a muffled rapping, a low moaning. Following the sound to the crypt, he unlocked the massive door and lifted his light, to see the imprisoned man fall unconscious to the ground. Had he not been rescued then, he might have turned insane, as some lost in the catacombs have. In a much higher way, had not Jesus risen from the grave, we should have been locked in eternal death, with no forgiveness for our sins, no comfort in the bleak, brutal hours of life, no strength in our weakness, no hope of heaven, nothing but the doom of hell — shriek and pound as we might. If those destructive enemies of God who like to laugh Christ away and with a superior smile try to reduce His resurrection to Palestinian fiction could live in any society that has willfully banished the Son of God, for instance, in the French Revolution or the Red Revolution or the Chinese Communist Revolution; if they could be brought face to face with the horror and hopelessness of men turned to beasts in their unbelief, they would indeed realize that the world without Christ is a living tomb, in which people may scream themselves hoarse and beat themselves bloody without being able to save themselves from sin, sorrow, and finally the doom of death. How true and necessary in a contradicting, Christ-denying world are the words of Saint Paul, *"If Christ be not raised, your faith is vain; ye are yet in your sins"!*

Praise Christ, however, worship Him, exalt Him, glorify Him — the crucified Savior lives! On that first Easter death died for Him as He *"brought life and immortality to light"* in the most magnificent of all victories. Should not the masses that keep their distance from worship and think of Easter only as an annual dress parade sincerely celebrate this day of death's defeat? In the early Church the resurrection anniversary was the festival for the reception of converts. With what greater force should this year's Easter, in a world of death and destruction, bring you the blessed, accepted hour for repentance and return to the redeeming, resurrected Christ! My beloved, if until this moment you have remained away from Jesus and against Him, may the Spirit gladden your heart, lead you to throw away false pride of self-justification, become poor in spirit, but rich in trust, and to approach your living Savior *"who was delivered for our offenses, and was raised again for our justification"!*

Come just as you are, even if, as some of you write, you lack the expensive wardrobe you think necessary for service! Remember that *"man looketh on the outward appearance, but the Lord looketh on the heart"!* A chaplain reports that while he was in New Guinea one Sunday morning a young officer appeared at the service — clad only in his underwear. After the worship he apologized, explaining that he had been wounded in battle, that his clothes had been cut away at the emergency dressing station, that he had had no chance to replace them and did not wish to miss church. When you have the living Savior you too know, *"He hath clothed me with the robe of righteousness."* My beloved, will this Easter, the day that defeated death, find you with Christ, for Christ, in Christ, *"the Resurrection and the Life"?* God grant that it will!

II

DEATH DIED FOR YOU ON EASTER

If you, by the Spirit's help, make Easter a time of soul resurrection from unbelief to faith, from denial to trust; if you believe the angel's proclamation: *"Why seek ye the Living among the dead? He is not here; for He is risen, as He said,"* then you should thank God with every thought, impulse, word and prayer that death died for you too; that through the living Christ the grave is

The Day Death Died

not life's goal nor the tomb its terminus. Rather, you can know with absolute certainty that there is a hereafter, an all-glorious, divinely prepared heaven, a life after this death, a resurrection after the decay of the body. This and nothing less our text promises us when it declares, *"He which raised up the Lord Jesus shall raise up us also by Jesus."*

How important this truth is in our massacre-mad world! Human life is too cheap today as death takes its daily toll by the tens of thousands. When a British air official is quoted as declaring, "We drop liquid fire on these cities and literally roast the population to death"; when the chairman of Foreign Affairs in our Congress is quoted as shouting, "From the emperor to the lowest Japanese ditchdigger — we'll hold the rats responsible for a million years"; when attacks on civilians daily become more numerous and more bloody — over the hysteria of war's hatred I want at least one broadcast to protest publicly against ALL inhumanity and brutality. Microscopic investigation reveals that shells like those which the enemy used at Iwo, where one of every three American marines was killed or wounded, were made of American scrap metal sold to Japan at huge profits. If we had only shown similar zeal in sending the Gospel to Tokyo, the number of Christians there could have been mightily increased, misunderstandings minimized, and spiritual fellowship enlarged. A listener near Philadelphia writes that two weeks ago Sunday a friend operating a large poultry farm sent to the near-by Japanese prisoner-of-war camp for two men who could help in an emergency. When the enemy soldiers arrived at the farm, they said, "We will do the work for you, but we must stop to hear a sermon on the radio." The poultry man objected that since he was paying them he certainly did not want them to stop until they finished the job. With that the two Japanese looked at each other, and one of them said, "We'll start, but we'll stop to hear the sermon all the same, even if you take it out of our pay." When they were asked what program they were so determined to hear, they replied that they had been prisoners of war in America for eighteen months but had never failed to hear the Lutheran Hour on Sundays. When the broadcast began, they stopped their work, and the poultry man listened with them. If on the first Easter Christ forgave the disciples who forsook Him, how can I hate those two Japanese? Rather do I want to help them! Chaplain E. V. Best in the South Pacific writes that on Easter morning word was brought that a Japanese Christian, a prisoner of war within a near-by stockade, wished to partake of Holy Communion. By special permission and with an official interpreter this man left the stockade to worship in the tent chapel. As a Navy quartet sang "Nearer, My God, to Thee," the enemy soldier and American fighting men worshiped together "about the broken body and shed blood of our Lord, who commanded us to *'do good'* to *'your enemies.'*" What a blessed Easter that was and how glorious this Easter can be for us, if, trusting Christ, we cling to the truth of our text, *"He which raised up the Lord Jesus shall raise up us also by Jesus"!*

Who else besides the Savior can offer us even a crumb of real comfort in these death-filled days? What assurance has any of you unbelievers who, when you take time to think of the end and the Judgment to come, often tremble in terror; you atheists who insist that man dies like a dog, but who, as the shocking deathbed scenes of some of your leaders reveal, are often gripped by horror? Can we discover the solution to the age-old question of the hereafter by consulting spiritist mediums? If you think that there is something in spiritism, read its books, and you will discover the denial of each truth for which Christ stands. Investigate its methods, and you will find fraud and falsehood. Keep away from spiritists! I know an easier and quicker way to destroy your happiness: stand in a cage of hungry, man-eating lions! Let a boa constrictor curl itself around you!

Can modern medicine give us any assurance that there is a life to come? Someone asked Dr. Chapman of the Steinhart Aquarium in San Francisco, "Can a fish frozen in liquid air come to life again?" and he answered: "If the fish has been frozen dead . . . it cannot revive. . . . No doctor has a formula for resurrection of the dead."

Can modern science restore life after *rigor mortis* has set in? A dean of Columbia University denies that one can even prove the reality of life after death. Indeed, he claims, man is far better off not knowing where he is going. Tell that to a passenger on a train! No one can have real, lasting happiness without being able to answer this question, "Where am I going after my life's journey?"

Can men of learning and wisdom produce any real, positive evidence of an existence beyond the grave? Nathaniel Hawthorne was writing a story on the discovery of a compound which would grant eternal life, when, in the midst of his work, he died. Similarly, every human author of any plan for immortality has collapsed in death.

Can the churches show searching men what happens to their body when it dies and is lowered into the grave? If they remain true to Christ, present-day preachers can bring immeasurable comfort, help, and guidance to groping multitudes. The curse of our age, however, is the denial of Christ's truth by smooth-tongued, mellow-voiced, but Bible-denying preachers. Listen to a leading Modernist as he says: "Yes, I believe in the bodily resurrection of Christ because I believe it is the simplest way out of it; but if any come to me and say they believe it was a vision, I have no quarrel with them. All I want to know is that a man believes that Christ made Himself known to His disciples, and I do not care whether He had a body or whether it was a vision. I do not expect to have a body myself."

Fellow sinners and fellow redeemed, on Easter, when, above all times, doubt and distrust are out of place, let us reaffirm the truth of our text, *"We also believe and therefore speak, knowing that He which raised up the Lord Jesus shall raise up us also by Jesus"*! Through this faith you have heavenly assurance that eternal death died for you on the first Easter. Believe this, trust it, build your hope for eternity on the Savior's promise, *"Where I am, there shall also My servant be"*! Don't rely on reawakening vegetation, the butterfly emerging from the cocoon, or on any other power of nature as proof for your resurrection! God give everyone of you the faith which moved Charles Reade, the British novelist. He had been a skeptic until he did what you unbelievers should do — read the Scriptures without the bias of prejudice and unbelief. Then, converted to Christ by the saving truth, he wrote these words for his own tombstone: "I hope for a resurrection, not from any power in nature, but from the will of the Lord God Omnipotent, who made nature and me. He created man out of nothing, which nature could not. He can restore man from the dust, which nature cannot. And I hope for holiness and happiness in a future life, not for anything I have said or done in this body, but from the merits and mediation of Jesus Christ. He has promised His intercession for all who seek it, and He will not break His word. That intercession, once granted, cannot be rejected; for He is God, and His mercy infinite. '*Him that cometh to Me I will in no wise cast out.*'" If only all dramatists, novelists, and journalists today would show that same loyalty to the Lord, thousands of our American youth, who avidly read their writings, could be saved from crime, lust, and hell itself.

Again, keep away from the thought that life after death is a sort of last-resort hope for the weak and womanish! If you ever go to Mount Vernon, home of our first President, stop before George Washington's tomb and read the inscription chiseled into its wall! Is it some smart, sophisticated line from unbelieving Voltaire, a sarcastic, skeptical reference to any other enemy of Scripture? You know better than that! The words carved onto this tomb are those of the Bible, yea, of Christ Himself, "*I am the Resurrection, and the Life; he that believeth in Me, though he were dead, yet shall he live.*" The faith of our country's father should be that of all its children today; or is America too proud to humble itself before the risen Redeemer? Has unbelief secured such a hold on our pulpits, schools, colleges, political leaders, that masses hesitate to join in the age-old confession of the entire Christian Church: "I believe . . . in the resurrection of the body," or in Job's centuries-older declaration, *"I know that my Redeemer liveth and that He shall stand at the latter day upon the earth; and though after my skin worms destroy this body, yet in my flesh shall I see God"?*

Christ, as our God, is able to keep His promise, take the body *"sown in corruption"* and raise it *"in incorruption."* I call your attention to two recent experiments. One was conducted by England's Ministry of Foods, which examined barley seeds from a jar that had stood in the British Museum for twenty-two years and previous to that in Tutankhamen's Egyptian tomb for 3,300 years. Careful investigation revealed that these thirty-three-century-old seeds still retained their vital properties. Indeed, London experts were able to make some of the grains sprout. Even more astonishing was the second experiment at the Army Air Forces Tactical Air Center, Orlando, Florida, where seeds grown from three small withered peas, likewise taken from the thirty-three-hundred-year-old tomb of King Tutankhamen, not only sprouted, but produced pestproof peas, far better in this respect than the present-day Florida crop. Now, if man can sow seeds in the ground after they have long reposed in darkened tombs, and produce notable harvests from them, cannot the Almighty, who made both seeds and men, resurrect our bodies committed to the earth and make them live again in glory?

See how definitely Easter is the day on which death died for you, how sure and simple your promise of eternal life is! Ask and answer these questions with me: Whence came death? From sin, for it is written:

The Day Death Died

"The soul that sinneth, it shall die." "The wages of sin is death." Is there no escape from this sentence? Thank God, there is through Christ, who defeated the grave! How did Jesus overcome death? He took away our sins. How could He remove our transgressions? He became the sinners' Substitute, transferred their iniquities to Himself, died to pay the penalty of their punishment, and then rose again to prove that He is, as heaven and earth testify, the Lord of life everlasting.

On Easter we see again that only through the atoning Savior can we have the promise of eternal life. The presiding judge of the United States Supreme Court recently suggested that bereaved parents find consolation by believing that if their sons die in battle they will automatically go to heaven; and to show this he quoted these words of one of Europe's most publicized churchmen in the First World War: "When a brave man has consciously given his life in defense of his country's honor . . . it is certain that death . . . assures the safety of that man's soul. Death on the battlefield," this church leader insists, "cancels a whole lifetime of sin; it transforms a sinful man into a saint." But Jesus never taught that you could earn your way to Paradise on a battlefield, as noble as such heroism is. Instead, He said, *"He that believeth on the Son hath everlasting life,"* and again, *"This is life eternal, that they might know Thee, the only true God, and Jesus Christ, whom Thou hast sent."* Heaven cannot be bought even with human life, but at the open grave it is given us by grace, through faith, *"without the deeds of the Law."*

Shakespeare could take a few sheets of paper, write one of his plays on them, and each sheet could become worth a hundred times more than its weight in gold. Leonardo da Vinci could select a bare plaster wall, paint his *Last Supper* on it, and produce a priceless masterpiece, which would not be sold for hundreds of thousands of dollars. Michelangelo could find a block of discarded marble and carve it into his world-renowned statue of Moses, which would command a fabulous price. But God, *"by Jesus,"* as our text emphasizes, can take our decayed, decomposed, buried bodies and resurrect them into the most magnificent masterpieces, the priceless treasures, the divine miracles that all believers will be in eternity; for here is the everlasting Easter assurance our text grants: the God who *"shall raise up us also by Jesus . . . shall present us with you."* We, as the eternally ransomed, are to be presented to Christ. Believe it, cherish it, hold tight to it! Come doubt, come temptation, come persecution, come death itself, cling to this triumphant truth! You, the quiet, unimportant people who look to Jesus; you, the sick, sorrowing, and soulburdened; you, the bereaved and brokenhearted; you, the opposed and the oppressed; you, the wan and the weak; you especially, but all who die in the Lord, shall have these glories: first of all, a resurrected body, as more marvelous than your present body as heaven is more wondrous than this earth; a new and radiant body — pure and perfect — free from the marks of sin, the ravages of age, the wounds of war, the mutilation of accidents, the amputation of disease.

There, in eternity, we shall also be without sin, without even one evil thought, with none of the envy, hatred, jealousy, covetousness, lust, desire which have made the world the madhouse we have seen these past years.

The Day Death Died

In the *"many mansions"* we shall behold beauty actually beyond all understanding or description here on earth. Now we have five senses: sight, hearing, smell, touch, taste. There, in heaven, we may have five hundred. Now we can discern colors only when at least four hundred million millions of vibrations of the air strike our eye in a second, but below that there may be scores of colors which will be revealed to us before the rainbow-encircled throne; for the Scripture promises, *"Now I know in part; but then shall I know even as also I am known."*

Resurrected *"by Jesus,"* we shall have no more sorrow. *"God shall wipe away all tears from their eyes,"* His unbreakable Word promises. How blessed that eternal homeland with no more pain or parting, no more sickness or sadness, no more want or woe, nothing but perfect, unending bliss beyond comparison!

There, before the throne in the celestial city, we shall meet again with those who have lived and died in the faith. What rapture of reunion for you gold-star parents to greet a son slain in the cruelty of a distant battle; for you orphans to meet long-lost fathers and mothers; you solitary husbands and wives to be restored to your departed helpmates! How true, even in war's blood and brutality, this exultation of our hymn "Earth has no sorrow that heaven cannot heal"!

There — and we ought to kneel down humbly when we hear this promise — *"we shall be like Him,"* our blessed Savior. We frail, sinful, selfish, human creatures, shall be so exalted, cleansed, and purified in eternity that we shall resemble our Redeemer in His holiness. Men have worshiped in thousands of different, anti-

Scriptural creeds, but never has one of these, with all their attractions and allurements, offered a single promise parallel to this golden truth, *"We shall be like Him."*

There, in the crowning glory, we and all believers shall be presented to Jesus. Neither kings nor emperors, czars nor presidents, have enjoyed a privilege as incomparable as this, by which we, resurrected in newness of life, shall see our Savior Jesus face to face, adore Him with the redeemed of all ages, with angels and archangels, cherubim and seraphim. We can only stammer before this stupendous miracle of divine love and ask — this is our prayer on the day death died for us — O God, keep us for Christ, for heaven, for the resurrection! Keep us in Christ even though we lose all else in life, even if we must be crushed and killed to remain faithful! Keep us through Christ in war and peace, sickness and health, life and death, now and until we behold Thee together with the Savior and the Spirit in the unending Easter radiance, for the sake of the resurrected Redeemer! Amen!

LOVE THAT WILL NOT LET YOU GO

"Go your way, tell His disciples and Peter that He goeth before you into Galilee; there shall ye see Him, as He said unto you!" SAINT MARK 16:7

CHRIST, OUR RESURRECTED, EVER-LIVING LORD: Where is there love like the deathless devotion with which Thou didst save us for eternity? Thou didst not only seek us when we were lost, plead with us when we turned away from Thee, Thou didst even die to atone for our sins and in the Easter triumph rise from death to give us life. With all our souls we thank Thee that the grave is not the end, and the decay of the body not the final chapter in human destiny, but that through faith which trusts Thy mercy, we have been freely granted the blood-bought assurance of the resurrection and the new, blessed life with Thee, the Father, and the Spirit. We praise Thee that although we sin much and often stray from Thy Word, Thou dost not forsake us, but in Thine endless compassion dost continue to call us back to Thee and to restore us to Thy grace. Through war and peace, pain and pleasure, youth and old age, life and death itself, keep us with Thee, O Jesus, our Savior and Sovereign! If need be, send us reverses to rebuke our pride, and help restore us to Thy love! Bless the broadcast today so that throughout the land many may be turned from themselves to Thee, from sin to salvation, from folly to faith, from hell to heaven! Mercifully guide America, its leaders and its people, to a holy reliance on Thy truth, a penitent seeking of Thy face, and a divine assurance of Thy power to save to the uttermost! Abide with us, Lord of love, for the day is far spent, and the world hastens toward its evening, when we need Thee more than ever before! Out of the depths we cry to Thee; from Thy high heavens do Thou hear and answer us! Amen!

EXPERTS are already discussing World War III. Despite the repeated promises of universal peace, despite the international conferences designed to banish bloodshed, men, whistling in the dark, show a courageous front but are sickened in their souls by the crushing fear that the shocking sacrifices of young American lives will not prevent another conflict. Even worse, military strategists are agreed that the next global struggle will be indescribably more destructive than the bloodiest we have known. Large cities, they predict, will be completely wiped out, not in days, but in hours; not by airplane armadas, but by swarms of superrobots with poison gases and new bombs a hundred times worse than the most devastating used thus far.

Because of this horrifying annihilation from the skies, authorities forecast that the coming conflict will send humanity deep down beneath the surface of the earth. Passing through plains and deserts on the way out here to the Pacific Coast, one can see thousands of holes, where gophers, woodchucks, rabbits and similar creatures have dug their dwellings. What a striking picture of proud humanity driven into the dust by the brutality of bloodshed! Essential defense and industrial plants will soon be built far underground, we are told, with subsurface living quarters, hospitals, schools, churches, recreation areas, and vast stocks of food. As soon as the first salvos of rocket bombs fly over the frontier to destroy homes and factories, the masses will scurry below like frightened animals retreating before disaster.

These dire predictions may be fulfilled unless men all over the world, including the United States and Canada, really repent and ruefully return to the Almighty. Yet, as they burrow into the bowels of the earth; as sorrow, worry, fear, suspicion, make many grovel in the dust of despair, those who have Jesus Christ, God's Son, as their Savior, can go up to new heights. The more deeply men dig themselves in, the higher you can be raised to heaven. Looking to the living Redeemer, who promised, *"And I, if I be lifted up from earth, will draw all men unto Me"*; following the appeal of His Word, *"If ye, then, be risen with Christ, seek those things which are above,"* you can have the heavenward, homeward vision. Imposing international treaties, signed and sealed with impressive formalities, may be discarded (we have fought one nation with which we made a perpetual alliance only twenty-five years ago); friendships may be formed only to be shattered (and some of you young folks know from your own experience how the war has produced unfaithfulness and broken marital promises); marriages may be solemnized only to be dissolved (experts are fearful that the postwar prosperity will reveal far more shocking depths of domestic debauch); political promises may offer prosperity but be crushed to pieces by adversity (remember how Nazi soothsayers lulled the German people into false security by the pledge that their cities would never be bombed!). Yet rising over human failures and falsehoods, you, the redeemed of Christ, with trusting faith in the Lord can always look upward to divine hope, because — and this is my message for you today — in Jesus you have

THE LOVE THAT WILL NOT LET YOU GO

during this life or the next. Hear this marvelous assurance in our text (Saint Mark, chapter sixteen, verse seven): *"Go your way, tell His disciples and Peter that He goeth before you into Galilee; there shall ye see Him, as He said unto you!"*

I

ON EARTH THE SAVIOR'S LOVE WILL NOT FORSAKE US

These are the pure, perfect words of the angel before the Savior's open grave. Our smart, sophisticated age likes to ridicule the angels; but these heavenly messengers should certainly not form the gibe of jokes. Because hundreds of Scripture passages mention these celestial servants, our broadcast believes that angels truly exist, as Jesus Himself directly declares that God has given them protecting, guiding charge over His children.

The angel at the open tomb gloriously fulfilled this mission! First of all he told the women early on Easter morning, *"He is risen."* How reassuring to have the report of the resurrection from an *angel's* lips! If we possessed only human accounts, we should be troubled by the same uncertainty which besets us when we consider any man-made claim; yet, because these sinless, superhuman servants of the Almighty, whose stainless lips constantly proclaim, *"Holy, holy, holy,"* announced the Savior's defeat of death, their testimony completely outweighs all blind, blasphemous contradictions.

Jesus *was* risen from the dead. He had kept His word, proved Himself God, shown that His self-sacrifice for the sins of mankind was accepted. How utterly different from the vain and empty boasting of infidels was His radiant resurrection! Three weeks ago, on a bridge over a Chicago park lagoon, a Detroit business man knelt, clutching a newspaper in his hand. He was a friend of Clarence Darrow, the Chicago attorney who delighted in denouncing the Christian faith. Before Darrow died in 1937, he promised that if he could return from the dead, he would come back to knock some objects from his friend's hand. Six times previously the effort failed. This year, too, the newspaper remained undisturbed; not even a breeze blew to move it. After a few moments Darrow's friend arose and declared, "I will be back next year and every year for the rest of my life!" Even if his children and his children's children should continue the experiment for a thousand years, the spirit of Clarence Darrow could never return. But Jesus — praise His divine power! — did come back; He fulfilled His promise, just as He always keeps His pledge.

The fact that Christ had risen was a summons to action. *"Go your way!"* the angel commands the women, the earliest witnesses of the resurrection. The first believers were not to stay in a cemetery, mourning for a dead Savior, but to go back to the world, testify to a risen Redeemer. Similarly Christians today must be ready to *"go"*; and the church that does not *"go"* is gone. If you know the agony Jesus endured when He suffered on the cross of sin and shame, transferring all your transgressions to Himself, paying the full penalty you should have suffered for your sins in hell, you cannot keep the glorious message of His mercy to yourself; you must *"go."* Therefore the divine truth calls out, *"Go your way,"* you preachers in America's pulpits, not the way of politics, not the way of popular applause, not your own selfish, Christ-condemning way, but the way of Gospel grace, blood atonement, and justifying faith! *"Go your way,"* the Holy Spirit directs, you churches of America — not the path of parties and theatrical performances, not the path of dinners and dances, not the path of socials and sensations, but the plain, hard, uphill approach to Calvary and the crucified Christ, God's Son and Mary's, the world's Redeemer and Restorer! *"Go your way,"* the risen Lord appeals to you Christians in America, not the easy, rolling road of recreation in the name of religion, not the wide road of card and cocktail parties, not the smooth road of compromise with unbelief and denial of Jesus, but the road of repentance, personal reliance on the Savior, and humble return to God!

These women, early at the grave, marvelous examples of the faith which should move our womanhood, were not left in doubt as to why they were to go. The divine messenger declared, *"Go . . . tell!"* If only God's angels would visibly stand before you and repeat this *"Go . . . tell!"* Stop for a moment to hear the triumphant truth that in Jesus men have a Savior who loved them with an intensity of affection which brought Him, God's own Son, down to a world of crime and corruption to be born in poverty, lowliness, persecution, to live for His fellow men, to help them, to befriend them in their needs and then by the miracle of His self-sacrificing devotion, willingly, knowingly, lovingly, unshrinkingly, to take the crushing burden, the eternal curse, the screaming guilt of their transgressions upon Himself, to be condemned in their stead, to suffer in their behalf, to die in their place, and then to rise again for their justification! Fall on your knees to thank God for this most magnificent mercy! Unto us poor, puny, frail, faulty atoms of humanity has been given the privilege of pointing men to the riven, but risen Savior, with the assurance that because He bore our sin, He offers not four fragile freedoms, but fourteen, full and final: freedom from fear, from sin, from hell, from doubt, from defeat by temptation, from despair, from overpowering grief, from spiritual failure, from the tyranny of an accusing conscience, from worry, from spiritual want, from crushing weakness, from Satan's control, freedom especially from eternal death!

What do we do with this marvelous message? May God forgive us! There is altogether too much hush-hush about the most glorious grace which God and man have ever known. Religion is being banished from many newspapers, except reports of ridicule, like the story of a cult founder who took thousands of dollars from credulous followers. He told them to inhale through the left nostril and exhale through the right. The Gospel is being pushed off the air. The Mutual System is the only major network which adheres to the real American policy of accepting Christian broadcasts like ours, and I trust that you express your approval of this policy to your station. While our soldiers laid down their lives to maintain freedom, including religious liberty at home, radio authorities who feature programs with suggestive, double-meaning situations and dialog stubbornly refuse to sell time at full commercial rates for broadcasting the Savior's Gospel.

Christ's message of salvation is being set aside in many churches. Is it too much to expect that at a time when our nation is confronted by issues of startling importance we should rely on America's quarter of a million churches to help keep us close to God, to proclaim the Redeemer's resurrection with a power and penetration hitherto unknown? Is it too great a demand, as we visualize the parade of our war cripples, men with only one leg or one arm, or in many cases none, men with their sight and their hearing gone, to expect that the preachers, exempted from the draft because they were to build the spiritual forces on the home front, lead our country in repentance and return to the Almighty? Yet during the war many of our pulpits became breeding places of unbelief, propaganda, sources for poisonous assaults on the Gospel. Not long ago a Middleborough, Massachusetts, six-cent daily newspaper displayed a half-page advertisement titled in large headlines, "Jesus was *not* the Son of God," a cheap, unscholarly rehashing of atheist arguments, written, not by a Communist Christ hater, but by a local preacher, who himself paid for the advertisement. If a soldier were guilty of the same disloyalty to his country this preacher shows Jesus, the military authorities would shoot him. If we want to keep progress and prosperity, the Church must keep Christ. New England should remember that particularly. It was founded 300 years ago by pioneers whose colony charters expressed their complete dedication to the Savior as the only Hope for sinful men; but New England has lost much of that faith. No other part of the country has produced and promoted as many sects which reject the redemption, deny Jesus' divine sonship, contradict the saving truth of the cross. Is there any connection between this apostasy and the unquestionable fact that large areas in the New England States have slipped backwards in population, in manufacturing, in wealth; that important sections of the textile, the shoe, and other industries have moved from New England and left large empty factories, with serious financial and social problems for peacetime? No state is so rich that, once dedicated to Christ, it can produce anti-Christian cults, build thousands of churches in which the inspiration of the Bible is ridiculed, the atonement rejected, the divine Deliverer reduced to the common level of all men, without paying a fearful price for such unbelief.

May our whole land learn this vital lesson! If the Gospel-preaching churches do not *"Go . . . tell"* now, while atheism, internationalism, materialism, skepticism, are all going and telling as never before, we may still suffer beyond measure. Our statesmen and diplomats may compose the best treaties which the human mind can produce; but if it is true — and Scripture says it is — that *"except the Lord build the house, they labor in vain that build it,"* how much more evident it must be that unless the Lord makes the covenant between nations, they likewise labor in vain that make it! Don't believe for a moment that without Christ and His blessing a thousand international assemblies can ever abolish war. The past centuries have witnessed treaty after treaty, but also conflict after conflict. It has been shown that from 1500 to 1942 England fought seventy-eight wars, France seventy-one, Spain sixty-four, Russia sixty-one, Austria fifty-two, Germany twenty-two, China eleven, the United States (for only 167 years and not counting Indian wars) ten, and Japan nine. Do you honestly see anything on the international horizon which promises that this frequency of strife will be reduced? As long as men can be sent into battle; as long as money can be made from bloodshed; as long as masses have evil, lust-filled, covetous hearts, those who exclude God from their procedures and programs can pledge themselves a thousand times to avoid war; yet a thousand times they will break their word and conflict will come. Therefore the churches should adopt one consuming postwar project: to follow the risen Lord's instruction by preaching *"repentance and remission of sins . . . in His name among all nations"* as it has never been preached before. Unless the Christian forces in the United States and Canada, the only actively belligerent nations in which not a single church has been destroyed by war, are mobilized for a program of world evangelism greater than any previously followed, sinister, sacrilegious forces will rise to unprecedented influence. If America wins this war without having masses contritely return to God, without having the churches rededicate themselves to *"go . . . tell"* the marvel of the risen Christ's mercy, we may suffer immeasurable disasters even in peacetime.

This puts the appeal squarely before every one of you; for those to whom the angel said, *"Go . . . tell,"* were not Apostles or professional preachers, but untrained women. They were to become messengers of the resurrection, just as God wants you Christian mothers and daughters to testify. If I could read you some of the records of remarkable conversions which God has given this radio mission, you would see that in many cases a humble, trusting woman, praying for her godless husband and living a consecrated life of radiance in the risen Redeemer, has been mightily used by the Holy Spirit in bringing her loved one to the Savior. If all believing mothers and daughters, before they engaged in social pastimes connected with their congregation, would first of all *"go . . . tell,"* the churches would experience phenomenal growth. If you men, with even wider opportunities for testimony to the risen Christ, would learn to speak about Jesus, unflinchingly tell friend and foe alike the story of His saving grace, the kingdom would come to us far more quickly. I ask you personally, have you told anyone that Jesus lives? A week has elapsed since the anniversary of the happy day when He defeated death, seven full days for personal testimony to unbelievers who surround you. To how many have you given this glorious assurance? You have had time for work, time for play, time for the radio, time for the newspaper, time for magazines, time for motion pictures, time for talk about the peace; but have you found a few moments to help win souls for the Savior? I cannot hear you answer, but God can. May His Holy Spirit give you who have kept your lips sealed the penitent desire to find His blood-bought pardon for keeping the story of His salvation to yourself! The Lord enrich you with the resolution: By Thy Spirit, O Christ of life and love, I will *"go . . . tell"!*

To whom were these women to bring the message of the open grave? The angel answers clearly, *"Go your way, tell His disciples!"* What matchless mercy! *"The disciples forsook Him and fled"*; yet Jesus still remembers them lovingly. They might run away from Him, but He returns to them. As the French, Belgian, and Dutch came back to rule their recaptured territories, they subjected to severe trials those who deserted their nation's cause during the years of Nazi rule. If Jesus had dealt that way with His disciples, they would have been destroyed; but His was the love that would not let them go. Bow thankfully before His deathless devotion! Everyone else and everything else may desert us, but not Christ and His mercy. Your letters show that your sons, your beloved wife or husband, are snatched away from you by death; but even the cross and the grave could not keep Jesus from coming to His disciples. George Matheson, a Scottish preacher, was torn by grief, because his sweetheart refused to marry him when he became totally blind. Then, it is said, he turned to Jesus and wrote the well-known hymn:

    O Love that wilt not let me go,
    I rest my weary soul in Thee.

One Sunday, later in his ministry, he suffered a collapse of memory; but turning to God in prayer, he found that though the powers of his mind might leave him, the love of Christ would indeed not let him go. After a moment of prayer he was strengthened to preach a strong sermon on an altogether different text. Similarly, Jesus will never desert you. Money, health, good name, may disappear; you may lose your loved ones, but not Christ. The disciples, fearful and faithless, had no right, outside the Savior's promise, to expect that He would return to them; but He did. You too may be so convicted of your own unworthiness that you feel God is through with you, that the Lord has cast you off; but you do not know the full measure of His mercy. You cannot sin too grievously, fall too low, transgress the divine Law too repeatedly, to be saved, if only with deep-rooted sorrow you plead, "Oh, come to me, Lord Jesus, forgive me and restore me!"

Suppose a committee of men had assumed charge of the resurrection publicity! They probably would have sent the first announcements to the Temple, to Pilate's residence, the high priest's palace, and the public centers of Jerusalem; but the angel directed the women messengers to the Savior's disciples. They, far more than the politicians and priests, needed the sustaining assurance that Christ was risen. The loving Redeemer thinks more of His humblest, simplest followers than He does of the mightiest unbeliever. He is more concerned about you who are His in faith, though you live far off the beaten path on an Alberta farm, a Texas ranch, or the Arizona desert, than about some of the imposing but godless figures who make international headlines.

Can you imagine what unbounded joy must have seized the disciples' hearts when they knew that the Lord whom they had deserted in His dying hour was truly resurrected? Likewise for us who are His, the whole earth contains no more basic and blessed assurance than that the Son of God, whom blasphemous men nailed to the cross, rose again as He had promised. Atheists may try to ridicule this truth, but in emergencies their bravado may fail them. Why is it that scoffers who never cross the threshold of a mission often clamor that their likeminded deceased relatives be buried by a Christian pastor? Is it not because they do not wish to take the chance of being damned by their unbelief? They fear that, after all, death may not be the end, that perhaps the Bible is right in describing the Judgment.

The highest evidence of this love that will not let us go is seen in two words of our text. The angel says, *"Go your way, tell His disciples* AND PETER." Glorious grace is expressed in that emphasis, *"and Peter."* Of the eleven remaining disciples, Peter had most reason to be ashamed of himself and least reason to expect the Savior's love. He had been the loudest in declaring that he would remain loyal at all costs. He had been the surest in repeating, *"Though all men shall be offended because of*

Thee, yet will I never be offended." He had been the bravest in starting a holy war for his Lord and cutting off the ear of the high priest's servant. Yet of all the disciples save Judas he had been most unfaithful. First he left his Lord and mingled with His enemies; then he denied that he knew Him; finally he cursed as he disavowed Him. Three times he repeated the fatal falsehood, *"I know not the Man."* He saw Jesus captive in the high priest's court, yet refused to raise his voice in His behalf. If the angel had given this instruction, *"Go . . . tell His disciples"* except *"Peter,"* we could understand why the overconfident, yet traitorous follower had been excluded; but — praise Heaven's limitless grace! — His love would not let even apostate Peter go.

Indeed, he is the one disciple whose name the angel mentioned and thus selected for special prominence. It is marvelous that the Bible contains general promises showing forgiveness in Jesus, radiant passages like, *"Behold the Lamb of God, which taketh away the sin of the world!"* or *"If any man sin, we have an Advocate with the Father, Jesus Christ the Righteous; and He is the Propitiation for our sins, and not for ours only but also for the sins of the whole world"*; or *"Though your sins be as scarlet, they shall be as white as snow."* In some ways, however, it is even more reassuring to read the individual, personal records in Scripture of heavy and willful sinners saved by the Savior's glorious grace. If your life has been stained by impurity, what comfort to know that David, penitently confessing his immorality, was restored to the Lord's grace! If some of you look back through long years of regret to a scarlet sin, what peace and promise to see the Savior refusing to cast a stone on a disgraced woman! If you have stolen, how strengthening to hear Jesus promise the penitent thief at Calvary that, through faith, pardon and paradise would be his! If you have lied, what assurance to find that Abraham, who had deliberately spoken an untruth, nevertheless, turning to his Lord, was forgiven. Above all, what uplifting, sustaining courage for you who were once ardent followers of God's Son, but who permitted yourself to be coaxed away from Him — and there are several million backsliding ex-Christians in the United States today — to know that proud, swaggering, boasting, self-confident Peter, who left his Master in the lurch and failed in the greatest emergency and opportunity ever confronting any man, could be singled out as the object of the resurrected Redeemer's special love and even be named by Him!

I pray God that you, once with Jesus, but now against Him, will return as Peter did, even in tears of repentance to the love that will not let you go. The Savior cherishes you though you hate Him; He clings to you though you run from Him; He wants to bless you though you curse Him. His mercy would have room even for Judas if he, truly repenting, had sought Christ for pardon; and certainly there is room for every one of you, no matter how black your transgressions, how frequent your iniquities, how cruel your unbelief, if only you come back to Him with sorrow for your sins, trust in His mercy, and the resolution to remain faithful!

Why then do you give the devil his way and object, "My sins are too many, too grievous, too constant, too vile, too destructive, too nasty, too bestial, too blasphemous, for His forgiveness"? Stifle these contradictions of our Savior's amazing grace by accepting Heaven's own unbreakable truth, *"The blood of Jesus Christ, His Son, cleanseth us"* not only from some sin, not only from small sin, but, thank God! *"from* ALL *sin"!* The Holy Spirit directs me to *"tell His disciples,"* and especially *you,* the unfaithful, the backsliders, the betrayers, the blasphemous, that God's Son suffered on the cross for your sins, atoned for your transgressions, paid for your redemption, freed you from death and hell's damnation; that you are saved by accepting Jesus and clinging to Him as your Redeemer. God grant that on this Sunday especially you unbelieving husbands or wives, parents or children, who should be united in Christ, will come to this faith!

Now what were these first witnesses of the resurrection to tell *"His disciples and Peter"?* The angel directed them to proclaim, *"He goeth before you into Galilee."* When they laid the Lord in the rock-hewn tomb, it seemed to His followers that everything was lost. Their hopes were dashed to pieces, their ambitions shattered, their predictions put to naught; yet in those darkest of days, they were to know that even though Christ had been crucified, His love would not forsake them. He was to go with them, yes, *"before"* them. I hope that today you will take these four words of Scripture, *"He goeth before you,"* as your life motto. Your letters reveal the hard roads many of you have to travel; but when the burden is heaviest, the afflictions most crushing, believe that Jesus goes *"before you"* and rejoice with Job, *"He knoweth the way that I take; when He hath tried me, I shall come forth as gold"!* Many of you have been journeying the long, weary road of sickness. Take heart as you realize, *"He goeth before you,"* since it is written

Love That Will Not Let You Go

of Christ, *"Surely He hath borne our griefs and carried our sorrows"!* Some of you toss in unrelieved agony; but remember, He was *"a Man of sorrows and acquainted with grief,"* as He bore in His own body the torture of all human wrong! Others among you will go to the cemetery this week and lay a loved one to rest. Push human bravado aside and look to Christ, who *"goeth before you,"* knowing the depth of your bereavement and providing the comfort your soul craves! No matter how hard or rough your road, how narrow and steep it becomes, how blocked by barriers it may be, *"He goeth before you"* to lead you, sustain you, overcome every obstacle and make a way for you when human strength and wisdom fail.

Sometimes, of course, we cannot realize that Jesus goes before us. Here in Orange, in the heart of California's citrus groves, two members of the congregation from which I speak to you volunteered to help in building a mission church near Long Beach. Day after day they hurried down to the construction of that house of God and gladly served without a penny of pay. One morning, as they hastened to this work of love, they were both killed in an automobile accident. Why did God permit this, while a hundred cars with infidels and scoffers roared safely over the same highway? We cannot find the answer, but some day we shall, and then we shall see that even this tragedy served a blessed purpose. One thing we do know now: Christ was with those two men when they went down into the valley of the shadow. As you turn your hearts to Him whose love will never let us go, believe that however completely you are crushed by sorrow, you can never drag yourself over any road of anguish on which your Savior has not gone before you! How much more blessed you believing sufferers are, with your major operations and your gnawing pains, than those who leap blindly into the dark, without the Lord's guidance!

Note that the angel announced, "*He*," the resurrected Christ, "*goeth before you* INTO GALILEE"! Few Christians realize what Galilee meant to the disciples. They had dreamed dreams of their Lord's world dominion; they had lived in the capital, Jerusalem, where they often had to shade their eyes against the Temple's glittering glory. Now all that was over, and they had to go back to the land of the half-breeds, the hinterland of the mixed races, which the proud citizens of Judea shunned except when they could make money there. Yet that despised territory our Lord, resurrected in power and glory, chose as the place where He would reveal Himself anew to His disciples. What a faithful Friend Jesus is when He selects the locality others spurn! What a Protector of the poor, Defender of the downtrodden, Friend of the caste-cursed He is! Thank God, you underprivileged folks who have no large, attractive, advantageously located homes: the resurrected Redeemer will come to you, too! Praise Him, you, the needy who have not enjoyed any of war's prosperity!

No particular reason is offered in our text for choosing Galilee. Perhaps the disciples were to make the Savior's resurrection known first in their own homes. Before they were to start out on missionary journeys to far-distant fields, their own loved ones were to be brought to faith. Our family circles are likewise the centers around which much of America's welfare and our own spiritual happiness revolve. Let Jesus rule our households! Let fathers, as priests of God, find time for Scripture reading and prayer with their loved ones, and the humblest dwelling will have more joy than the most ornate has without the Savior. Keep the cleansing Christ in our families, and we have hope, assurance, guidance for whatever tomorrow may bring.

II

IN HEAVEN THE SAVIOR'S LOVE WILL BLESS US FOREVER

There, in Galilee, the disciples were promised, *"shall ye see Him,"* the crucified but now victoriously living Savior; and they did see Jesus. The brief accounts of the Gospels tell us in short, simple language, *"Then were the disciples glad, when they saw the Lord."* How glad, we shall never know. Their sorrow was turned to joy; their bereavement to rejoicing; their despair to triumph. The risen Redeemer, whom their own eyes could behold, who talked with them, walked with them, ate with them, had proved Himself their God, possessed of power over death itself. Why should they tremble in terror any longer? Why should they cower before their enemies? Beholding their living Lord, they knew that every promise He had made them was as sure and certain as His own victory over the grave.

It will not be given to us to meet the Savior face to face here in this world, as they did; but the angel's promise, *"There shall ye see Him,"* holds a far higher happiness for us. Only for forty days did the death-conquering Christ remain on earth before He ascended into heaven, but we who trust Him with true faith shall see Him throughout eternity. There His love will never let us go, even for a brief moment's parting. Because He rose from the dead we shall rise, too. Errorless Scripture promises, *"We shall be also in the likeness of His resurrection."* There, before the throne, not as vague, cloud-like spirits, but with heavenly bodies and with a sense of sight incomparably sharper than our present vision, we shall behold our Savior in His celestial beauty. Even now we can join Job in exulting, *"Yet in my flesh shall I see God."*

Who can measure the magnificence of that mercy? Our own eyes shall behold Him before whom the holy angels shield their faces. The Deliverer, whom the sacred hosts now adore, before whom the ransomed saints and martyrs in the ten thousand times ten thousand bow humbly, to whom our own departed loved ones in the faith will sing their heavenly hallelujahs — Him our resurrection eyes shall see in far clearer vision than earth ever afforded. Fellow sinners and fellow redeemed, is it not worth giving up everything you possess, selling all you have to be assured of that priceless privilege? Yet thank God daily that to secure this highest and holiest blessing even the omnipotent God can give you, you need only trust Christ's full power to save, humbly accept Him as your only but all-sufficient Redeemer!

The disciples should have been sure that Jesus would meet them in Galilee, for He had told them that He would. You too, looking to heaven, likewise have the angel's promise, *"There shall ye see Him,* AS HE SAID UNTO YOU." Jesus never fails; He always keeps His word. *"Heaven and earth shall pass away"* before one syllable of His promise remains unfulfilled. When He declares,

"Where I am, there shall also My servant be," when He asks His Father that all believers *"be with Me where I am,"* know that this shall come to pass *"as He said unto you"!*

Can you not see that the most important issues in your life are to know what Jesus has *"said unto you,"* to trust His promise for the piled problems and the multiplied miseries of this age, to know your Bible, read it, memorize it, love it, and live it? Make time for the Word of Truth with its winsome, wondrous Savior! Then, as you cling to the love that will not let you go on earth or in heaven, the Holy Spirit will strengthen you to raise your right hand in the oath of eternal allegiance and to declare, "O Christ, Redeemer and Ruler of my soul, my love will never let Thee go. So help me God!" Amen!

JESUS CHRIST — OUR LIFE IN DEATH!

"Set thine house in order, for thou shalt die." 2 KINGS 20:1
"He that believeth on the Son hath everlasting life."
                                                    SAINT JOHN 3:36

LORD GOD OF THE NATIONS: We come before Thee in this hour of national crisis, when death has taken our Chief Executive, to beseech Thy continued guidance of our country. May his sudden departure from life remind us that we are to number our days, apply our hearts to eternal wisdom, and be reconciled to Thee through faith in Thy Son, who gave Himself for us on the cross and rose again to seal for us the assurance of everlasting life! Make us penitent, contrite, sin-confessing! Give American men and women the courage which comes not only with the vision of victory, but also through the knowledge of Thy Son, their Savior! Let not this sudden death delay the day of reconciliation among all nations, particularly through the preaching of the Gospel of Thy Son, Jesus Christ, our Lord! Humbly we invoke Thy blessing upon the new President and ask that Thy Spirit direct him always to follow Thy will and execute his office according to Thy Word. Show us that our country's hope and help are in Thee, more than in armies, industries, and human leaders! O God of all grace, continue to be with us, as Thou wast with our fathers, for Jesus', our Savior's, sake! Amen!

Jesus Christ — Our Life in Death!

TODAY the body of President Franklin Delano Roosevelt is lowered into the earth at Hyde Park, New York. Perhaps never before has the departure of one man been so widely and impressively commemorated as the death of our thirty-first Chief Executive. Not only in these United States, but also in at least fifty allied nations and in the few remaining neutral capitals official and personal mourning reigns. Troops on the march to victory have halted in memory of their commander in chief. Business and commerce have stopped. Flags flutter at half-mast. Commemorative exercises throughout the country are attended by millions. Telephone and telegraph communications pause to pay tribute to the deceased leader. Radio hushes the louder music to tell his life's story. This broadcast extends the sympathy of its international audience to Mrs. Roosevelt and the members of the bereaved family.

Far more vital, however, than all public rites and ceremonies is the fact that our President's death speaks to us individually and should teach necessary lessons. For us, as American Christians, the issues raised through this burial are not political. We recognize the vast dangers confronting us and understand how easily our policies may become the playthings of foreign diplomats who have publicly attacked our democracy. Yet, if we dedicate ourselves to triumphant trust in the Almighty, through His Son we can have the assurance of continued divine blessings. I am sure the heart of every American believer who read President Truman's request to the newspapermen at Washington, "Pray for me," beat with gratitude to God for this reliance on the Lord. No man has ever assumed the Presidency in a more critical time, and — no matter for whom you voted or whatever your politics may be — you would not meet your duty toward Heaven and your country if you were not to remember our new leader in fervent, repeated intercession. To President Truman this radio mission pledges its sincere support and the assurance of earnest intercession.

Yet we leave to the Congress and our federal officials the political questions as to our nation's future course which this unexpected death emphasizes, just as we leave to those who knew him best all temporal and secular lessons to be drawn from the memories, administration, and achievements of our deceased Chief Executive. Today, our public buildings draped in black and the nation pausing in silence, I, a minister of Christ's Gospel, have but one purpose, a goal which, particularly in dark moments like these, can bring us guidance, truth, and love. As I ask you to join me in beholding both the cross on which the Son of God died to defeat death and the open grave where our Savior rose to guarantee you life, I pray that the Holy Spirit will help you grasp the eternal, indestructible, all-victorious comfort and assurance in this magnificent truth:

JESUS CHRIST — OUR LIFE IN DEATH!

To learn this marvelous message of mercy, let us study two words of God's unbreakable Scripture, the first from the Old Testament (Second Kings, chapter twenty, verse one), *"Set thine house in order; for thou shalt die"*; and the second from the New Testament (Saint John, chapter three, verse thirty-six, *"He that believeth on the Son hath everlasting life."*

I
WE MUST ALL DIE IN TEMPORAL DEATH

The reign of Hezekiah, to whom these first words were addressed, in some way was parallel to the administration of our departed President. The Israelite monarch ruled more years than most of the other kings, and no one else has occupied the White House twelve years, as did our deceased Chief Executive. Hezekiah's dominion was marked by the most brutal and bloody war Israel had ever known, and since 1941 our country has been engaged in its costliest struggle. In Hezekiah's day Israel came in contact with the great world powers, through foreign alliances on a larger scale than ever before — the same situation these days present. That Israelite sovereign held sway over imposing wealth; and never before have we had as much money in our treasuries. God gave this Old Testament ruler the victory when He miraculously intervened to defeat the Assyrian enemy, and one of these next Sundays I hope to show you how marvelously the Lord has interposed His power to control even the weather, the raging sea, the drifting snow, and grant us victory.

In the midst of these triumphs the Almighty suddenly spoke to Hezekiah, and he became *"sick unto death";* but Jehovah saved him, prolonged his life, and permitted him to live fifteen years after that fatal malady had seized him. In 1921 Franklin Delano Roosevelt was also seized by a dread scourge, infantile paralysis. Many of its victims die in consequence of its physical penalties, but, though crippled, he lived almost twenty-four years more and gave the nation a remarkable example of conquest over a serious handicap.

Finally, to Hezekiah came the fulfillment of the divine warning, *"Set thine house in order, for thou shalt die"*; and on Thursday death came, as it must to all men, to the President of the United States. The hand that signed more legislation than any previous Chief Executive became lifeless and rigid; the voice that spoke to many more millions than any preceding President is silenced in the grave; the mind that conceived far-reaching plans, admired by friends and criticized by opponents, functions no longer. The man whose authority drafted millions of men for war, spent billions of dollars in bloodshed, whose name is blessed or cursed throughout the world, is no more among the living.

Can you not see, then, that if presidents pass away, you, too, in the infinitely smaller circle of your influence, are doomed to decay? You may fight against this as you will; you may belong to a sect like that which selected a baby girl for immortality but soon conceded its own defeat by returning the child to its mother; you may picture death as distant and delayed; you may boast of your good health, your exceptional strength, your long years of sound life; but be assured of this inevitable, inescapable truth, once spoken to Hezekiah, on Thursday addressed to President Roosevelt, and in God's own time to confront you: *"Thou shalt die."*

Laugh at this now if you dare, but the moment will come when your ridicule may turn to remorseful screaming. Postpone this, if you insist, but remember, its truth will confront you more surely than night follows day! Dismiss the thoughts of your end as something distasteful now, but don't forget you are doomed! You are under a death sentence which can never be commuted.

Jesus Christ — Our Life in Death!

Your body, active and energetic, will become cold and still; your strength, your motion, your voice, your senses, your thoughts, will be gone forever, and your physical frame, under the doom of decay, will disintegrate and return to the ground. You may be a millionaire; you may be high in the present Congress; you may be a department head in a large university; you may be a public figure of renown, but before God and man I tell you that you are marked by death. President Roosevelt had enjoyed the counsel of the nation's highest medical authorities; world specialists could hasten to help him; no lack of finances ever restricted him from enjoying the latest and best cures. But he died; and here is the first lesson his death would teach every one of us, high or low, rich or ragged: *"Thou shalt die."*

The end approached suddenly at Warm Springs, Georgia. The President was not in a hospital bed nor on an operating table when his summons came; he was sitting quietly, having his portrait painted. His previous utterances, his scheduled plans, show clearly that he had no premonition of the appointed hour, no knowledge that last Thursday was his last day. This should warn us that our final hour may likewise come swiftly and unannounced. Every day more than a hundred thousand human beings, who came into the world just as you and I did, will leave it just as you and I will, many of them with only a few minutes' or even a few seconds' notice. Don't rely on your youthful strength, your unbroken good health to keep you among the living! A virus so small that even high-powered microscopes can hardly detect it may suddenly lay you low. Accidents, at work, on the highway, at home, can quickly snuff out the flame of your life.

The second lesson every one of you should learn, as you stand in spirit at the President's casket, is this: since death may come upon you unheralded, so live in faith that you will be prepared to meet your Maker! At night when Dr. Horatius Bonar, author of many beloved hymns, applying to himself the Scriptural warning, *"Take ye heed, watch and pray; for ye know not when the time is,"* said his prayers, he would draw aside the curtain and, gazing up into the starry heavens, say, "Perhaps tonight, Lord?" Mornings, as he arose, he would look out into the breaking dawn and declare, "Perhaps today, Lord?" Do you mark each day's beginning and end in that way? Don't expect any special signs and indications from the Almighty that your end is drawing close! Many of you, past middle age, have these warnings right in your own bodies — the lines in your faces, the glasses for your eyes, the hearing devices for your ears, the dental work in your mouth, the increasing visits to the doctor, your decreasing energy, your increased tiredness — all these are unmistakable warnings, if only you will heed them, that every day brings you closer to your last resting place, a lot in the cemetery.

Don't wait for the eleventh hour and a deathbed conversion! It has well been said that Scripture contains one record of a brand plucked from the fire in the last hour, the penitent thief crucified with Christ, so that none will despair, but that the Bible offers only one of these last-moment conversions so that none will cheat himself by thinking that he can live his life in sin and then just before death come to his Savior. You may never have that chance. Often the end comes so swiftly that thought and reason perish quickly. About a week before

Jesus Christ — Our Life in Death!

he died, President James Knox Polk told a Christian pastor: "If I had supposed twenty years ago that I should come to my deathbed unprepared, it would have made me an unhappy man; and yet I am about to die and have not made the requisite preparation. I have not even been baptized. Tell me, can there be any ground for . . . hope?" Then the full grace of the Lord Jesus Christ came into his heart. He publicly confessed the Lord his Savior; he was baptized, received the Lord's Supper, and with unwavering confidence in his Redeemer went to a blessed eternity. But who knows whether you will have a week to reflect before you die? Now, while you have the chance — and this appeal is directed to you stubborn older men and women who know that you should be with the Lord but have continually cast His mercy aside — ask yourselves, "Who knows how near *my* end may be?" hear the warning of our text, *"Thou shalt die,"* and prepare to meet the grim Reaper!

President Roosevelt's death left much of his work unfinished. He had prepared a speech which he was to deliver last Friday. Even that was not granted him. He had spoken confidently of the years beyond this fourth term, but God gave him hardly three months of its four years. The United Nations Conference at San Francisco was to have been the crowning achievement of his career, but he was never to see or hear it. Learn, therefore, that death waits for no man. If the leader who had planned a program of peace for the world was cut down even before peace was declared, we must be ready to leave our far smaller tasks interrupted and unfulfilled. Only one great work was ever truly brought to an end on this earth and that was the self-sacrificing, sin-atoning ransom and redemption wrought for each of us when the Son of God, bearing our iniquities, dying our deaths, at Calvary cried out, *"It is finished!"* Because He completed our rescue from ruin, we can leave life with everything else incomplete and with the sense of our own insignificance but of His all-sufficient majesty. Millions of soldiers die on the battlefields of this war; many more civilians perish in consequence of its bombings and terrors; the greatest of the great suffers a cerebral hemorrhage and fades out of existence; but the earth moves on, the tides rise and fall, day breaks and ends, just as though there were no millions of new gravestones every year. How infinitesimally minute even the strongest of men are! But how glorious and almighty is our God! When John Bacon, the British sculptor, died, his will specified this inscription for his plain burial tablet:

> WHAT I WAS AS AN ARTIST
> SEEMED TO ME OF SOME IMPORTANCE
> WHILE I LIVED;
> WHAT I REALLY WAS AS A BELIEVER
> IN CHRIST JESUS
> IS THE ONLY THING OF IMPORTANCE
> TO ME NOW.

Some of you think that you are important, with large but unfinished tasks before you. As they lower the remains of our President into his grave, realize how insignificant you are! Stand beneath the Savior's cross to cry out, *"He must increase, but I must decrease"!*

The President's death came during a great crisis. Some commentators believe that this was the worst possible hour for a change in the administration. The delicate plans for a new world, problems of dealing with our enemies, grave national issues, are at stake, and many wish that Franklin Delano Roosevelt, who began these negotiations, could end them. Here too we are reminded that God Himself says, *"My thoughts are not your thoughts, neither are your ways My ways."* The Lord has shown us that no man is indispensable for our national blessing, that the United States needs — far more than capable leaders and an efficient Congress — the Almighty Himself. This sudden death, then, should call America to repentance and to the realization that God, eternal, unchangeable, omnipotent, rules our land, that for national progress, prosperity, and a peace which will not prepare for further war we need Him of whom it is written: *"Thou changest not"; "Thou canst do all things"; "Our times are in Thy hand."* May the Holy Spirit grant us the recognition of the Lord's power over life and death, when even the Chief Executive of the world's greatest nation is told, *"Thou shalt die,"* and quickly collapses! If from eternity President Roosevelt could speak to us today, I feel sure that he would plead: "America, give God a greater part in your hopes, your plans and actions! Recognize the risen Redeemer as Him who can *'do all things'!* Beseech the blessing of the Holy Spirit on the lawmakers, the judges, the officials, of this nation and its forty-eight States!"

The fact that every one of us, no matter how we may otherwise differ in race or religion, color or class, will hear the inevitable summons, *"Thou shalt die,"* should make us think thoughts of eternity. The last words of the President, as far as the newspapers record, mentioned the pain in his head; but what his thoughts were after the power of speech left him no one knows. Others who have recovered from ordinarily fatal diseases state that passages of Scripture, thoughts of eternity, went through their minds. With so much energy and money devoted to tell people how to live, should we not take time during health and happiness to learn how to die, to realize that there is a hell (not only in the vulgar profanity of men and — God forgive them! — of women), horrifying beyond all word or thought, a place of endless punishment for those who willfully reject the Lord Jesus; and that there is a heaven, purchased for us by our Savior — the celestial realm with our Father's home and its special places prepared by Christ for those who accept Him as the Deliverer from death?

For president and pauper, for millionaire and miser, for the high and mighty as for the down-and-outer, this rule holds: *"It is appointed unto men once to die, but after this the judgment."* That is why God told King Hezekiah, *"Set thine house in order; for thou shalt die!"* That is why the Lord would have me tell every one of you, even those in the prime of health, the exuberance of youth, *"Set thine house in order!"* That means more than making a will, keeping any money accounts you have straight, destroying evidences of the sin that you want to keep from your survivors, making provision for your wife and children. No; setting your house in order means making it right with God, preparing for the moment when you breathe your last. A few weeks ago in Cambridge, Massachusetts, a man died who was a dear, devoted friend of this broadcast, a humble believer, who, with his wife, had read the Scripture through more than sixty times. So that he could delve into the full depth of divine truth, he had devoted seven years of his spare time to learn Hebrew and Greek, in which God's Word was originally written. He had made minute preparation for his end, and when his final breath faded, he departed with joy, leaving behind a detailed plan of his burial service, including the Scripture to be read, the hymns to be sung, and the text he desired for the strengthening of the bereaved. Death had no terror for him because, having set his house in order, he was prepared to meet his God.

I have prayed the Holy Spirit to arouse some of you from your fatal indifference, blindness, selfishness, and sensuality, and make you ask: "How can I prepare my house? How can I meet the inevitable *'Thou shalt die'* with the promise of eternal blessing?" Listen closely as I tell you! Position and power cannot provide a way into eternity. Franklin Delano Roosevelt will not be saved because he was President of the United States, nor will you have the assurance of life after death because you are president of a corporation, president of a bank, president of a university, president of a city council, even president of a religious denomination or of a Christian congregation. President Roosevelt will not be saved because he was commander in chief of the American forces. People like to tell us, of course, that death on the battlefield is an automatic entrance to paradise, but you cannot find this in the Bible. Again, a man is not rescued from eternal ruin by having believing parents, churchgoing children, or friends on earth and in heaven who pray him into paradise. God Himself reminds us that *"no man can redeem his brother."* Nor can we earn our own way into heaven by our exemplary actions, our charities, our kindness to our fellow men, our bravery, our heroism. In the hour of national visitation when death has cast its shadow over the length and breadth of the land, we ought to be honest enough to come before our heavenly Father not with the deceit and hypocrisy which leads us to pretend that we are good, not with the shame and falsehood which denies our iniquity, but with the open confession that we have sinned grievously, repeatedly, willfully, thanklessly, and stand condemned by the Almighty for lustful thoughts, cruel ambitions, hate-filled longings, sentenced by the sin in which we were born and in which our lives abound. When we in our own sight become less than nothing, we have truly begun to set our house in order, to prepare for the Judgment to come. Then we have taken the first step toward victory over the grave.

II

THE BELIEVERS WILL LIVE IN ETERNAL LIFE

The second step is indicated to us by the assurance of our second Scripture passage, *"He that believeth on the Son hath everlasting life."* There is a blessed eternity, then, as God's Word testifies here, when it speaks of *"everlasting life,"* and when it reinforces this truth not in ten but in hundreds of other passages — a glorious, radiant, certain life to come, far too marvelous for our poor powers of understanding. The believer's body is placed in the grave, but it remains there only until the day of resurrection. Then it comes forth, not lamed by paralysis, pock-marked by disease, broken by accident, worn out by old age, ravaged by war, but a new, perfect, heavenly body.

All this is not guesswork, pious hope, wishful thinking, theological imagination, the blind refuge of fear-stricken men and women. Some of the mightiest minds have humbly accepted this Gospel guarantee. Think of Michael Faraday, for example, that learned British chemist and physicist, who stands in the forefront of the world's greatest scientists. Weighing the evidence of survival after death with his critical, analytical mind, he comes to the conclusion: "It is permitted to the Christian to think of death; he is even represented as praying that God would teach him to number his days. Words are given him: *'Thanks be to God, which giveth us the victory through our Lord Jesus Christ!'* And though the thought of death brings the thought of Judgment, it also brings to the Christian the thought of Him who died, who rose again, the Son of God, who *'brought life and immortality to light.'* "

Yet, we do not rely on men's opinion for proof of the resurrection. We trust Jesus. He has promised, *"Because I live, ye shall live also."* Again, *"Where I am, there shall also My servant be."* Again, *"In My Father's house are many mansions. . . . I go to prepare a place for you."* Again, *"This is life eternal, that they might know Thee the only true God, and Jesus Christ, whom Thou hast sent."* Again, *"He that believeth in Me, though He were dead, yet shall he live."* Again, *"God so loved the world that He gave his only begotten Son, that whosoever believeth in Him should not perish but have everlasting life."*

These repeated reassurances are endorsed by Christ's own resurrection. Only two weeks ago the Christian Church stood in spirit before the open grave to see that our Lord, proving Himself the mighty God, the accepted

Atoner, the Victor over death, has conquered the grave for every believer. Never lose sight of this truth — and if you have not heard it before, pay doubly close attention now! Our pledge of eternity is not a hit-or-miss proposition which may or may not hold true for us! Rather, take heart, you, the afflicted, suffering from fresh sorrows of recent bereavements, and know: this is the positive, unchanging truth based on God's justice, His faithfulness, His love! Jesus died — O love beyond compare! — to pay the penalty of your sins, remove each charge against you, blot out the handwriting recording your transgressions, ransom you from the ruin of your own rebellion against God, free you from the dominion of death. Now, because He, the Redeemer of the race, did this for all men, your iniquities have been removed, your breaking of God's holy Law punished and paid for. As soon as you believe His promise of plenteous grace; as soon as you humble yourself so that you become nothing, but Jesus everything; as soon as you cling to Christ as your loving, living Redeemer, your sins no longer exist. They have been completely canceled; and — here is the highest happiness — when your sins are blotted out, the dominion of death, the gruesomeness of the grave, the doom of decay are broken. As the Son of God rose from the dead, so you shall rise from the dead, all contrary blasphemy and atheistic ridicule nothwithstanding.

You should agree, then, that as the nation mourns the departure of its leader and thoughts of death are brought close to each one of us, above all else we ought to be sure of our own resurrection. Thank God, in the mightiest, most merciful, most magnificent message the

Jesus Christ — Our Life in Death! 207

radio can ever proclaim, I tell you in the name of the living Savior, this triumph over death can be yours now and forever. You cannot earn it; you cannot buy it; you cannot secure it by exchange or for reward. It is a treasure so costly that a whole lifetime of pain and penance, service and sacrifice, would not be long enough to purchase its blessing. Yet, in His endless grace, our heavenly Father offers it to every one of you, free, without condition, without credential, without restriction, to be received by humble, sincere trust in the Savior's atonement, by victorious reliance on His redemption. Here is the promise of our text, the pledge that neither wicked men nor hell's devils can ever destroy: *"He that believeth on the Son hath everlasting life."*

Mark this: *"he that believeth"!* It is your guarantee that you can come to Christ for eternal life, just as you are, sin-conscious, sin-burdened, sin-soiled. Don't let this glorious grace pass unaccepted! — As soon as you cling to Jesus in that true faith, you have everlasting life. A radiant existence begins for you on earth, which continues unending in the heavens of divine beauty, incomparable majesty, unimaginable splendor.

Great Americans have believed on the Son of God and received eternal life. In the cradle days of our country Benjamin Rush, who risked his life and property as he placed his signature below the Declaration of Independence, bade final farewell to his wife, when death approached, with these words: "My excellent wife, I must leave you, but God will take care of you. By the mystery of Thy holy incarnation; by Thy holy nativity; by Thy baptism, fasting, and temptation; by Thine agony and bloody sweat; by Thy cross and passion; by

Thy precious death and burial; by Thy glorious resurrection and ascension, and by the coming of the Holy Ghost, blessed Jesus, wash away all my impurities and receive me into Thine everlasting kingdom!" Today too some of America's leaders have the same assurance of a blood-bought immortality. It is our hope that Franklin Delano Roosevelt died in Jesus. The last sermon he heard was a Christ-centered Easter message at Warm Springs, which clearly stated the reality and blessing of the Redeemer's resurrection.

It is likewise our prayer that you will accept the Son of God; for with what incomparable comfort this faith can fortify us! You need this triumphant trust in the Savior. Recently a mother in Norwalk, California, wrote to me: "I have just received a telegram that my only son died from injuries received from a flame-thrower explosion on New Caledonia. I prayed two long years for his safety and really prayed with tears and agony. He was brought up in the Lord, and only two days before that telegram came, his chaplain wrote that my boy, Elton, had said all was well with his spiritual life. He was my very life, and it seems to me that God let them kill him. The devil, or something, says to me: 'God forsook Elton, and you too. God doesn't love you; your prayers are in vain.' I keep seeing Elton's broken, mangled body before me, and I am on the verge of collapse. Please help me!" It is particularly for the bereaved, the brokenhearted, like this California listener, that Christ has promised, *"He that believeth on the Son hath everlasting life."* Don't let the vision even of your departed dear ones blot out the picture of the cross, the resurrection grave, the open heavens! Learn to rely on *"the Son*

Jesus Christ — Our Life in Death!

of God," to trust Him fully, to say, *"Thy will be done!"* to hear Him promise, *"What I do thou knowest not now; but thou shalt know hereafter,"* and then to kneel before Him with the victorious resignation that explains, "Whatever God ordains is good!" When you believe the truth of every divine promise you have heard today; when you begin to realize that one moment in heaven, face to face with Jesus, is worth more than centuries of the best years life can give on earth, you will realize that God let your consecrated, Christ-dedicated sons, brothers, husbands, meet death so that they could the longer enjoy the hallowed bliss and beauty with their Redeemer. Then, washed in the blood of the Lamb, resurrected in celestial radiance, you will understand in higher knowledge that your hours of agony or the crushing anguish of sickness your loved ones endured are *"not worthy to be compared with the glory which"* has been revealed in you.

Why, then, do some of you dally and delay, when you can have the assurance of life eternal through faith in Christ and when our country needs this trust above all else? Few words in our language are more deeply tragic than these: "Too late!" Because you may not be on earth next Sunday to hear this broadcast appeal for repentance and return to God, accept Christ as your Savior now! Before your radios, in this moment, wherever you are, repeat after me these words: "O Jesus, crucified for me at Calvary, resurrected for me from the grave, Savior of my soul, Thou art my Redeemer from this moment throughout eternity."

If the Son of God rules your heart, don't delay in bringing Him to others! The most sorrowful letters we receive come in answer to those we send our military men by request of parents who ask us to help their loved ones; yet, when we write words of encouragement and mail faith-building tracts and books, the letters and packages sometimes come back marked, "Addressee deceased." Give us the name of anyone whom we can help before it is too late and he has lost the only hope of avoiding hell and entering heaven men can ever know!

Let this thought linger with you: *Only "he that believeth on the Son of God hath everlasting life"!* There is no other way to heaven than by Jesus, who clearly and pointedly proclaims, *"I am the Way, and the Truth, and the Life; no man cometh to the Father but by Me."* As you realize with President Roosevelt's burial that death, which can take the highest and the lowest, must snatch you from the land of the living, which will you choose, life or death, heaven or hell, salvation or damnation? Oh, let the answer re-echo across America and Canada today: "Lord Jesus, *'to whom shall we go? Thou hast the words of eternal life!'* We are Thine and Thou art ours forever — in life and in death." Amen!

THEY CAN'T TAKE CHRIST AWAY!

"They say unto her, Woman, why weepest thou? She saith unto them, Because they have taken away my Lord, and I know not where they have laid Him. And when she had thus said, she turned herself back and saw Jesus standing, and knew not that it was Jesus. Jesus saith unto her, Woman, why weepest thou? Whom seekest thou? She, supposing Him to be the gardener, saith unto Him, Sir, if thou have borne Him hence, tell me where thou hast laid Him, and I will take Him away. Jesus saith unto her, Mary. She turned herself and saith unto Him, Rabboni! which is to say, Master."

SAINT JOHN 20:13-16

HEAVENLY FATHER: Rise up to rebuke the enemies of Thy Son, our blessed Savior, and bring to naught the proud plans by which boasting unbelief would rob us of our Redeemer! We are surrounded by scoffers who seek to discredit Thy Word, subtle, yet satanic foes of our faith, who cunningly question the truth of Christ's atoning love. Therefore we plead: Send us Thy Spirit to make our hearts burn with flaming zeal for Jesus, to help us remain ever faithful to Him at all cost! We are firmly convinced that no power on earth or hell can tear us from our Redeemer, if only with penitent hearts we trustingly cling to Him! Show those in anguish over their sins that even our transgressions, black and blasphemous though they may be, need not separate us from His love, since, if we have Him, all our iniquities have been washed away forever by His cleansing blood! Therefore increase our faith! Draw our country closer to Thee! Direct the President, the Congress, and those in authority! Guard our military youth on distant shores and send them back to us soon! Endless thanks be to Thee, almighty, all-loving Father, for Thy marvelous mercies in Jesus and for the answer Thou hast promised us for prayer made, as this petition, in His saving name! Amen!

We can lose everything we possess. Money may be taken from us. Nazi officials know that. When the tide of battle turned against them, they hid $100,000,000 in gold bars, hundreds of sacks filled with coins, and a lavish collection of art treasures in the concealed chambers of a salt mine deep in the earth. Yet only a few days ago alert Americans discovered this fabulous fortune, practically the entire German gold reserve, and seized it all. Even far greater sums may be taken from us. American financial experts no longer bother about hundreds of millions of dollars. Even billions — of public money — make little impression on them. A Chicago University professor, whom many regard as a national authority, recently declared that the federal budget should contain "a margin of about seven billion dollars to play around in." If so-called money geniuses keep on playing, our national reserve may play out. People can lose their health, as the 16,000,000 Americans hospitalized last year understand. They can lose their power, influence, empires, as Nazi officials are now forced to admit. They can lose their learning and reason, as hundreds of thousands of our mentally disturbed countrymen have. They can lose their dear ones, as 250,000 American gold-star families know too well. They can lose even their own lives, we see, as a President planning a new world is snatched away, or a war correspondent, who had just written a description of our impregnable defense, is shot down. But thank God with me today, as flags flutter at half-mast over America, one priceless possession can never be taken from us, and that is the glorious Gospel of our Lord Jesus Christ. You may

They Can't Take Christ Away!

be deprived of your good name, property, investments, home, happiness, friends, family; but believe with all your heart

THEY CAN'T TAKE CHRIST AWAY!

This is the divine assurance guaranteed us by our text (Saint John, chapter twenty, verses thirteen to sixteen): *"They say unto her, Woman, why weepest thou? She saith unto them, Because they have taken away my Lord, and I know not where they have laid Him. And when she had thus said, she turned herself back and saw Jesus standing, and knew not that it was Jesus. Jesus saith unto her, Woman, why weepest thou? Whom seekest thou? She, supposing Him to be the gardener, saith unto Him, Sir, if thou have borne Him hence, tell me where thou hast laid Him, and I will take Him away. Jesus saith unto her, Mary. She turned herself and saith unto Him, Rabboni! which is to say, Master."*

I

WE MAY THINK THAT THEY CAN TAKE CHRIST AWAY

This Scripture again takes us back to the Savior's resurrection. I hope that none of you thinks I am devoting too much time to His victory over death — the central, pivotal, crucial point in all human history. Here is hope, comfort, strength, joy, eternal life itself; and as the first day of the week was chosen the Lord's Day because Jesus rose from the dead on Sunday, so every sermon preached in every house of God should point to the open heavens, where the risen Christ rules with the promise, *"I am the Resurrection and the Life; he that believeth in Me, though he were dead, yet shall he live; and whosoever liveth and believeth in Me shall never die."* The only people who dislike believing in an existence beyond the grave — and one of every four Americans, so the Gallup poll tells us, denies a future life — are those who are cowed by their conscience, terrified by their sins, afraid of a just and holy God. When Moffat, courageous missionary of Christ to Africa, once spoke to a noted Negro chief in the interior of that black continent, he mentioned the resurrection. "What," the native ruler demanded, "what are these words about the dead? The dead rise?" "Yes," Moffat answered, "all the dead shall rise." That was too much for the chief. Placing his hand on his breast, he turned squarely to the missionary and declared: "I love you much. The words of your mouth are sweet like honey; but the words of the resurrection are too great for me. I do not wish to hear about the dead rising again. The dead cannot rise. The dead shall not rise." "But why?" Missionary Moffat dared to ask. "Why must I not speak of the resurrection?" Raising his arm in a wide sweep, as if grasping a spear, the black leader cried, "I have slain many thousands, and shall they rise?" He was afraid to meet his enemies; similarly many of you fear eternity because you dread facing the people whom you have cheated, slandered, polluted, injured. You are terrorized by the thought of standing before your God.

This broadcast, however, proclaims what Scripture clearly, repeatedly, forcefully, teaches: first, that as surely as this world exists, there is a hell, the destination after death of all whose crimes against Heaven have not been forgiven and removed; second, that as truly as the Almighty lives and reigns, there is a heaven of unspeakable glory, with a personal, prepared place for every sinner who clings to his Savior, the Lord Jesus Christ; third, that as certainly as every person on earth is bound either for heaven or hell — eternal light, joy, life, or everlasting darkness, sorrow, death — Scripture recognizes no third, half-way, intermediate place of purging and preparation. After death it is only heaven or hell; but it is positively *either — or* for every one of you.

Mary Magdalene, the woman Jesus had healed, was first at the garden grave in the hush and darkness of the resurrection morning. Let me emphasize again what I have tried to stress continually in these messages: our country and our churches need women of her steadfast devotion to Jesus, not the whisky-drinking, profane-speaking, risqué-storytelling, freethinking, Bible-mocking, family-neglecting, purity-despising women whom the moral letdown of the war has produced in too large numbers! We read of sweeping, but complicated plans for rebuilding this nation; but far more effective for America's welfare than any ambitious, economic or social program is the spiritual help believing women can offer. Give us God-fearing, Christ-exalting, home-loving, clean-living, Scripture-reading, church-supporting mothers, sisters, daughters and, under the Spirit's guidance, we will have better families, better churches and, therefore, a better country.

Tears were in Mary's eyes when she returned to the Savior's grave. That Sunday morning, the beginning of the third day since Jesus had been crucified, was marked for her by searing sorrow; yet before evening what radiant rejoicing surged through her soul! Thus in a single day the Lord can fulfill His promise, *"Your sorrow shall be turned into joy."* Perhaps this fourth Sunday in April has dawned with heavy anguish for some of you. There may be trouble in your own family, quarrel, drunkenness, unfaithfulness, crime. Your conscience may be burdened with remorse over your own sins, your spirit torn by fresh wounds over worry, your heart broken by bereavement. You may have spent the first hours of this Sunday in unrelieved torture; but if you heed God's Son as He pleads with you, *"Come unto Me, all ye that labor and are heavy laden, and I will give you rest";* if you meet Jesus in trusting faith as He speaks comfort to you, before this day is past your reverses can be changed to rejoicing just as Mary Magdelene's were. My beloved, He is a compassionate, helping, sustaining Savior. Look to Him and learn this for yourself!

However, approach Jesus with much more than the sympathetic sorrow Mary showed when she came to mourn at His grave! The Son of God does not want sympathy now; He does not need it. He lives, a million times more assuredly than you or I live, and He rules with *"all power . . . in heaven and in earth."* I am sick of reading how mealy-mouthed Modernists speak of Christ in condescending sympathy, saying in effect: "Poor Jesus! He tried His best. Too bad that He failed and they crucified Him! What a wonderful effort He made!" That kind of talk will send souls to hell. As Mary was soon to learn, we have a living Leader, a risen Redeemer, a victorious Jesus, an all-powerful Christ, an eternal Savior.

When Mary came to the sepulcher the second time, after the first hasty visit, in which she saw the stone removed, the tears ran down her cheeks. She was gripped

They Can't Take Christ Away! 217

by a double sorrow; not only had her Lord died, but, so she thought, they had removed His body. In her agony the angels, whom she did not recognize, asked, *"Woman, why weepest thou?"*

What marvelous mercy the Lord Jesus Christ offers His own! He always tries to dry your tears, no matter what sorrow may overtake you. When you sob convulsively, His love would give you calm and quiet. If the heaviest of life's blows strike you, clasping the Savior's hand more tightly, you can be spiritually rich in poverty, strong in faith despite human weakness. You can find soul gain in earth's loss and — as unbelievable as this is to scoffers — inner pleasure even in pain. Are you doing right, then, when Jesus, seeking to remove the cause of your suffering, asks you, *"Why weepest thou?"* and you turn away from Him, try to master your own afflictions without Him, or resign yourself to stolid defeat? Not long ago an elderly Philadelphia woman collapsed from lack of food. For years she had lived alone in a three-family house, without light or heat and with practically no furniture. At the hospital attendants discovered that she had sewed $5,618 into the lining of her clothes; yet she starved in the midst of plenty. "How senseless!" you exclaim; yet this is not nearly as foolish and fatal as some of your own mistakes. Your souls are famished for spiritual nourishment. You need help, hope, happiness, and all the time you have Christ's comforting Word close at hand. You are not far from churches which preach His glorious Gospel. You have free recourse to prayer, but you spurn this divine source of strength. You keep your souls sickly, starved, and separated from the Savior. In this very moment He wants me to ask some of you, *"Why weepest thou?"* and to direct you, *"Cast . . . all your care upon Him; for He careth for you."* Believing the Lord Jesus, *"let us . . . come boldly unto the Throne of Grace that we may obtain mercy and find grace to help in time of need!"*

Mary Magdalene was inconsolable, however, for she told the angel, *"They have taken away my Lord and I know not where they have laid Him."* It did not occur to her worry-weighted soul that Jesus' grave was empty because He had arisen. She took no time to recall His own words and to learn that He had kept His promise by defeating death. That would be far too great a miracle for her. Similarly many of you do not grasp Scripture's wondrous pledges. Death has entered your household; and in the grief which grips your soul you forget the Savior's consolation, live on, sorrow on, mourn on, as though you never had the assurance, *"All things work together for good to them that love God,"* as though Jesus had never promised, *"Be thou faithful unto death, and I will give thee a crown of life";* as though His Word had never guaranteed, *"Because I live, ye shall live also."*

Again, many of you, like Mary, who even at the open grave rejected the very thought that her Redeemer, despite His repeated pledges was resurrected, refuse to accept the wondrous assurance of full, free, and final forgiveness in Christ. "That may be all right for others," you conclude, "but not for me with my screaming sins and treacherous transgressions; I am beyond the limits of His grace." Stop blinding yourself to His blessed, all-embracing love! Ask the Spirit to help you learn Mary Magdalene's lesson! Though our Lord had returned to life, she actually thought that someone had taken His dead body from the rock tomb; that the Christian faith was finished, the Gospel glory gone forever, just as many surveying the present hostility to Jesus are apt to repeat, "*They have taken away my Lord.*" Many point to ten thousands of churches partially or completely destroyed by air raids, Christian schools ruined, preachers of the Word killed, promising missions stopped, the enmity to God's Word increased, and they cry out, "This bloody conflict and its subsequent savagery are taking '*away my Lord.*'"

Others are gripped by the godlessness of this age. They remember that one of the last acts of Congress which Abraham Lincoln signed, shortly after the Civil War, ordered that the motto he endorsed with all his heart, "In God we trust," be inscribed on our coins; but they look in vain for similar trust now after the Almighty has granted victory in this struggle. For this reason their voices are frequently raised to lament, "'*They*,' the godless, are taking '*away my Lord*' from this blessed land."

Again, the increase of atheism brings fear to many. Make no mistake! — godlessness is growing. It is becoming more firmly entrenched in government, labor, education, entertainment, even in some churches, than ever before! Therefore believers, recalling how in this generation the Red revolution changed churches into theaters, burned Bibles, dragged pictures of the Savior through the filth of muddy streets, persecuted Christians, and murdered preachers, often cry out, "The atheists are taking '*away my Lord.*'"

American schools have often become centers of skepticism. Ten American colleges, founded before the

Revolution, still exist: Harvard, William and Mary, Yale, Princeton, Washington and Lee, Columbia, Brown, Rutgers, Dartmouth, and the University of Pennsylvania. Each, except the last, was begun to train ministers of Jesus Christ, and the tenth, the University of Pennsylvania, developed from a charity school established by George Whitefield, the evangelist. These colleges and universities owe their existence and continuance to Christ, the Church, and the Bible; but today every one of them supports men who systematically try to tear our youth away from the Savior's altar. Our public educational system is being saturated with unbelief. Listen to this, especially you throughout New York: in a book by Dr. George D. Stoddard, commissioner of education in your State, bearing the title, *The Meaning of Intelligence,* this man, whose salary comes also from taxes of Christian citizens, ridicules our faith, labels as "man-made concepts" the Biblical truth of hell-fire, original sin, and divine revelation. He infers that those who accept these truths are "feeble in mind." No wonder a *New York Sun* columnist protested: "No, Dr. Stoddard! You can't teach my children any such hokum, and that is one reason why I, a taxpayer, paying for the upkeep of public schools, send my children to private schools. I don't want to expose them to your intellectual jungle!" Confronted by educational atheism, aghast at this assault on the Savior sponsored in many of our schools, high and low, Christians may be inclined to cry out, *"They have taken away my Lord."*

Violence keeps on rising. Late bulletins from FBI headquarters in Washington report that last year 158 heavy crimes were committed every hour in the United

States, almost three a minute. Each day of 1944, on the average, witnessed 28 killings, 30 instances of rape, 120 highway robberies, 150 cases of brutal assault, 555 automobile thefts, 749 cases of burglary in homes or business, 2,176 occurrences of larceny, besides thousands of smaller crimes. Not a few of those who remember God's truth that *"righteousness exalteth a nation; but sin is a reproach to any people,"* throw up their hands in horror at this reign of lust and lawbreaking to lament, *"They have taken away my Lord."*

Still others focus their attention on religion. Sunday schools are in decline. A Washington authority predicts that if the present rate of decrease continues, the Sunday school will be dead in thirty years. Church leaders admit that they find "ignorance of Christianity's basic teachings about God and man" among young and old. Believers often listen to Christless sermons from Christless pulpits; they see Bibleless teachings in Bibleless theological seminaries; they notice anti-Christian leaders in larger church bodies; they find that the fashionable, widely publicized, highly paid, publicly acclaimed preachers are usually those who reject the Redeemer, deny His deity, attack His atonement, ridicule the resurrection, cast suspicion on Scripture; and as they behold denominations wavering when they should stand fast, leaders compromising when they should confess the Crucified, church officers living in utter worldliness as though they have no living Savior to follow, these bewildered, burdened souls repeatedly cry out, *" 'They,'* the wolves in sheep's clothing, *'have taken away my Lord.'"*

II

BUT WE SHOULD BELIEVE THAT THE LIVING CHRIST ALWAYS REMAINS WITH HIS FAITHFUL

Thank God, however, that while sin, war, crime, unbelief, and apostate churches may attack our faith as never before, and while we in the United States must be prepared for fiercer assaults on our Gospel than this country has yet witnessed, no agency of earth, hell, or both combined can take Jesus away! Men have tried to remove this Redeemer. They have even boasted, as Roman tyrants did, that His name has been destroyed. Three hundred years after Christ an emperor sat on Rome's throne who, once a believer, had rejected redeeming grace. He was Julian, known to history as "the Apostate." With the venomous hatred such men often show after Satan has coaxed them from the truth, he resolved to put the Savior away forever by proving Him a falsifier. Cunningly he planned his program. Jesus had predicted that Jerusalem's Temple would be destroyed and left without one stone on the other. Julian determined to brand this an utter falsehood by rebuilding the sanctuary. Then the Bible would be exposed as a book of lies. What happened? Who won — Julian or Christ? Read this verdict of the historian and skeptic Edward Gibbon, who concedes, "Whilst the governor of the province urged, with vigor and diligence, the execution of the work, horrible billows of fire, breaking out near the foundation with frequent and reiterated attacks, rendered the place, from time to time, inaccessible to the scorched and blasted workmen, and . . . the undertaking was abandoned." Our Lord and His truth could not be taken away, even by a Roman ruler with the resources of a world empire at his disposal.

The Nineveh that enslaved God's people is gone; the Babylonia that destroyed His Temple is gone; the Antioch that set His Law aside is gone; the Rome that murdered the Savior's followers is gone. Nero and Diocletian, fiendish foes of the faith, are dead; Voltaire, Tom Paine, Ingersoll, are returned to dust; but Christ can never go down to defeat. The outward splendor of our worship may be lost; but its inner glory, Jesus, can never be destroyed. False creeds may momentarily rise at the expense of Christianity, as in England, where, we are told, spiritism, increased 200 per cent in four years, now claims three million followers and three thousand churches, with its spokesman none other than Britain's Chief Air Marshal. Instead of the peace and prosperity politicians have promised us, we may meet reverses and rebuke. It may be that our international course, influenced strongly by atheists, is headed toward hostility to the Savior and persecution of His followers. Yet even opposition will be for our blessing. The reign of bloody terror under which European churches suffered now appears to have been destined for their good. The head of the Russian Orthodox Church explains that during the czarist regime the churches had grown too rich, too soft. "When the revolution took away our wealth, we had to find our souls. I thank God for persecution. . . . When Stalin closed the seminaries, he did a good thing, for the seminaries were corrupt." Listen, too, as that authority warns, "I see in the Christian churches of America many of the signs of decay which I saw in the churches of Russia before the revolution — considerable wealth, absence of conviction . . . an easy-going religion . . . nominal church loyalty which is not backed by personal character and conduct." Yet all the might and money mobilized by men and devils cannot take our Lord from us. He lives to help us live! He will keep His promise: *"Lo, I am with you alway, even unto the end of the world." "I will never leave thee nor forsake thee."*

Mary Magdalene was to learn that blessed lesson; for while she was mourning the supposedly departed Christ, He was actually there. We read, *"She turned herself back and saw Jesus standing, and knew not that it was Jesus,"* even when He spoke to her. Why? Perhaps because it was still dark. Besides, her eyes were filled with tears, her mind was blinded by grief.

We need not be surprised at this misunderstanding, for we ourselves do not always recognize God. The Almighty spoke to us in the war; but do we understand and acknowledge His grace? He speaks to us in our individual sorrows; but do we see Him? Because He loves us with a deathless devotion, He punctures the bubble of our false pride and makes us humble, helpless, so that we rely on Him. How often, we, like Mary, refuse to welcome Jesus in the hour of our affliction!

Christ's first words to Mary Magdalene asked, *"Woman, why weepest thou?"* the same question of comfort the angels addressed to her. You see, there is a happy harmony between all parts of the Bible, whether spoken by the Lord or His messengers. No contradictions can be found in Scripture, because it has one purpose: to comfort and sustain believers with the blood-bought hope of salvation. Therefore Jesus — and never has there been a Friend, a Helper, a Comforter, like Him — again asks

They Can't Take Christ Away! 225

Mary, *"Why weepest thou? Whom seekest thou?"* just as He wants every searching sorrow in your life to stop and end in Him, the Son of God.

Mary, who previously had spoken with the Savior, knelt before Him, served Him, watched Him die on the cross, should have welcomed Jesus immediately. Instead, we read, she, *"supposing Him to be the gardener, saith unto Him, Sir, if thou have borne Him hence, tell me where thou hast laid Him, and I will take Him away."* The morning light perhaps was not yet clear enough, the tears in her eyes too heavy, the uncertainty in her soul too deep, for her to recognize her risen Redeemer. Many others, of more profound knowledge, have, in similar mistake, classified Christ as a mere human being. They regard Jesus as an unsuccessful leader, a failure, a sad and sorry figure, simply a man among millions, when in truth He is their God, their Redeemer, their Victor over death.

That blessed assurance soon came to Mary, for in one of the most moving New Testament records we are told, *"Jesus saith unto her, Mary."* He knew her though she did not know Him. He called her by her name, even if she thought He was the gardener. Praise His limitless love! He knows you too, and He calls you by name. You may be a number in the Army or in the nation's vast social security system; no one else may pay the slightest attention to you; but in Christ's sight you are precious, possessing a soul worth more than the whole world. He knows and names you from your first breath until the last. He knows you now, when you have money, friends, good times, and He will know you later when everything may be lost. He died, paying the complete penalty for all transgressions, not only for the world generally, but for you individually. His thoughts went out to you when they crucified and killed Him. Your salvation was uppermost in His mind when at Calvary His bleeding head dropped in death. And when your last hour comes, He will be with you, if you love Him, and no one can take Him away as He comforts, upholds, sustains you in your final moments and guides you into the eternity He purchased for you with His blood. Despite your doubts, denials, thanklessness, broken faith, He still asks you to be blessed by trust in His self-sacrificing love. He knows every one of you. He loves you, He wants you, He awaits you with that personal, individual love which enables you to put your own name into any one of Scripture's thousands of promises, assured of its benediction. Now and whenever you hear the Gospel grace, He is calling you by name, you, among the down-and-outers, and you, as a Florida woman reminds me, among the up-and-outers, the idle, idolatrous rich. As He, living in eternal power and majesty, now promises you, *"Fear not; for I have redeemed thee, I have called thee by thy name; thou art Mine,"* God grant that He is yours today and forever!

When Jesus spoke to Mary, *"she turned herself"* to Him; and when the Savior, through this broadcast, now speaks to you, drop any selfish ideas, any futile plans, any sinful desires! Turn wholly to the living Christ! No one will ever know how glorious the Lord appeared to Mary in that flash of recognition, just as no one can tell you how radiantly the Savior will stand before you when you truly believe Him. Turn to Him now and behold His divine person, both God and man; virgin-born, yet eternal! Hear His glorious message, Heaven's promise of forgiveness, life, and salvation, which makes you too exclaim, *"Never man spake like this Man!"* Witness His heavenly wisdom as He leads you, sometimes along the hard way, sometimes the rocky road, but always on the right path, to pardon and peace! See His life of love, never stained by a single sin, always the perfect pattern of mercy, with compassion even for His enemies! Touch His riven hands, His feet, His side, remembering that He was wounded for your transgressions, bruised for your iniquities! Recognize His surpassing devotion, which sought you out when you avoided Him, which even now intercedes for you at the throne of heaven! Behold Him in His radiant resurrection, offering the assurance of your own life after death, the pledge of His power to destroy even the grip of the grave! Then, with a prayer for Mary's faith, cry out in triumphant recognition, *"Rabboni! . . . Master!"* Fall down before Him, your God and Savior, your Lord and King, your Resurrection and Life, your All-in-all! Declare: "O Jesus, Thou art in truth the Master of my life, in whom I live and move and have my being. Thou art the Master of my heart, for Thou hast purchased me with Thy blood, and I am no longer mine but Thine. Thou art the Master of my salvation, for Thou didst save me when I was hopelessly lost in sin." When you have Christ in that faith, no enemies, no persecution, no sorrow, no death can ever take Him from you. Rather, you can exult triumphantly, and I ask you to believe this, to memorize it, to repeat it, to live it: *"Who shall separate us from the love of Christ? Shall tribulation, or distress, or persecution, or famine, or nakedness, or peril, or sword?*

... Nay, in all these things we are more than conquerors through Him that loved us. For I am persuaded that neither death, nor life, nor angels, nor principalities, nor powers, nor things present, nor things to come, nor height, nor depth, nor any other creature, shall be able to separate us from the love of God, which is in Christ Jesus our Lord." Fellow sinners and fellow redeemed, clinging to the cross in this victorious faith, cry out, "They can't take Christ away from me nor me away from Christ!" — God give you all that courageous confidence for the Savior's sake! Amen!

WITHOUT CHRIST WE FAIL

"If ye will not believe, surely ye shall not be established."
                                                    ISAIAH 7:9

LORD GOD, RULER OF THE NATIONS: As we set ourselves to the task of helping to rebuild a war-ravaged world, teach us ever anew how completely we depend on Thy blessing! Therefore we humbly invoke Thy benediction on the conference of the allied nations and the efforts to establish a just, lasting peace. Rebuke all selfishness, suspicion, greed, envy, in their deliberations, and let no plans or programs contrary to Thy Word be accepted! Direct especially the course of the United States, its new President and the Congress, toward peace! Teach us to understand that without Christ, Thy Son and our Savior, who on the cross atoned for our sins, we can do nothing good! Fill our country with real repentance over our individual and national sins, but strengthen many throughout the land with His pardoning, sustaining, renewing love! Again we plead, in this hour of victory keep our military men from cruelty and brutality, especially toward civilians, women, and children! Make us all realize more fully each day what a marvelous, merciful Savior Jesus can be for every one of us, and how we can best promote the interests of peace by following in His footsteps, living by His Spirit, helping our fellow men according to His example! Hear us and bless us for His sake! Amen!

In his syndicated column a few days ago a national writer and radio reporter mentioned a New York hotel which received this letter of complaint from a patron dissatisfied with the fact that the menus, restricted by rationing, continually offered only the same food: "See the Bible, the Book of Hebrews, chapter thirteen, verse eight, about your daily menu." People who still read this columnist's words took their New Testaments and turned to Hebrews thirteen, eight, to find, *"Jesus Christ the same yesterday and today and forever,"* used as the profane protest against the sameness of the bill of fare. Now it is bad enough when an infidel makes light of a beloved passage exalting Christ, the changeless Son of God; but it is doubly damnable when a newspaper writer, sometimes acclaimed America's Number One Columnist, deliberately calls this scandalous, sacrilegious misuse — and these are his very words — "clever and funny." God have mercy on America when a man, whose words are published in many large newspapers, is paid for featuring blasphemy, profanity, scoffing, ridicule of the Redeemer as "clever and funny"! Anyone who degrades Christ and debases Scripture is a national menace. Lord Macaulay was right when he told the British Parliament that he who says a word against the Christian religion is an enemy of the state. It is about time that you red-blooded American believers, hundreds of thousands of you, tell your newspapers that if they continue to print columnists' sneers at Jesus and the Bible, they can count on your opposition. Write us for details describing this recent ridicule of the Savior! Determine now to help show scoffers that loyalty to the Lord is not dead in America!

Unbelief and irreligion do not hesitate to direct

bitter, cutthroat attacks against Christ and His Gospel! Here in San Francisco, for example, a professed atheist is suing a local broadcasting company because it refuses to accept his program attacking God. The station declares — and we agree 100 per cent with its officials — that godlessness is contrary to the best interests of the United States. Yet a newspaper in New York, clear across the continent, comes to the defense of this West Coast atheist. Have you ever heard of a newspaper protesting against the un-American, discriminatory practice which bars Gospel broadcasts like ours from many stations in this so-called Christian country?

This bold, blatant ridicule of Jesus, publicly promoted, is one of the most destructive dangers threatening America today and menacing its plans for tomorrow. This nation will never be able to carry on successfully without Christ or against Him. We may plan programs based on money, might, men, modern science, international agreement; but if we neglect God, omit Him, oppose Him, reject Him, all these proposals are doomed to failure. With representatives of almost half a hundred nations meeting here in San Francisco to form plans for a warless age, may the Holy Spirit lead them and us to understand clearly that our world, our nation, our blueprints for the future, require, as President Truman implied, divine blessing; that to solve even private problems, individual difficulties, we must have God; that — and this is the message for today —

WITHOUT CHRIST WE FAIL

Hear this warning in Heaven's own Word, when the Lord through His Prophet declares (Isaiah, chapter seven, verse nine), *"If ye will not believe, surely ye shall not be established."*

I

A TIMELY WARNING TO OUR COUNTRY

By Jehovah's command Isaiah spoke these words to King Ahaz during a time which in many ways strongly resembles our twentieth century. Like our age, that was a period of drawn-out war. Is it not strange, if evolutionists are right — but they are wrong! — that in the 2,600 years since Isaiah men have made no progress whatever in banishing bloodshed; that war, far from being outlawed, has steadily become more hideous and brutal; that at the height of culture and civilization, when according to the advocates of man's ape ancestry all strife should have vanished, history's most shocking, horrifying, widespread conflicts raged, not between Kaffirs or Bushmen, Hottentots or Igorots, headhunters or cannibals, but between the world's most advanced and polished peoples; that, with far wider destruction even than the massacres of Attila or Genghis Khan modern slaughter has blasted to death civilians, women, invalids, old folks, babies, by the tens of thousands.

Again, the age of godless Ahaz and of God-fearing Isaiah was heavily scarred by unbelief, rejection of the Lord and ridicule of His truth. Superstition, sensual cults, service to hideous Moloch, reigned rather than the simple, saving faith in Jehovah. That war did not bring Judah closer to God; and the second world struggle has not led America nearer to the Almighty. Instead, we witness a chaos of cults, a confusion of conflicting creeds, which have only one thing in common, and that is, they all denounce Christ and discredit His Word. The victories God gave us should have taught us how much we owe Him. Our pulpits should re-echo the Redeemer's praise; our churches should be overcrowded; our homes should eagerly and daily commune with our Father in prayer; yet it is unquestionably true that masses in our country are farther away from the Lord now than they were before the war started, because they have been coaxed astray through the luxury, lust, and abundance of money supplied by the struggle which has taken almost a quarter million lives.

The age of Isaiah was like ours notably in its plans to establish security and create a warless world by treaty and international alliances. Ahaz, regarded by many of his subjects as a shrewd politician, sought to strengthen his cause through a covenant with the godless, cruel Assyrians. His formula for security was an alliance between the Big Two, Tiglath Pileser at Nineveh and himself at Jerusalem. But when his plans were completed and his ambassadors had met the Assyrian monarch, God, who knows every secret agreement, all private diplomacy, had seen the danger of this federation and sent the Prophet Isaiah to give worldly Ahaz and his courtiers the warning of our text, *"If ye will not believe, surely ye shall not be established."*

Today, in this city of San Francisco, a United Nations Conference meets to establish world-wide security by agreement and treaty. Although no voice of prayer is heard in its meetings, I ask every one of you to pray, not that the resolutions here passed will eliminate war and promote an age of perpetual peace, for Holy Writ warns us that this is utterly impossible, since until the end of the world, and in a sign of the beginning of that end there shall be *"wars and rumors of war,"* but rather that the Christian delegates to this convention will heed

Isaiah's warning, *"If ye will not believe, surely ye shall not be established."* Ask your heavenly Father to fortify many with the faith in Jesus, since without Christ we must fail! Ask the Lord of the nations to prevent the San Francisco conclave from becoming just another in a long line of pretentious, glittering, glamorous gatherings of the internationally powerful, which in the past have failed to prevent strife just as pathetically as a tissue paper dam would restrain the ebb and the flow of the rip tides here at the Golden Gate!

There is a clear-cut danger that despite its aggregate of men, money, majesty, might, this San Francisco meeting will fail in preventing bloodshed and in reaching other much-to-be-desired objectives. The perils to our peace, which stem from the disregard of faith in God, are, first, the greed, envy, suspicion, and hatred among nations. Countries are like people; and commonwealths, like criminals, are often swayed by lust for power, desire for dominion, the mania for money, the curse of conquest. Why, if this were not so, would the demand by certain groups for more votes in this assembly be so insistent? The League of Nations collapsed not because the United States refused to participate, but because leaders selfishly worked for their own people's interests, as nations always will. Show me one large country that has not planned systematically and selfishly for its own growth in territory and might! How have great empires been established? All of them by conquest, cruelty, killing! As long as one world power represented at San Francisco unjustly holds another's territory, sanctions its own bloody aggression, and is supported by other friendly forces, there can be no hope that this meeting will succeed. Let the peoples who have persecuted and oppressed others restore the rights and freedom of these depressed masses; then we can begin to talk about a just and righteous peace. But don't expect anything like that as long as powerful private interests can continue to make money by holding others in subjection! Isaiah's words should be painted in large, legible letters on each hill in San Francisco, *"If ye will not believe, surely ye shall not be established."* The one hope we have for better international understanding is faith in the Lord Jesus, reliance on the power of His Word to change the hearts and lives of men, particularly the leaders in human affairs whose decisions can send almost fifty million men into war and almost ten million of them into their graves. The Gospel of a Savior who never grasped the sword, who, instead of cursing and killing His enemies, pleaded and died for them on the cross, has made pagan armies, bent on suicidal slaughter, lay down their arms; and — let a columnist sneer at this truth and pervert it into profanity — *"Jesus Christ the same yesterday, and today, and forever,"* can today give millions rebirth with the promise of peace and blessing. Yet there is no room for the Crucified in the hearts and lives of many world figures; and as true as He is the Son of God, the verdict recorded throughout the past will be repeated in our day, *"If ye will not believe, surely ye shall not be established."*

The second danger threatening this international assembly is the disregard of the claims of morality which often characterizes powerful countries. God's holy Word plainly declares, *"Righteousness exalteth a nation, but sin is a reproach to any people";* yet it is clear that some of the nations invited to build a better age have bloodstained records. They have directly or indirectly killed millions in cold blood; by persecution and starvation they have savagely attacked small nations; they have wantonly opposed the spread of the Gospel, the printing and distribution of Bibles, the freedom of worship; they have practiced the "might makes right" delusion. Should their principles and programs prevail, we can expect only further bloodshed. If power politics continue, if the Big Three or Four constitute themselves rulers and policemen of the world; if the rights of minorities are ruthlessly crushed; if, for example, Poland, to restore whose boundaries this war started, is ruthlessly ripped apart; if poor, frugal, God-fearing Finland, whose children, according to a competent observer in our own Church, are often starving in the slow death of malnutrition, could first be regarded as a martyr when foes overran its boundaries, but later called an enemy because the Finns continued to fight for their liberties against our ally — then Isaiah's warning will be fulfilled: *"If ye,"* people and nations, *"will not believe"* in God's demands for righteousness, justice, truth, and honesty, then *"surely ye shall not be established."* No matter how many votes are given each delegation, no matter how large and elaborate, how well-planned and well-financed, the proposed world organization may be, to have divine blessings, each nation must come before the Lord with clean hands.

The third danger threatening this conference is the greatest menace of all, the tragic fact that some of the men commissioned to make a new age lack trust in God or are even militant atheists. A few have even the blood

Without Christ We Fail

of Christians, persecuted and oppressed, man-hunted and massacred, on their consciences. In their territory and under their direction, ministers of the Gospel have been mowed down with machine guns, churches closed or converted into recreation centers, Bibles destroyed and their distribution prohibited, the walls of public buildings used as billboards for attacks on Scriptural faith, images of Christ slopped through the gutter. Now, when God's unbreakable Word warns, *"If ye will not believe, surely ye shall not be established,"* does anyone in this audience actually expect a better world should this rebellion against the Almighty prevail and the principles of applied atheism persist? Are you one of those who laugh off everything I have said and claim, "As long as we can rely on powerful allies, we are safe and secure"? But are we? In 1917 we shook hands with the Japanese in a pledge of friendship and federation; twenty-five short years later they began shooting down American boys, often with American metal. What guarantee have we that some of today's friends will not likewise be tomorrow's foes?

Recall what happened to Ahaz and his kingdom! When he refused to believe, Isaiah's warning was fulfilled; he was not established. He was victorious, just as we have been; but when the war was won with the Assyrians' aid, Judah was crushed into paying them tribute. Then in the days of his own son Hezekiah, the Assyrians overran Judah and encircled Jerusalem. On tablets dug out of the mounds at Nineveh, we read how the Assyrians boasted that they had destroyed the kingdom of Ahaz. They almost did, until Judah repented and returned to Jehovah. Then with no human allies whatever, but with God's help, the Lord's people, contrite and humble, witnessed the most striking of all recorded victories. In a single night an angel cut down 185,000 Assyrians before Jerusalem's walls. When Israel believed, it was surely established.

You in this radio mission are not primarily responsible for faith or denial in Europe, Asia, and Africa; but you are personally, individually, and collectively responsible for Christian faith in your own country. Therefore it must be of constant concern for you that this beloved land, which, as I have often reminded you, was discovered, founded, and colonized by men and women devoted to the Lord Jesus, should strenuously strive to keep Christ in the United States and His enemies out of our boundaries. Pray and work that America gets and keeps right with God!

At the same time, more deeply than in sackcloth and ashes, we should repent for our manifold and repeated transgressions of the Almighty's will, for our disregard of His divine blessing. Despite the visitation of this Second World War and its call for contrite hearts, listen to these shocking figures which I have compiled from data furnished by Government agencies, public opinion polls, expert investigations, and other reliable sources:

1 of every 29 Americans does not believe in a personal God.

1 of every 27 Americans is a criminal actively at work.

1 of every 23 Americans is afflicted with venereal disease.

1 of every 16 Americans between the ages of 40 to 50 is a liquor addict.

Without Christ We Fail

1 of every 12 American children is illegitimate.

1 of every 6 American marriages ends in divorce.

1 of every 5 American mothers annually practices prenatal murder.

1 of every 4 American families suffers the consequences of a major crime.

1 of every 3 American marriages is childless, many willfully so.

1 of every 2 Americans, almost, indulges in some form of gambling.

1 of every 2 Americans is not a member of any kind of church.

1 of every 2 American church members neglects to attend church regularly.

Can you not see, then, that the appeal re-echoes through our land, "America, repent and return to God in Christ"? During crises of the past our people were directed, not only to pray to our heavenly Father but also to beseech His grace and goodness through the merits of the Lord Jesus. In an hour of national need President John Adams issued his second proclamation for a day of humiliation and prayer, asking — and these are his own words — "that the citizens on that day abstain, as far as may be, from their secular occupations, devote the time to the sacred duties of religion, in public and in private; that they call to mind our numerous offenses against the most high God, confess them before Him with the sincerest penitence, implore His pardoning mercy, through the great Mediator and Redeemer, for our past transgressions, and that through the grace of His Holy Spirit we may be disposed and enabled to yield a more suitable obedience to His righteous requisitions in time to come; that He would interpose to arrest the progress of that impiety and licentiousness so offensive to Himself and so ruinous to mankind; . . . that He would put an end to the effusion of human blood and the accumulation of human misery among the contending nations of the earth by disposing them to justice, to equity, to benevolence, and to peace." I firmly believe that if in our time this had been the sincere, repeated prayer and pleading of every American, from the highest to the lowest, it would not have taken more than three and one-half years to win the European war; indeed, if the German people had followed the Savior, instead of the Nazi ideology, and prayed with the same repentance and reliance on God and His Son, the war doubtless could have been avoided.

Years ago Missionary David Cargill landed on the Fiji Islands. When savage cannibals, armed with murderous clubs, rushed out threateningly against him, he cried out in the few words he had mastered in their language: "My love to you! My love to you!" This immediately disarmed the natives, won their interest and respect. In fewer than fifty years the Fiji Islanders were brought to Jesus, and they have never engaged in a war of their own since. What do you suppose would happen if Americans, Germans, Japanese, British, French, Italians, peoples of all nationalities, filled with the love of the Savior who died for them on the cross, would stifle the propaganda of profiteers by bloodshed, *"obey God rather than men,"* and rush to each other with the yearning cry: "My love to you! My love to you"? We should be much nearer peace than any international conference which excludes Christ can ever bring us.

Without Christ We Fail

Hear these words of Heaven's truth once more: *"If ye will not believe, surely ye shall not be established."* On the basis of this sacred statement, I tell you, although I am no prophet: If the allied powers' meeting in San Francisco gives room to claims of national selfishness, condones or compromises the sins of any people, passes resolutions which in letter or in spirit contradict God's Word and discredit Christ, it will ultimately fail. Send for a copy of this message today; file it for future reference and see if we are right!

II

A PERSONAL WARNING TO EVERY ONE OF US

There is also a personal warning in the Prophet's words. Without Jesus we must fail in finding peace for ourselves and salvation for our souls. We, too, often try to follow Ahaz' formula for success in the smaller circles of our lives by relying on wealth, wisdom, worldly means of building our happiness; but there is no substitute for faith. Money, position, honor, education, even in their highest attainments, offer no escape from life's frightening forces. A few days ago one of the foremost financial figures in this country, yes, in the world, sat down in his palatial New York State summer home to pen a startling note. Declaring that he enjoyed everything life could offer, he wrote, "I have no troubles of any kind, nor am I in bad physical health." Hundreds of millions of people would have envied him, since he was president of the powerful First National Bank of New York, with assets of much more than a billion dollars. A man of great wealth, he was educated; he had a Ph. D., an LL. D., and a Phi Beta Kappa membership. He earned wide political recognition as president of the Bank of International Settlements, which regulated finances after the First World War. He had social acclaim, international medals and citations — in short, he had everything money could buy, influence secure, or merit receive; but he had no faith in Christ. After he had finished his note, this leader in world finances, bank president, university trustee, member of exclusive clubs, placed a 32-caliber revolver at his temple, pulled the trigger and destroyed himself. He had just written, "I have suffered from a melancholia that steadily gets worse." This world figure was afraid to live, while you, perhaps poor, unimportant, with no college degrees, yet with your Savior, can confidently face the most crushing blows.

Notable family connections cannot bestow peace and blessing. Recently a distinguished woman died in Washington, D. C. She was an authority on genealogy and had written books to trace the lineage of well-known people through the centuries. She belonged to the Daughters of the American Revolution, the Colonial Dames, the Order of the Crown, Dames of Magna Charta, Barons of Runnymede, the Society of Mayflower Descendants, the Women's National Press Club, and many other exclusive groups; but when the undertaker arrived at her home, twenty cats trailed him about the place, until, to his own horror, he came upon a hidden niche with a casket in which reposed the remains of her mother, who had died in Saint Louis thirty-three years ago. Evading the law which requires burial of dead bodies, this social figure for a third of a century had spent long hours of the night gazing at the mummified remains of her mother through a small window in the

Without Christ We Fail

hermetically sealed mahogany coffin, which bore a name plate with the death date, March 13, 1912. The Washington clubwoman and authoress, despite her family connections, was afraid of death's separation. In Christ, however, you need never fear death.

The problems and sorrows now confronting many of you, which eventually will stare every one of us in the face — the weight of sickness, the frequent burden of fears, the dread of death, the terror of hell, and that question which sin-burdened souls yearn to have answered with positive assurance, *"What must I do to be saved?"*—cannot find solution and relief in any man-made scheme, as ingenious as it may be. If even expert minds cannot solve ordinary economic issues, how can men alone give us light on the problems which perplex our soul? When we entered the war, food administration executives urged the highest possible production of chickens and eggs. American farmers and poultrymen co-operated energetically; but less than a year ago, our storehouses bulging with millions of dozens of surplus eggs, the appeal was issued to reduce the supply by killing many hens. At that time newborn chicks by the thousands were smothered and vast stores of eggs bought at federally-subsidized prices left to spoil. Now, however, a serious egg shortage exists in our country, and the cry for more and more production is insistently raised. I cite this merely to impress you with the fact that if a large corps of scientifically trained experts, with Government millions at their disposal, cannot regulate even a commodity like eggs, how in the name of reason, not to make the higher appeal to God's truth, can any human schemes remove your soul's pressing sorrows?

Our text cries out to you too, *"If ye will not believe,*

surely ye shall not be established." You need faith, trust, confidence, in Jesus Christ. The Prophet, with the message of peace and promise he always brought, directed King Ahaz, and every one of us, to the virgin-born Savior, whose name was to be *"Immanuel," "God with us."* Truly, Christ — and He alone — is our Hope, our Assurance, our Guarantee of grace, our Deliverance from death, our eternal Redemption! Never was there love like His, a devotion unto death, which made Him, the sinless Son of God, become the sinners' Substitute on the cross, the eternal Ransom for ruined lives, the everlasting Atonement for all vile and vicious transgressions, the divine Reconciliation between God and man, who *"made peace through the blood of His cross."*

Have faith in Jesus, for *"with God nothing shall be impossible!"* He can use heaven's resources to support and sustain you in any need. As your Savior, who Himself bore your sins on Calvary's cursed tree, He offers you free salvation by faith; full salvation, with no transgression too heavy to be removed; final salvation, as He completes your redemption, satisfies the demands of His Father's justice, and pays the whole price of your redemption; sure salvation, with no doubt or uncertainty that He is able to *"save . . . to the uttermost."* As your best Friend, He promises, *"I will never leave thee, nor forsake thee"*; and with Him constantly at your side, you need never tread life's bitterest pathway alone. As the Sovereign of your soul, He overrules the evil threatening your life, and makes *"all things work together for good"* because you are His.

If you have humble, contrite, sin-confessing faith in Jesus, you will surely be established. Your hope for heaven, your assurance of pardon will be built on a

Rock, immovable, eternal. The devil will work overtime against you, but you can always repel him with this unfailing defense: *"'Get thee behind me, Satan,'* in the name of the Lord Jesus!" Your own flesh will coax you to take the easier way of compromising His truth, but His Spirit will help you, as Christ's, to *"fight the good fight of faith."* The world will tempt you, and sadly you will feel your own weakness and inability to stand fast; but as you look to the cross, the Crucified will reassure you, *"My grace is sufficient for thee; for My strength is made perfect in weakness."* Trouble will surround you, but your crushed spirit can always find new guidance, strength, hope, in the merciful Redeemer, who today promises every one of you believers, *"Let not your heart be troubled. . . . My peace I give unto you!"*

Whatever comes, sickness, nervous breakdown, pain, poverty, imprisonment, persecution, loss of money, business, or good name, family trouble, unfaithfulness, desertion, temptation, an accusing conscience, the surrender to sin, or in the deepest sorrow, the death of a loved one, death for us ourselves — with faith in God's Son and the world's Savior, we, as redeemed and restored children of our heavenly Father, will be unchangeably established, in earth and in heaven. May God's Holy Spirit put that faith into the hearts, lives, and actions of those in attendance at all international assemblies! May He keep America close to Jesus, and away from the antichrists! May He fortify the American pulpit with preachers *"determined not to know anything among you, save Jesus Christ, and Him crucified!"* Above all, God give every one of you across the country this firm, fortifying faith in Jesus, our only but all-sufficient Savior, without whom we fail! Amen!

THE VICTORY IS THE LORD'S

"Thine, O Lord, is the . . . victory." 1 CHRONICLES 29:11.

ALMIGHTY GOD: With unspeakable gratitude for victory, we join the Psalmist in declaring, "Thine, O Lord, is the greatness and the power and the glory and the victory and the majesty," for Thou hast given us the triumph over our enemy, and without Thee we would have gone down to defeat. Keep our country ever thankful to Thee for Thy protection, ever humble and penitent in recognition of its own sins, always eager to follow Thy ways! Guard us against pride and the overbearing falsehood that we alone won our victories! Look down with Thine especial love on the young men who must still serve with the armed forces! Shield them with Thy might! Keep us just and merciful toward our enemies, and especially make us all honest and contrite in the confession of our own transgressions! Direct our thoughts to Thy Son, whose triumph over sin, hell, and death offers every one of us the far greater promise of victory in both earth and heaven! Through Thy Spirit give us that inner soul peace which Jesus secured for every one of us, through the shedding of His blood at Calvary! Use this broadcast, and every message of Thy Gospel grace, in bringing many to the faith which trusts Him as the Savior from sin, and help us walk obedient to Thy Word of Truth! Draw us ever closer to the Christ of endless compassion, and by the sustaining comfort of Thy grace put peace into our anxious hearts, peace into our strife-torn souls, peace into our sin-marked lives! Grant us this victory of faith for Jesus' sake and for our blessing! Amen!

The Victory Is the Lord's

ONE of the most eventful weeks in world history has just ended. Benito Mussolini, the Fascist leader who six years ago ruled Italy with an iron hand, was savagely slain. Adolf Hitler, who at the height of his dictatorship held sway over more than 200,000,000 people, is said to have died by his own hand. Berlin, the proud Nazi capital, was captured, and in a startling climax, after five and two thirds years of fighting, practically all the German army surrendered and the official announcement of V-E Day is expected momentarily.

Our gratitude goes out especially to our American soldiers, who recently have borne the brunt of the attacks. We cannot measure their devotion merely by repeating the fact that they have suffered 1,000,000 casualties. We should enter military hospitals to see our sightless men, with white canes and Seeing-Eye dogs, learning to grope their way through a darkened world. We should step into amputation wards, where week after week hundreds of young men have had artificial limbs attached to stumps of arms and legs. We should talk to specialists teaching large classes of the deaf, whose ear drums have been broken by artillery fire. We should ask nurses about those victims of war's cruelty mercifully kept from public view, the battle-fatigued, the mentally disturbed, the physically wrecked, the basket cases, the spiritually deadened. We ought to picture, as closely as we can, the quarter million of our young men who left home never to return, who lie buried in foreign soil, or unburied in the ocean's depth. Nor dare we forget the civilians, driven by overwork, who have gone down to an early grave, the physicians and nurses who overtaxed their energies. All these, humanly speaking, won the European war for us at the cost of their lives, while the average American, far from battle, in a homeland unscarred by enemy shells, made more money than ever before.

What can we give you veterans who gave us victory? Medals, bonuses, pensions, memorial exercises? As we resolve, the Holy Spirit helping us, to stand by you in word and deed, to keep you from selling apples on street corners, waiting in bread lines, or marching on Washington in unemployment armies, we pledge you: We will work and pray that, under God, your sacrifices have not been made in vain. We will strive to protect the liberties at home which you have defended abroad. We will do everything within our power to help the United States turn gratefully, humbly to the Lord.

To Him, the Almighty, we give our highest thanks. Not human ingenuity and self-sacrifice but His power and love, we declare, is responsible for our constant triumph.

THE VICTORY IS THE LORD'S!

Therefore I ask you, across the continent and out on the high seas, soldiers and civilians, to join me in proclaiming these glorious words of David (First Chronicles, chapter twenty-nine, verse eleven), *"Thine, O Lord, is the . . . victory."*

I

OUR NATIONAL VICTORIES COME FROM HIM

No doubt should remain in the heart of any American that God made the surrender of our enemies possible. He enriched us with the resources necessary for our triumphs. He gave us the wind and the weather required for the forward march of our forces. He guided

The Victory Is the Lord's

our leaders, through the costly mistakes of well-trained enemy forces, to smashing triumphs. If He had not greeted the Nazi invaders with one of the coldest winters in Russian history; if He had put gasoline inside the German boundaries and essential war material within our enemies' reach; if He had not endowed the minds of American inventive and industrial genius with the ability required to produce radar and superior instruments of war, the struggle in Europe could still go on its bloody way. The official records of the United States War Department present the testimony of two high-ranking officers who agree that a "miracle" was largely responsible for the American success in North Africa. When our troops approached the shores of that continent, their transports were threatened with two violent storms, either one of which could have wrecked the heavily loaded fleet. General Marshall, Chief of Staff, reveals that the officers commanding the ships prayed frankly and publicly. Then, in answer, the miracle occurred. The two approaching storms appeared to neutralize each other, and our men could be landed safely, with the sea off Casablanca calmer, as an experienced observer noted, "than it had been for sixty-eight years." When our fighting men invaded Sicily and another great storm threatened destruction, who suddenly made the Mediterranean, in the words of the late Ernie Pyle, "smooth as a table top"? When a third of a million defeated British troops were trapped at Dunkirk, who enshrouded them with a fog so that they could return home safely? When, after the disaster at Dunkirk and the collapse of France, England was so close to defeat that its cabinet met secretly to consider the possibility of flying to Canada, who kept Hitler from crossing the Channel when, according to English admission, "the plight of the defenders would have been hopeless," since Great Britain at that time had at home only one completely equipped infantry division, only 300 light tanks, fewer than 100 field guns, and hardly 500 planes, while Germany had more than seven times as many — who if not the same God whose help in Christ can strengthen you? When the German officers commanding the bulge into Belgium figured on the continuance of fog to keep our planes grounded, who suddenly gave our bombers sixteen days of clear weather in which to rout the enemy? I testify publicly that God did all this, and that America should be on its knees to thank the Almighty, who still *"maketh wars to cease unto the end of the earth,"* who *"breaketh the bow and cutteth the spear in sunder, . . . burneth the chariot in the fire."*

When our fighting men return, ten thousands will be able to recount marvelous records of rescue and tell us how God saved them after many harrowing days on life rafts, when lost in enemy territory, or as they lay helpless beneath destructive fire. They, who saw the war in the blood, the tears, the agony of the battlefields, know, as every one on this side of the Atlantic should realize, that *"Thine, O Lord, is the . . . victory."* Therefore the entire nation, officials, churchgoers, citizens, young and old, should pause, worthily to praise the Almighty. It is an insult to the Lord that masses are celebrating these triumphs with drunkenness and debauch, without a thought for the Triune God. If this conquest of the powerful Nazi military machine does not bring us down on our knees in grateful acknowledgment of our heavenly Father's help, this country can sustain terrifying losses.

If we would give the Lord proper thanks, America must show itself really repentant over its own sins. This war has not been marked by a national day of humiliation. Who among our civil leaders has called us to repentance? Who among our mighty military men has told us that we must get right and stay right with God? We have lived on, rich and secure, in smug, satisfied, self-righteous pride, as though America had no faults to confess, no wrongs to admit, no evil to reject. We must trust in the Almighty, instead of relying on men. The decline of power usurped by Europe's dictators, their death, and the brutal disgrace to which Mussolini was subjected, should teach us in the United States pointed lessons. When you read how the boastful tyrant, whom certain churchmen acclaimed as his country's deliverer, whose statues dotted Italy, vainly offered his captors an empire if they would release him; how he, whose word was absolute law for 60,000,000 people, shook in terror as he and his latest mistress faced a Communist firing squad; when you find, further, that the mob near Milan brutally broke his jaw, dashed out part of his brains, kicked and spit at his corpse, hanged his body by the heels at a filling station, and then buried him in a potter's field, don't say simply, *"How are the mighty fallen!"* Pray that America be brought closer to humble trust in God and farther from proud reliance on men! When some of you recall that less than four short years ago Hitler, shouting in Berlin's Kroll Opera House, declared: "Germany can no longer be subjugated. She is so strong that no combination of powers could ever prevail against her!" and when this week you learn that the German dictator is reported dead, his country ruined, and the very place where he screamed his haughty defiance of the world captured by the Russians, resolve that you will personally pray and work to keep out of authority in our country men who thus set themselves above the Almighty!

As the Lord has helped us in the past phases of this war, so may America, clinging to Christ, have the assurance for the future, *"Thine, O Lord, is the . . . victory!"* Doom and disaster steadily move in more closely on the Japanese. A hundred times more dangerous to our continued progress are the forces of irreligion in the world about us and inside our own boundaries. With the destruction of Fascism and Nazism, but, at the same time, with the steady rise of godless Communism, many Americans are wondering whether we have overcome one enemy only to face far wider opposition to our national and Christian ideals. We stand before deep-rooted postwar problems: a $300,000,000,000 debt, social upheaval within our shores, serious labor complications, grave economic issues; but Communism, the radical brand, which refuses to recognize the Redeemer, is crashing its way from one triumph to another. In the last election before the war, the French Communist vote totaled less than 1 per cent of all the ballots; in the first election after the war, last week, it had risen to 25 per cent; and that is only the beginning. Christless Communism is beginning to overshadow Finland; it has engulfed the Baltic countries, Latvia, Estonia, and Lithuania; it rules public affairs in Rumania, Bulgaria, Hungary, and northern Italy; it seeks control of power in

The Victory Is the Lord's

Austria and Denmark; and even Berlin is scheduled to become a Communist capital. The menace steadily moves closer to us. Whatever else the years after the war will bring, we may be sure that Christians in our beloved country will meet this opposition to their faith on a tremendously large scale.

Other forms of godlessness will increase in the first flush of postwar prosperity; for, unbelievable as this is, the victories Heaven gave us in bloody battle have not brought us closer to Christ. How, then, can the ease and luxury of peace do this, if people who hardly sought the Lord, even though battlefield dangers threatened their loved ones, will utterly forget Him after the peril is past? Remember what happened to America after World War I! That was the time when Modernism secured control of many denominations; when the crime figures began to skyrocket; when juvenile delinquency and divorce started their shocking upswing; when many churches, tired of the plain but powerful Gospel, first featured fads and fancies, instead of simple, saving truth in Jesus Christ. The Second World War is more than four times as costly and destructive of human lives as the First. How terrifying, unless the Almighty Himself graciously intervenes, will be the increase of evil after this far heavier and wider bloodshed!

In what way, then, can we overcome the tremendous anti-God forces which arise from within our country? Can men sitting around a conference table curtail these dangers? Can we go forward through concession or compromise with unbelief? Can new laws, new economic systems, really pave the way for a better tomorrow? Can new political philosophies, internationalism, world organizations, guarantee us sure hope? Can atheism, favored by the territorially largest nation on earth, hold out promise for improvement? We must be frank and fearless in proclaiming that none of these proposals, nor a dozen others, such as the planned peace-time drafting of our high-school graduates, or the policing of the world — even the best program which scientific research and ingenuity can produce — will meet the full demands of tomorrow. What this war-torn world needs, what our beloved, God-blessed nation needs, what you and I need, is, first of all, the rebirth in faith which makes us new creatures, gives us a new heart, a new soul, a new desire to serve our fellow men instead of destroying them. The old, selfish, lust-filled, blood-crazed, bestial side of human nature, which can rejoice when it is reported 300,000 civilians have been killed in a single city, should disappear, while we must learn to love mankind, to hate war, to maintain peace, as far as in us lies, with everyone.

I have been trying to tell you what Jesus taught when He told Nicodemus, *"Ye must be born again."* Unless this new life in Christ comes to masses in our world through regeneration and the trusting faith which looks to Him, there can be no hope that wars will decrease and hatreds diminish. In fact, without Christ recognized and revered as the Rescuer of the race, we must be prepared for the far more savage and widespread massacre which, military experts agree, will mark the next wars.

Only personal trust in the Lord Jesus as the Savior from sin can assure men of the answer to David's prayer, *"Create in me a clean heart, O God, and renew a right spirit within me."* You and I can be reborn into that renewed existence only by confessing our fatal failures to obey God's will, our lustful desires, sensual emotions, by admitting that even in our best and highest moments we are hopelessly below the divine requirements, and by trusting our Savior's power to save to the uttermost. Therefore, may our sin-convicted, grace-gripped souls now trustingly testify of Jesus: "He, the holy Son of God, transferred all my transgressions to Himself; He assumed all my guilt; He endured all the curse of my godlessness; He suffered its full punishment; He completely atoned for every evil thought, impulse, word, plan, or deed in my life; He was crucified to secure my release, ransom, and redemption from the doom of sin, death, and the devil; He — O love beyond height and depth, beyond knowing and telling! — willingly, lovingly gave His sinless life on the cross to forgive, cancel, remove, all my sins and thus make me, who was a child of wrath, a child of God, with a new heart, a new spirit, a new, heaven-born desire to follow the Redeemer, who never raised His arm in warfare, never advocated bloodshed among men."

If the present triumph of our arms is to be followed by a triumph of truth, be sure of this: We must have Jesus uppermost in our hearts and lives — not the counterfeit Christ of the brash unbelief in control of many fashionable, financially prominent churches, firmly intrenched in divinity schools graduating Bible-questioning, truth-denying preachers, but the Scriptural Savior, God's Son and Mary's, who, with a love that passes our understanding and description, suffered Himself to be nailed to the cross and there died to restore us, our sins removed, to His heavenly Father. Because only He can make better men, a better nation, a better world, America must go back to faith in His love, back to His cross, His blood, His atoning death, back to His Bible,

His unbroken promises, and His sustaining Spirit. We need Him today more than ever before. Preachers of His Word, forget all side issues, point your people to the Crucified and lead them to declare, *"Thine, O Lord, is the . . . victory"!* Christian congregations and Christian homes, rededicate yourselves to this royal Redeemer! Realize that you are the bulwarks for a brighter tomorrow! Find more time for Jesus, show more love for Him, bring greater sacrifices for His cause, and constantly cling closer to His grace! My countrymen, use every possible means of keeping America's course in harmony with Scripture and away from contradictions to its truth! The Holy Spirit make us not only just in our dealings with our defeated, destitute enemies, but also merciful! Our Lord Himself said, *"Do good to them that hate you, and pray for them which despitefully use you and persecute you!"* If we learn to follow Christ's way instead of the rule-by-force delusion, we shall be much happier, much safer, much nearer true peace and blessing.

II

OUR PERSONAL VICTORIES COME FROM HIM

Far more than national victory comes through faith in Jesus. Turning to Him in trusting faith, each one of us can exult, " *'Thine, O Lord, is the . . . victory'* in my soul and mind and body." By God's remarkable grace the war has left millions of Americans practically untouched. The heaviest hardship they have experienced in the bloody conflict which has cost more than 10,000,000 fighting men their lives — and only the Almighty knows how many tens of millions of civilians — is higher taxes, rationing and similar restrictions. But another war is being waged in which every one of us is engaged daily, the

The Victory Is the Lord's

struggle against the legions of hell, which seek to destroy us. How terrifying to lose this conflict, to be separated everlastingly from God, completely barred from heaven, forever sentenced to hell and endless punishment for unforgiven sin! People think that they suffer misery on this earth; but, oh, what anguish beyond comparison divine wrath will inflict in the next world on those who have spurned the Savior's mercy and rebelled against His redemption! No sacrifice or self-denial, no payment or penance, no prayers or privations, not the longest catalog of good works and sparkling virtues, can give us the victory over vice, the escape from punishment, and the promise of Paradise. In ourselves we are hopelessly lost, defeated by evil, headed for hell. What glorious grace, then, that you can kneel before the cross of Christ, trust His eternal truth, and declare: *"'Thine, O Lord, is the . . . victory'* over my sin. Thou hast cleansed me with Thy holy, precious blood. Thou didst give Thyself for me, take my place, suffer my punishment, die my death, and rise again for my life. Despite my thanklessness, my selfishness, my uncleanness, my dishonesty, my treachery, Thou didst love me until the bitter, brutal end on Calvary's cross. And because Thou hast paid the full price for my redemption, I have no more sins in Thy Father's sight; they have been completely removed. With thankful heart I repeat, *'Thine, O Lord, is the . . . victory!'"*

Your sins forgiven, you can conquer every surrounding enemy of your soul. Many of you will face opposition in peace far worse than the war brought you. Don't deceive yourselves by the false hope that when an armistice is signed, your troubles disappear! However, humbly beholding the saving Christ, you can exult, *"Thine, O Lord, is the . . . victory'* over my troubles and afflictions." If men can rise over heavy handicaps to positions of world leadership, surely you, with the Savior who told Saint Paul, afflicted by the thorn in his flesh, *"My grace is sufficient for thee; for My strength is made perfect in weakness,"* can find divine guidance from grief to glory. Premier Ismet Inonu of Turkey is deaf, but he defeated that heavy affliction and piloted his country safely through the war's diplomatic difficulties. China's Chiang Kai-shek suffers from chronic rheumatism and a fractured twelfth vertebra, which at times forces him to wear a steel brace; but this has not prevented him from leading his country upward. Josef Stalin has a withered left arm; yet he has become the dominant figure of world affairs. Now, if men, often without Christ, can overcome handicaps, how much more can you, with Christ, for whom nothing shall be impossible, find that your afflictions have become advantages, realize that you, as a child of God through Jesus, have Heaven's own assurance of sorrows turned to joy, of sickness, loss, reverses, mightily transformed into mavelous blessings of your Father's love! No matter how often and savagely the blows of adversity may strike you to the ground, relying on your Redeemer, you too will never be defeated. You can always, lifting trusting eyes to the Crucified, say, *"Thine, O Lord, is the . . . victory!"* If you actually mean what you say, you can learn how to live in joyful peace despite torment and torture at their worst.

All foes of your faith are defeated when the Savior's constant companionship sustains you. Searching His Word, deepening your faith as you receive strength and

The Victory Is the Lord's

guidance from the Spirit, you can say, "*'Thine, O Lord, is the . . . victory'* over my temptations, my doubts, my indifference, my enemies, my self-seeking flesh, the hostile, sin-loving world, — the complete and final victory even over death." No one but a Christian knows how to die, and no one but a true believer in Him who has overcome death for us can have light and strength in the hour of bereavement. A Pennsylvania mother wrote me last week that within two years her husband died and both of her sons were killed in action. Yet, instead of the bitter, scathing attacks on God's love that some of you send me, she wrote in a resigned, faith-filled spirit, which thanked the Lord for having brought her dear ones to Christ; and joyfully she looked forward to the blessed reunion with them before the throne of the Lamb. Do you want that triumphant trust, even when confronted by death? Then come to Jesus, just as you are, sin-burdened, worry-weighted, grief-gripped! Lay your transgressions at the foot of His cross! Keep none of them back! Confess them all! Admit that you are lost without Him! But then cry out in exultant confidence, "*'Thine, O Lord, is the . . . victory'* over death for me!"

My beloved, during these days when our nation celebrates its smashing victories, and when we gird ourselves to defeat our enemies from without and within, may all of you, whatever your race, color, condition may be, humble yourselves to be exalted in Jesus and, clinging with constantly deeper trust to Him, the Son of God and the Savior of your soul, cry out: *"This is the victory that overcometh the world, even our faith!" Thanks be to God, which giveth us the victory through our Lord Jesus Christ!"* Thine, O Savior of endless compassion, is and ever shall be the victory! Amen!

FAMILIES OF AMERICA, STAND BEFORE THE LORD!

"Keep therefore the words of this covenant and do them, that ye may prosper in all that ye do. Ye stand this day, all of you, before the Lord, your God; your captains of your tribes, your elders, and your officers, with all the men of Israel, your little ones, your wives . . . that thou shouldest enter into covenant with the Lord, thy God."

DEUTERONOMY 29:9-12

GOD OF OUR FATHERS AND OF OUR CHILDREN: As we thank Thee again for the victories in Europe and plead for a speedy end of all strife, we praise Thee for the fathers and, today especially, for the mothers who bring their children to Christ and win spiritual triumphs through His saving love. We thank Thee for the sons and daughters who, despite the heaped temptations in these godless days, cling closely to Jesus and overcome encircling evil. Forgive us, for the Savior's sake, the sins committed in our homes, all the selfishness, impurity, unfaithfulness, hatred, unbelief, in our family circles! Show us again that the blood of Jesus, Thy self-giving Son, can cleanse us of the most terrifying transgressions; that the Holy Spirit can stifle the selfishness which causes strife, by making us new creatures with a deep desire to live in Christ's love! Help us prepare our homes for the return of our dear ones now in distant battle-scarred lands by receiving the Redeemer into our households, reading His Word, raising our hearts to Him in prayer, making our homes temples of His grace and truth! Bless us, Father, through Thy Spirit, with faith and fervor for Christ, and by His presence make our

Families of America, Stand Before God! 261

earthly dwellings foregleams of the eternal radiance in Thy many-mansioned heavenly house! Keep us always in the faith, and when our last hour comes, bring us to the place of eternal rest with Thee, which Jesus, our Savior, prepared for us! May our loved ones here be reunited with us there, through Christ, who is the Resurrection and the Life! Amen!

Today is the first Sunday in almost six years on which the gunfire of mighty armies is not heard in Europe. Praise God for that! Thank the Almighty, as the President reminds the nation, for the victory which has kept our country from being bombed into the rubble of ruin that marks Germany! Acknowledge His protection by which millions of our American fighting men overseas will return safely to their homeland! Glorify Him without whose help we would have gone down to defeat, because this gruesome business of killing and destroying on a scale fiercer than men have ever known before is finally over in Europe! Pray God that the prisoners of war, the inmates of horror camps, the victims of bestial cruelty, may be sustained and restored; that the missing may be found, the wounded healed, the homeless sheltered, the destitute supplied, the hungry nourished, the bereaved comforted! As Jesus, the Son of God, pleaded on the cross for His crucifiers, so may we have the faith, the courage, the love, to intercede for those who were our enemies, asking especially that they be kept from despair!

This Sunday should also be a day of prayer for our own beloved land, as we entreat the Holy Spirit to change the hearts of our remaining enemies, to give us total peace, and to prevent our nation from being swept into another world war after a few years' recuperation from the losses of this struggle. Having last week told you, "The victory is the Lord's," today I declare, "The peace is the Lord's!" Be clear on this: No group of men, even the most high-minded, sitting in conference sessions, can alone establish international harmony; no alliance of the world powers, even on the most unselfish principles, can itself avert war; no military machinery policing the earth, even the most powerful, can remove all bloodshed. We need Him of whom the Psalmist says, *"The Lord will bless His people with peace."*

Today, then, America should be close to God *"in spirit and in truth."* His mighty benedictions in the past and the necessity of His heavenly help for the future should bring every one of us on our knees in penance, prayer, and praise. As never before in this generation, every church throughout the land should resound with the glorious Gospel of Jesus Christ. Since the God-fearing family is a basic unit for blessed peace, progress, and prosperity both in body and soul, every American home should this day dedicate itself to the Redeemer, in whom alone we have hope and assurance. Therefore on this second Sunday in May, which by praiseworthy custom has been set aside to remind us of the importance of motherhood, and the Christian home, we ask:

FAMILIES OF AMERICA, STAND BEFORE THE LORD!

That is the lesson we should draw from our text (Deuteronomy, chapter twenty-nine, verses nine to twelve): *"Keep therefore the words of this covenant and do them, that ye may prosper in all that ye do. Ye stand this day,*

Families of America, Stand Before God! 263

all of you, before the Lord, your God; your captains of your tribes, your elders, and your officers, with all the men of Israel, your little ones, your wives . . . that thou shouldest enter into covenant with the Lord, thy God."

I

OUR FAMILIES SHOULD STAND BEFORE THE LORD

These words were spoken through divine direction by one of history's mightiest military and civil leaders, Moses, the man of God; and they were uttered in a national crisis, similar to our present situation. Just as America has enjoyed a series of startling victories, so Moses had led the children of Israel through the heat and blister of the desert, with one triumph after the other, as the well-organized Egyptians, the swift Amalekites, the powerful Bashanites, the militant Amorites, all went down to defeat before the irresistible power of God's strength. But just as we still face a fierce and fanatical foe, so Moses, standing on the brink of the Promised Land, declares to his countrymen that cruel and crafty adversaries lie in wait for them on the other side of the Jordan. How can they overcome these well-equipped armies opposing them? In the same way that we can vanquish the Japanese and any other enemy which may arise against us from without or within. Be sure of this: the World War is over in Europe, but the world revolution, the attempt to overthrow the existing order, the fatal folly of making the state supreme and dictatorial, will not be over for a long time! We have not the slightest reason for believing that the work of the Christian Church in Europe, Asia, or in our own United States will be easier and smoother in the years ahead. The Bible warns us that those who are Christ's must expect persecution, oppression, worldliness in the churches, cold, formal lip worship, the falling away from the faith — all this and much more in the bloody, war-filled last days. Regardless of what politicians promise, who among you, knowing God's Word, can doubt that these times are upon us, and that Jesus will soon return in His triumphant second coming?

Listen carefully, then, as Moses tells Israel and America how to face the future with promise and confidence! He does not rely on armed forces, although he has military men; he does not trust his own ability and diplomacy, although the ages since have never seen his equal in national leadership; instead, he does what every statesman in America should do today — he directs his people to the Lord and assures them, *"Keep therefore the words of this covenant and do them, that ye may prosper in all that ye do."* What appeal, I ask you pointedly, does our country need for its question-weighted future, if not the same plea that our divinely endowed land would remember the covenant with God made by our founding fathers; that our people, enriched as none other on the face of the earth, express their allegiance to the Lord Jesus Christ, God's Son and their Savior; that, led by the Holy Spirit, they, humbly repentant of their sins, walk in Heaven's way? With a staggering national debt which has grown at the rate of $100,000 each minute; with shocking problems of an impoverished world, economists will propose many programs for postwar prosperity. God bless all good plans and rebuke all efforts that would selfishly lead the masses into further misery! But here is the Almighty's own direction for national peace and

Families of America, Stand Before God! 265

well-being: *"Keep . . . the words of this covenant* [the worship of the true and triune God] *. . . that ye may prosper in all that ye do."*

Therefore after many victories and before their final conquest, Moses told his people, *"Ye stand this day, all of you, before the Lord, your God."* Can you not hear the echo, "O people of America, *'ye stand this day, all of you, before the Lord your God'* "? The triumphs which the Almighty granted impose a heavy responsibility, asking us to show our gratitude to Him from whom all our blessings, and notably the most recent, have come. America for Christ, and Christ for America — that should be the cry resounding throughout the land. While statesmen labor to build the political structure of a new world, we who love the Lord Jesus should strive by our faith and consecrated life to lay the necessary spiritual foundation, deeper trust in the Savior, who says, *"Behold, I make all things new,"* and whose verdict still holds, *"Without Me ye can do nothing."* We regard it as essential for divine blessing on our land that there be no actions or decisions against Jesus in our Congress and in our courts, nothing opposed to His will in our national and international affairs. We plead that He reign in the hearts and lives of multitudes now far from the cross and His love; that He who, as the Church last Thursday observed, visibly ascended to heaven to reign in majesty at the Father's right hand, gloriously rule our churches and quickly overrule those who rise up against Him.

Note that when Moses summoned the people to reconsecrate themselves, he told Israel, *"Your captains of your tribes, your elders, and your officers"* shall *"stand . . . before the Lord."* He wanted the leaders, civil and military, to show their allegiance to the Almighty. Today, too, He asks that public officials and soldiers, officers and enlisted men, stand humbly and gratefully before Him. Indeed, every fighting man to whom the end of the war in Europe means the escape from the danger and death of bloodshed should live in constant praise of the Lord. How encouraging to read that during the war the American Bible Society distributed almost 7,000,000 Testaments and Scripture portions among our armed forces! God grant that, with the peril past, you soldiers and sailors will continue to read your Bibles as you did under hostile fire; that you will faithfully and reverently say your prayers, just as you did when you expected your end any moment! If the men in America's armies and navies come back to us influenced against Christ and the Bible, by their contact with foreign unbelief, growing atheism, brazen sin, we will have won the war, but unless the Almighty graciously intervenes, we will lose the peace and the promise of His blessings. Stand by your men in the fighting forces especially now!

It should not escape our attention, however, that at the same time Moses asks the leaders and the warriors to assemble before Jehovah, he also, in the same appeal, says, *"All the men of Israel, your little ones, your wives"* should *"stand this day . . . before the Lord your God."* He puts the family on the same level of importance with the rulers and soldiers. He knows that the home must be brought to the Almighty if his people are to face the future with assurance. May the Holy Spirit give us the same conviction! What shall we gain if, having won the war, our country loses truth, honesty, decency, the fear of God, and the love of Christ in its homes? Of what benefit are social securities if we lack stability in our families? How can we hope to right the evils of the globe if we have not set our own houses in order? What is the United States profited if it takes over the trusteeship of Pacific islands but forfeits the trust in masses of its own youth?

Our families, fathers, mothers, children, should follow Israel in standing before God. But do they? Today is Mother's Day. — How many American mothers will receive no flowers, no gifts, no cards, not even a loving thought, from their children, because their sons and daughters — proud, self-sufficient, sometimes too successful — have forsaken their mother, deserted their father? The world frowns on this thanklessness, but God's Word puts a curse on it when it thunders out this denunciation: *"Cursed be he that setteth light by his father or his mother. And all the people shall say, Amen."*

Many of our homes do not stand before the Lord because parents neglect their little ones. Not only have more parents than ever before cruelly deserted their offspring, but masses of our boys and girls, their fathers absent, their mothers preoccupied or unconcerned, live on without discipline, counsel, and especially spiritual guidance. We are told that one of the first diamonds ever found in the South African fields was picked up by a farmer's child who placed it on a shelf as a curious, interesting stone. Some months later a peddler came to the farmhouse, spied the gem on the shelf and, recognizing its real nature but concealing its value, asked the mother what she would take for it. Pointing to her little boy, she answered laughingly, "It belongs to him, not to me." Cunningly the peddler offered the lad a set of wooden soldiers in exchange, which he gladly accepted. The peddler hurried to Capetown and sold the diamond for a large sum to a jeweler. He, in turn, received $125,000 for it on the European market, and today it adorns a royal neck. "The poor child," you say; but not as poor as many American little ones whose parents, against better knowledge, permit them to make their own decisions concerning their soul and to suffer eternal losses far greater than the exchange of a crown jewel for wooden soldiers.

If American families are to help form the blessed foundation we need for individual and national happiness, they must stand before the Lord in banishing the strife and quarrel that mars many a household. Unbelievable as this may seem, our country has many homes in which the husband never tells his wife that he loves her, often because he no longer has any affection for her; because wives, their early infatuation turned into hatred, steadily plan to oppose their husbands. What heartless, selfish battling and cursing often reigns under roofs where peace in Christ should be supreme! How about your dwelling? It was recently announced that a new apparatus has been perfected by which every word spoken within a building may be overheard three miles away. A small, sensitive device is attached to the outer wall and another apparatus beamed toward it with the result that entire conversations may be recorded. What if such a device were directed to your home? Would it pick up words of devotion or angry snarls, blessing or cursing? Above all, what does the Almighty, who perceives even the unspoken thought, hear within the walls of your house?

Families of America, Stand Before God! 269

Some families should stand faithfully before the Lord but are degraded by drunkenness. A Washington, D. C., newspaper quoted a British surgeon who said, "I see no reason from the medical point of view why a man shouldn't get roaring drunk once a month," and then sent its reporters to see whether the man on the street agreed. The paper published six answers from soldiers and civilians — and they all declared that periodic drunkenness was a good thing. But the Bible says this sin, if unforgiven, leads to hell; and many of you wives, beaten, cowed, and cursed by alcohol-soaked husbands, feel that hell can start on earth.

Families often fail to stand before God because of impurity and marital unfaithfulness. In 1712, when it was predicted that Whiston's comet would appear in the skies over London, people in that city thought that the Day of Judgment had come; and when the comet streaked across the sky on October 25 of that year, more than 7,000 couples living out of wedlock hurried to be married legally. We are 233 years closer to the Day of Judgment than those frightened Londoners were, and a comet is a plaything in comparison with World War II; yet have you noticed any decrease in the sins of the flesh, any real evidence of widespread repentance and return to God in Christ? Every family weakened by the ravages of vice, devoted to selfish childlessness and the support of anti-Biblical birth control, torn apart by divorce and desertion, reduces our national strength. Go to your public libraries, ask for the Cambridge Ancient History volume on Assyria, and you will find that eminent authorities ascribe the sudden and unexpected downfall of Nineveh to the reign of ruinous lust. History thus supports the inspired truth that *"sin is a reproach to any people,"* a crushing reproach from the Almighty Himself, which recalls the smouldering ruins of Sodom and Gomorrah. The Lord give our blessed land a million more voices to warn against the savage assaults of sensuality!

All these sins that weaken the home, provoke divine wrath, and undermine the nation, stem from the first and most fatal domestic weakness — rejection of God. American households, unscathed by war, more comfortable and commodious than ever before, often have no room, no time, no love, for the Savior, particularly today, when money is easy and plentiful, when short-sighted men pat themselves on the shoulder and say: "We won the war. We don't need God." What happens to faithless families when calamity and sorrow break upon them? The Associated Press reports "dozens of new suicides" daily in Berlin. Unbelief always fails, leads to despair, and tears others down to destruction with it. But indescribably more harrowing and horrorful even than the brutal end of a scoffer is the eternal punishment in the hereafter for rejecting God and denying Christ. Jesus Himself said, *"He that believeth not shall be damned."* And who are proud pulpiteers, that they dare to question the Savior's truth, contradict His Word, deny that there is a hell? Don't gamble with eternity! Don't take a chance with your soul! Don't listen to any man, however powerful and popular he may be, who questions or opposes one sentence spoken by the Son of God! Rather realize, with all your heart and soul that faith in your Redeemer is the supreme need for yourself and your dear ones; that in truth a peace-filled nation must have Christ-filled families which stand reverently before the Lord.

II
OUR FAMILIES CAN STAND BEFORE THE LORD

Now some of you, dissatisfied with conditions in your house, disturbed over your own sins and sorrow, but urged by the Spirit, have been asking: "How can my family and I stand before the holy God with our transgressions of His Law, our failure to do His will? How can we change things in our home, so that love and peace and joy reign supreme?" What a privilege it is for me to answer and, in the name of the crucified, resurrected, ascended Savior to bring every one of you — with no restrictions of race, poverty, color, class or condition — the message of marvelous mercy for the whole world, and in this moment especially for you! You can stand before God; your home can be blessed beyond the gift of wealth and comfort by the astonishing, limitless love your heavenly Father offers you in Jesus, His own Son. We are grateful to parents who rear us, husbands or wives who sacrifice for us, men who help us, soldiers who defend us, policemen and firemen who risk their lives for us, nurses and doctors who aid in curing us; but how can we begin to thank our gracious Father for the endless grace He has showered on us!

Pause for a moment to see what the Lord has done for you! First of all, He created you and endowed you with the marvel of your senses, which a million scientists could never reproduce. He loved you with an unquenchable devotion, which when you were lost in sin — and every one of you is, without His Son — decreed an eternal plan for your salvation. He sent prophets to proclaim it, inspired writers to record it. He gave the Bible to preserve it for you. In the breath-taking, sense-staggering climax of His love the Father sent His own dearly beloved Son into this world of wickedness and woe for you. With a compassion too divine for us to understand, the all-merciful, self-sacrificing Jesus died on the cross amid soul torture and agony a million times more cruel and crushing than the horrors of this war. Then, in the mightiest mercy which even He, the all-powerful God could show, He accepted Christ's atonement as the payment for the penalty of your sins, as your ransom from ruin, your rescue from hell. He offers you *full* salvation, with no sin you have ever committed too grievous to be forgiven, no blasphemy too brutal to be removed, no impurity too foul to be cleansed, if only you have faith in the Savior's sin-removing blood and His atoning death. God promises you *free* salvation, with your redemption entirely Christ's work and no part your own contribution. He pledges you *certain* salvation, so sure that you can exult, *"I know whom I have believed, and I am persuaded that He is able to keep that which I have committed unto Him against that Day."* He grants you the constant companionship of the risen, ascended Redeemer and the glorious guarantee of His intercession for you now before the throne of eternity. He sends you His Holy Spirit to teach, enlighten, and strengthen you in the faith. He assures you of comfort in every distress, lightening for every burden. He can change your sorrow into joy, and by the marvel of His mercy transform afflictions into blessings. Daily your heavenly Father supplies you with everything you need for body and soul. He guarantees you through Christ a prepared place in heaven. He, whose Word will never be broken, can marvelously resurrect your dead, decayed body and by the final magnificence of His mercy make you and all believers like unto the risen Redeemer.

With these blessings, unspeakably greater than earth's highest benefits, to be accepted by personal, penitent faith, acclaim and acknowledge Him your divine Deliverer now! The powers that be waited two days after Germany's complete surrender before they announced it; but for the sake of your soul don't wait a moment longer before announcing your peace through the blessed Redeemer! Now, before your radios, cry out, "O Jesus, Thou art mine from this moment and, Thy Spirit helping me, forever!" Life is too dangerous to exist even one unnecessary moment without Christ, the risk of losing our souls in hell too terrifying to permit any postponement of accepting Him. Come to Him now in contrition and confidence!

Then, as His faith captures the hearts of your family, you can *"stand this day, all of you, before the Lord your God."* The family that has this trust is divinely blessed with peace and happiness, strengthened with courage when afflictions strike it, comforted when bereavements burden it. Such Spirit-filled homes are the surest hope for a peace-filled nation, God's own guarantee of a radiant reunion for parents and children in the better homeland.

May all of you therefore on this victory Sunday gratefully resolve to follow the Apostle's plea, *"Let the Word of Christ dwell in you richly!"* Fathers, God and man give you the first responsibility for bringing Christ into your family. Find regular and reverent time to read the Bible and to beseech God earnestly with your loved ones! Get away from thoughtless, hastily spoken prayers! Booth, the famous Shakespeare tragedian, tells us he spent thirty years learning how to pray the Lord's Prayer. He maintained that hardly one in a thousand understands the rich content of this petition. This intercession should not merely be recited in your family circle; together with the prayers which each member of the household directs to the Almighty in Jesus' name, it should come from humble and believing hearts!

Mothers, this is your day. Make it a truly blessed, holy day by standing before the Savior and promising to serve Him even in the common, everyday household tasks! The mother of Ziegenbalg, the mighty missionary to India, left as her legacy to her children a worn copy of the Bible. "Take it," she told them on her deathbed, "read it, follow it! Every page is stained with my tears." Mothers of America, are you reading the Word with such devotion? Are you helping to bring up your children *"in the nurture and admonition of the Lord"*?

Sons and daughters, give God's Son the leadership of your life! Everything else for which you work and strive, the comforts and pleasures and riches of life, last their brief moment and then disappear; but your soul is eternal. How many minutes each day do you spend preparing for eternity? Don't let the worship of Christ be a crowded side issue in your home! Devote ample time to daily devotions, family Scripture reading, prayers, and hymns, morning and evening! Give God thanks at each meal!

Young people who look forward to marriage, remember that the most essential blessing for your future is the presence of the never-failing Redeemer! Don't consider a lifelong union with an unbeliever! Don't hope that after the wedding you can convert a scoffing husband or an infidel wife! I wish you could see the letters sent me by disillusioned people who thought they could start a happy marriage in a house divided against itself by unbelief, but who failed dismally. Choose a real, consecrated, confessing Christian as your life mate! Here in San Francisco, a few days ago, a young marine, home for a short furlough, learned that the Navy nurse to whom he was engaged was stationed somewhere in this vast city of three quarters of a million people. They had planned to marry on this furlough, but his frantic effort to find her during two days of telephoning were of no avail. Suddenly he remembered: "This is Sunday. She will be in church as usual," and the Lord led him, of all congregations, to this very Saint Paulus Church, which serves 1,100 of our servicemen and servicewomen. Sure enough, there was his beloved, worshiping her Lord. A few hours later they were married in the church by the pastor, the best place and the best way for believers to enter wedded life. — Will you meet your loved one in a night club or in church, in a public dance hall or in a Christian young people's gathering?

Husbands and wives, stay close together in Jesus during these trying years, when the forces of hell are loosed, as they seek to destroy happy families! You married men away from home, get down on your knees daily to ask God for strength to resist temptations! You war wives, flee enticements! Ask Christ to keep you pure and clean and healthy! You need the Savior, especially when your own human selfish nature whispers: "Why not have a good time? Why not get a divorce? Higherups, even in Government circles, do." If ever it seems that your marriage is at the breaking point, cling wholly to the Lord! Spurn Satan's temptation! Jesus can save your home even in the last moment. When the earthquake shook San Francisco and the flames gutted its houses, military authorities had placed sticks of dynamite beneath the church from which I speak to you. To keep the fire from spreading, they planned to blow to pieces this beautiful structure of a pioneer Pacific Coast congregation because they thought the hydrants were empty and the water supply gone. But just before they were ready to light the fuses, the pastor cried out, "Wait, let me try the hydrant before the church!" They laughed at him but finally gave their permission, and suddenly a stream of water gushed from the pipes. One reservoir high in the San Francisco hills was still functioning, and its water saved not only the church, but also the buildings for blocks around. Similarly, if men or devils whisper to you: "Destroy your home! Leave your husband! Run away with some other woman!" stop to recall that a Power higher up — no matter how unbelievers may ridicule it — can save your soul, your home, your happiness, and at the same time bring blessing to those around you!

Families of America, I repeat the words of Moses: *"Ye stand this day, all of you, before the Lord your God . . . with all the men of Israel, your little ones, your wives . . . that thou shouldest enter into covenant with the Lord, thy God."* As you look with me to the ascended, victorious Christ, the Pardon for our sins, the Source of our strength, the Assurance of our redemption, the Pledge of our heavenly reunion with all believers, resolve now, throughout the length and breadth of the land:

> Then here will I and mine today
> A solemn covenant make and say:
> Though all the world forsake Thy Word,
> I and my house will serve the Lord.

Amen!

COME, HOLY SPIRIT!

"When the day of Pentecost was fully come . . . they were all filled with the Holy Ghost. . . . And the same day there were added unto them about three thousand souls."
ACTS 2:1, 4, 41

HOLY SPIRIT, ENLIGHTENER, COMFORTER, SUSTAINER: Shed Thy power on us through our broadcast as once on this day Thou didst descend on Christ's first disciples! Neither by our own human reason, mental or physical strength, can we believe in the Lord Jesus as our atoning Savior and come to Him. Our sins muddle our mind, destroy our desire for the divine Redeemer, blind us to our own destruction, crush our consciences. We need Thee to show us that we are lost without Jesus, to create faith in His sin-bearing love within our hearts, to sanctify our lives, to preserve us in the truth. Therefore come, Holy Spirit, to millions in our blessed country, to multitudes in our churches, to many in the armed forces, who need Thee now with double urgency! Descend on our war-torn world with increased power, and by strengthening men's hearts with the Savior's inner peace bring outward peace into our beaten, bloody age! Repeat the miracle of the first Pentecost by enlightening the souls and minds of America's preachers! Fill them with the heavenly wisdom required to proclaim only Thy revealed truth and to know nothing save Christ, and Him crucified! Without Thee we cannot call Jesus Lord, but with Thee we are born into a new faith-grounded life. Therefore, come to us, bless us, guide us to our Deliverer, keep us with Him! We pray in His saving name and by His unfailing promise! Amen!

A FEW years ago on the night before Easter, so it is reported, a new play opened in one of Moscow's leading theaters, a blasphemous comedy entitled "Christ in Tuxedo." A packed house saw the first act, with a scene featuring a church altar arrayed like a saloon bar, with bottles of beer, wine, and vodka. Fat priests sat around the altar raising their arms in drunken toasts. Nuns squatted on the sanctuary floor playing cards. It was just another of those degrading, damnable exhibitions of atheism which repeatedly marked the Red rebellion against the Savior, and which, despite frequent and increasing attempts to whitewash this horror, should make every American Christian pray and work with redoubled force that such ruinous godlessness may not overtake our beloved country. The second act featured Comrade Alexander Rostovzev, a Moscow matinee idol, a dyed-in-the-wool disciple of Marx and a sneering enemy of Jesus. You can imagine, then, how the audience roared, when Rostovzev walked out on the stage impersonating Christ, dressed in a flowing oriental robe and carrying a large New Testament. Soon after his entrance he was to read two verses from the Sermon on the Mount, remove his Palestine gown, and cry out, "Give me my tuxedo and top hat!" Rostovzev, as directed by the script, began to intone slowly: *"Blessed are the poor in spirit, for theirs is the kingdom of God. Blessed are they that mourn, for they shall be comforted."* Then, instead of following his cues and putting on the tuxedo, he stopped as though paralyzed. An uneasy silence gripped the spectators when the smooth, suave actor, his whole body shaking, started to read again:

"Blessed are the meek, for they shall inherit the earth. Blessed are they who hunger and thirst after righteousness, for they shall be filled. Blessed are the merciful, for they shall obtain mercy." He finished the forty-one remaining verses of Matthew's fifth chapter before a stunned audience. Backstage other actors in the cast, perhaps thinking that he was drunk, coughed, called, and stamped to urge the star of Moscow's stage on with his forgotten blasphemies. But Rostovzev was no longer a blasphemer. Christ's Word had conquered and converted him; for there, before the footlights, he who had reviled the Crucified, now made the sign of the cross in the Russian Orthodox tradition and cried out in the prayer of the penitent thief, *"Lord, remember me when Thou comest into Thy kingdom!"* That was too much for the management. The curtain was lowered, someone announced that Comrade Rostovzev had taken ill suddenly; the performance was canceled. But how the heavens must have re-echoed with the special praise of angels, who rejoice when one sinner is saved!

That startling change from blasphemer to believer was the work of the Holy Spirit, the same enlightening God who took Saint Paul, bent on destroying the early disciples, and made him the mightiest Apostle of all; the same faith-bestowing God who has called every disciple of Christ from the darkness of sin into the light of our Lord's marvelous mercy; the same gracious God who now appeals to you, the unsaved, on the way to hell without Jesus, and would put you on the sure road to heaven with the Savior.

That Holy Spirit, believers throughout the world, even in Japan, honor today, on Pentecost, the birthday of the Christian Church. Because every one of us should personally have the same Spirit who this day descended on the disciples, join me across America today in this Pentecost prayer:

COME, HOLY SPIRIT!

Learn the divine blessings He can give you from our text (the Book of Acts, chapter two, verses one, four, and forty-one), *"When the day of Pentecost was fully come . . . they were all filled with the Holy Ghost. . . . And the same day there were added unto them about three thousand souls."*

I

COME WITH THY BLESSINGS FOR OUR FAITH!

Pentecost, as its name indicates, fifty days after Easter, was a holiday in Jerusalem, a sort of Thanksgiving Festival on which the earliest wheat harvest was presented to the Lord. What a happy day for giving the Father the firstfruits in the harvest of human souls won for Christ and His Church! The disciples, obeying their risen Lord's command, had stayed in Jerusalem since the ascended Savior left them ten days before. How much they would have missed if, driven by a desire to make money, they had gone back to their fisher boats in Galilee! How much many of you lose every day because you refuse to follow Christ's design and direction for your salvation!

Nobody knows the place where the disciples assembled; but it must have been some unimpressive, out-of-the-way room, perhaps that unmarked upper chamber in which Jesus Himself had instituted the Lord's Supper. You see from this again that the Almighty performs His miracles without the fanfare, pomp, and ceremony which often impress blinded men. Newspapers report that the allied nations' conference in San Francisco cost the United States one and one half million dollars; but the Pentecost miracle demanded not a single shekel. No press agents, paid feature writers, photographers, were present with the disciples, as publicity men cover important meetings today; but the power of Pentecost, shown in that small and at first unnoticed gathering, inestimably exceeded the influence of all our generation's international conferences, which, one after the other collapsing, as the late David Lloyd George, Britain's World War I Prime Minister, correctly stated, too often were only "pre-arranged blather."

While that hunted band of believers prayed and worshiped together, it happened. Christ kept His Word to them, as He, the Son of God, will fulfill His promises to you. He had pledged His followers, *"Ye shall receive power, after that the Holy Ghost has come upon you,"* and now, in fulfillment, the Holy Ghost came. At first nothing unusual was to be seen, but a strange noise, *"as of a rushing mighty wind . . . filled all the house where they were sitting."* No twenty-one gun naval salute has ever had the force of that reverberating, gale-like, rushing sound from heaven; for it was the Comforter, the Sanctifier, coming into the souls of His servants. A few moments later little fiery flames appeared and descended on each of the disciples. They were men of different stations and positions in life, but each of them needed the Holy Spirit fully to believe, worthily to accept Christ as his Savior; and here, descending gently on each one as a blaze of purifying fire, came that enlightening, sustaining Spirit, whom we worship as our God.

I make neither apology nor defense when I declare that the Holy Spirit, in the fullest sense of this exalted term, is our God. Large churches may deny this, unbelievers laugh at it, many who call themselves Christians ignore it, supporters of sects and schisms pervert it — and may Heaven forgive us! — many otherwise sincere people neglect it; but this cannot change the eternal truth, clearly revealed in the Bible, which calls the Holy Spirit God, gives Him divine honor, ascribes divinely blessed work to Him, and makes Him, together with the Father and the Son, our true and Triune God. The Father created our earthly life, but the Spirit creates us anew in the heavenly life. The Son died for our redemption, but the Spirit brings the message of His mercy into our hearts. You may not hear much of the Spirit in many modern churches, but this omission helps account for the fact that, while with His help Peter, a Galilean fisherman, could preach a heart-searching sermon, which won thousands of converts for Christ, many a highly paid D. D., Th. D., S. T. D., without the Spirit has never been able to bring a single soul to the Lord Jesus. Today is set aside in many places as a special day of prayer for ministers and missionaries. God knows they need fervent intercessions! Ask especially that, with the Holy Spirit's help, many American pulpits stop serving as propaganda points for the denial of our Lord, many American churches become more than community forums and social centers, many American preachers more than leaders of polite society!

Only God could show the mighty Pentecost power

Come, Holy Spirit!   283

which the Spirit exercised on the first disciples. Think of it! A short week and a half before, these men were so saturated with ambition for earthly power that they asked Christ immediately before His ascent the political question when He would make Israel a world power again — strangely enough the very issue which modern, but misguided pulpits often discuss, rather than the answer to the personal and pointed question, *"What must I do to be saved?"* Now, when the Holy Spirit filled their lives, He purified them and, as Jesus had promised, guided them into all truth. Read Peter's address on Pentecost, his first recorded sermon, and you will notice that he does not spend his time discussing various theories of the millennium, nor advancing his own opinion on the political future of his countrymen, nor speculating on vague issues of prophecy, nor featuring a dozen different moral side issues, which so crowd and clutter many sermons today that no room remains for the one imperative issue, the salvation of souls blood-bought by Christ. Illumined by the Spirit, Peter, who before had manifested ignorance, weakness, and often only a hazy understanding of our Lord's self-sacrifice for the atonement of the world, finds his faith purified. The blinders drop from his eyes; the mist of error vanishes; he sees Jesus and His saving Word with a clearer understanding than he ever had before. The New Testament gives us only twenty-three verses of his sermon, but fifteen of these are direct quotations from the Old Testament and Peter's own explanation of them.

This, then, is the first Pentecost blessing in the faith of believers: the Holy Spirit leads them, not to tradition, not to human keys to the Bible, not to church council decrees, not to their emotions, but back directly to the source of all truth, Sacred Scripture. May you who love the Lord Jesus find a powerful lesson here! If you are dissatisfied with your spiritual life; if the joy and fervor of your faith are disappearing; if your heart is riveting its desires on earthly schemes; if you doubt your Savior's grace, with deep sincerity pray today and every day: "Come, Holy Spirit, come to cleanse, refine, purify, guide, teach, my heart as Thou didst the disciples'! Bring me back all the way to the Bible with its beauteous, bountiful promise of my redemption!" Again, if, as is often tragically the case, some of you Christians find your interest in God's Word waning, hear yourself laugh at jokes about Scripture, admit that you find no time any more for real, personal study of Holy Writ, and if this weighs heavily on your conscience, it will not help you to run to a psychiatrist who tells you: "Stop going to church!" "Don't read the Bible!" "Don't say your prayers!" "Don't think about religion!" Instead, get down on your knees and pray, "Come, Holy Spirit," and that Teacher of eternal truth, who opened Peter's understanding to explain Old Testament passages better than any scribe or religious authority of his day, will create a burning love for God's Word in your heart, a sustained desire to delve deeply into its teachings, a holy reverence for its heavenly wisdom.

However, the Spirit does more than explain the Bible to Peter; He leads this wavering disciple to the crown and climax, the center and circumference, of Scripture — Jesus. It has become fashionable in certain circles to practice a hush-hush policy regarding the Savior's name, just as though the Son of God never came down to earth.

Peter, wavering and weak of faith, tried that. He fell so low two months before Pentecost that he lied and cursed, claiming that he did not even know Jesus; but the twenty-three recorded verses of his powerful Pentecost appeal show that he refers to Christ directly and indirectly eighteen times, each time clearly as the Savior of the world. You, His twentieth century disciples, know that you need more than outward religion, church membership, Bible class enrollment, congregational offices and honors; you need atonement for your sins. Without Jesus, you know, you can never have that. Yet you realize all too keenly that a hundred hostile forces try to crowd Him out of your life and that too often they succeed. You long for a closer walk with God's Son, a deeper trust in His mercy; but too often you surrender to sin. What can you do? What if not to pray: "Come, Holy Spirit! Bring me ever nearer to my Savior! Strengthen my faith! Increase my trust! Stir my soul into flame for the Redeemer, who loved me and gave Himself for me!" By God's grace the same Sanctifier who put Christ uppermost in Peter's life will crown Him Lord for you.

Even more startling is the faith-bestowing power with which the Spirit leads unbelievers to Jesus. In the crowd of thousands soon gathered before the disciples were many scoffers and sworn enemies of our Lord, some probably who were directly involved in His crucifixion. Peter did not spare their feelings, just as no real Christian pulpit today will gloss over popular sins to make people feel good. Instead, Peter told that hostile mass directly and unhesitatingly, *"Ye have taken and by wicked hands have crucified and slain"* Jesus of Nazareth. Publicly he accused them of their savage sin of murdering Christ, and then the Holy Spirit began His blessed work in their hearts. He convicted them of their terrifying transgressions, and three thousand of them cried: *"What shall we do?"*

More than ever before we must pray: "Come, Holy Spirit, to prick the hearts of the self-righteous and self-satisfied who smile at evil, shake hands with hellish forces, acclaim atheism, and stubbornly seek to defend evil!" Today, in their blind, petty, human way, selfish, greedy men strive for world domination; nations seek the advantages of power politics and spheres of influence; but our Lord warns us that someone exercises a rule far greater than all the allied nations will ever exert. Our Lord has told us who this ruler is. Do you want to know his name? Listen and be warned — it is Satan. Three times in four chapters of John's Gospel, Jesus — and He never makes a mistake — calls him *"the prince of this world."* His rule was never any wider than today, when in history's most civilized age at least ten million men have been killed on the field of battle, many more millions of civilians destroyed, cruelties and atrocities beyond description practiced, and perhaps a hundred million made homeless, while, with all this agony, people can cry, "Hurrah for war!" and gloat over their blood money. Hell, not high ideals, rules masses. For multitudes the prince of this world is still the devil, as crime, vice, impurity, falseness, lying, greed, covetousness, profanity, sacrilege, increase to shocking proportions, and at the same time the sense of sin is dulled, its destruction ignored, its enticement even glorified. Read some of our magazines, and you will be led to think that the girl who pooh-poohs purity but is smart enough to escape the consequences of her affairs, is made the ideal for American young womanhood. Study the glowing newspaper tributes paid atheists, whom the Bible, on the contrary, calls *"fools,"* and you will find that men who sneer, "There is no God," are often held up as models of achievement. Great numbers within our borders are losing their sense of sin, its hideousness, its soul-destroying, damning guilt, because the war loosened new hounds of hell over the land.

Therefore, we pray for you still far from Christ, who, with your private, personal, concealed transgressions, long for a peace which your position, your money, your influence, your friends, your college degrees, your self-confidence, can never give, "Come, Holy Spirit, to convict them of their guilt, to show them that every violation of God's Law can ruin their lives, blast away the happiness of others, and send their souls to hell!" Unless you know that in your sins you are hopelessly lost, deserve God's wrath and eternal punishment, you can never realize the need of the Savior's pardon.

Then the Holy Spirit can continue His blessed work in you by bringing you the glorious assurance of redemption. On Pentecost three thousand souls were brought to Christ for His full, free forgiveness; and today, because Scripture itself testifies, *"No man can say that Jesus is the Lord but by the Holy Ghost,"* I tell you, who want pardon for your sins and peace for your souls: Fall on your knees and plead: "Come, Holy Spirit! Lead me to the Lord Jesus! Show me beyond question, as Thou didst show those three thousand, that He, my God, is also my Savior; that with a love surpassing my poor powers of understanding, He transferred my transgressions, their guilt and punishment, to Himself, freed me forever from their curse, saved me from eternal damnation, restored me to the Father!"

God grant that this will be a real Pentecost for you as the power of the Spirit descends on your lives! Don't make the mistake of which Aaron Burr, later vice-president of the United States, was guilty. Despite the appeal of his grandfather, Jonathan Edwards, Burr left Princeton University an unbeliever. Once, when he was ready to accept Christ, the president of Princeton told him to think the matter over carefully so that his judgment would not be too hasty. That was bad advice; and Burr, a brilliant student, left college, telling God, as he later explained to his friends, "that if He would let me alone, I would let Him alone, and that settled it." But later in life, after receiving high honors, he was charged with murder, betrayal, and fraud. He left this country, and when he returned, an old, broken, friendless man, he admitted, "Sixty years ago I told God that if He would let me alone, I would let Him alone, and God has not bothered about me since." May the Holy Spirit refuse to let you alone, but instead prod your conscience, terrorize you by the guilt of your sins, call you to the comfort in Jesus, and guide you to your sure salvation!

The power of Pentecost is not past. The Spirit, our almighty God, can still perform wonders. The amazing blessings with which He has remembered this radio mission are in some ways even more startling than those first conversions. There, in Jerusalem, the crowd could see the disciples; but what shall we say when — all praise and honor to the Lord — we broadcast the message of repentance and return to God in His Son here in Saint Louis and a hundred, a thousand, five thousand miles away truth-seeking souls actually turn to their Savior

Come, Holy Spirit!

without ever having seen the speaker? An image maker in Costa Rica heard the broadcast and came to Jesus; a listener in Argentina who never before knew the Gospel until our broadcast brought it to him gave his life to the Lord. A man in Chile, 6,000 miles away, tuned in and wrote: "In the name of Christ I beg you, What must I do to join your Church?" A cabaret singer in Ecuador, living in sin and unbelief, listened to our message of the Redeemer's love, fell on his knees in repentance and faith, and dedicated his voice to sing hymns of praise to God. A Chinese young man in the Dominican Republic, a Cuban student in the West Indies, a sailor in the South Pacific, learn the Gospel of grace and plan to give themselves to Him in the ministry. In our own country a soldier saved from suicide for Christ; a profane bartender, repentant and reborn into a new and radiant life; a New York atheist converted; a scoffing Texas woman made a humble worshiper; a murderer in a Minnesota penitentiary baptized; a convict in a Michigan prison led to his Savior; an Indiana spiritist medium recalled to her Redeemer — these are only a few of the startling miracles the Almighty has permitted us to see in our mission of the air. Dr. Bertermann, our radio secretary, has prepared a booklet, which we shall be happy to send you, bringing the very words of many who have come from the darkness of unbelief into Christ's marvelous light. Write for a copy today and read this witness to the Holy Ghost's startling power! Above all, however, stop resisting the Spirit! Hear, read, study, the Bible, through which the Comforter can come into your soul! Follow His invitation to accept and acclaim God's Son your own Redeemer! Do it now!

Rebuilding with Christ

II
COME WITH THY BLESSINGS IN OUR LIFE!

When the Holy Spirit thus enriches you with faith, He will bless you with new life. You will be reborn a new creature in Christ. See how completely Pentecost changed those first disciples! After the crucifixion they feared the men who had killed their Lord; but when heavenly fire purged their souls, fright gave way to love, and they yearned for the salvation of their countrymen. If sullen, passionate resentment fills your soul, if you want peace in your home, pray, "Come, Holy Spirit, grant me Thy forgiving love," and, reborn in your Redeemer, you will learn that Jesus' command, *"Love your enemies,"* can truly be obeyed. No matter how savagely revenge-mad men may denounce you, you will be ready to befriend the destitute masses even in enemy lands as soon as possible.

Peter and the other disciples had been cowards, shamelessly deserting Christ and full of fear hiding themselves behind locked doors; yet when the Holy Spirit descended upon them, all fright disappeared. You too may be afraid to stand up for your Lord; you may keep your lips sealed when your mouth should be open, testifying that *"Jesus Christ . . . is our Hope";* but when the Spirit takes mastery over your life, this terror will vanish as the fog before the sun. That is why sixteen-year-old girls in Rome's blood-stained arenas, faced with the horror of being torn to pieces by panthers, tigers, lions, could bravely sing their hymns of praise to the Savior. Pray, "Come, Holy Spirit!" and as in answer He enters your heart, He will strengthen you with the courage in Christ to face the worst that life or death itself may bring.

Come, Holy Spirit!

Pentecost gave those unlearned disciples the wisdom required to preach the Gospel; it enriched them even with instantaneous knowledge of many hard, foreign languages. The Holy Spirit can grant the same enlightenment today, although this need is not nearly so great now since the Bible has been translated into more than a thousand different languages. If you hesitate to speak out for Christ because you have never attended a theological seminary and it is not easy for you to talk publicly, then pray, "Come, Holy Spirit!" As we are told of the Apostles, *"The Spirit gave them utterance,"* so fitting thoughts and expressions shall be given you. The very words you need will be placed in your mind and on your lips.

See what the gift of the Holy Comforter did for the Church! On Pentecost morning one hundred and twenty believers, on Pentecost evening three thousand one hundred and twenty! And that was only the beginning! Preaching Christ crucified, the Church moved as a mighty army, and wherever the Gospel was proclaimed the fortresses of paganism, idolatry, and superstition collapsed. Tertullian, leader of the second-century North African believers, could tell the heathen world: "We [the Christians] are a people but of yesterday; yet we have filled every place belonging to you — cities, islands, castles, towns, assemblies, your very camps, your tribes, companies, palaces, forums. We leave you your temples only." Soon after, in the third century, Emperor Maximianus could write officially that almost all his empire "had abandoned the worship of their ancestors for the new sect," that is, the Christian faith. The historian Gibbon, an enemy of Christianity, admits that the onward rush of the Gospel "finally erected the triumphant banner of the cross on the ruins of the Capitol" in Rome. That forward march was led by the Spirit and was marked by the shedding of much martyr blood. When you read today that some of our large denominations show an annual decrease in membership or some a gain of only 4 or 5 per cent over a ten-year period; when the International Sunday School Council in America estimates a loss of four million in Sunday schools during a recent ten-year period; when many of you know better than I can tell you that you belong to dwindling, decreasing churches which do not have the pure, powerful Gospel and therefore not the Holy Spirit, you can understand first why it is necessary to plead as never before in our generation, "Come, Holy Spirit, reform, restore, rededicate apostate churches to Christ!" and then to realize that God may permit the days of persecution to overtake His Church in this country as they have in Germany and Russia and other European nations.

See what the Holy Spirit did for the world at large when the Apostles, led by Him, spread the message of the crucified Savior! In the words of their own enemies, they *"turned the world upside down."* They began to put into men's hearts the Gospel principles which would fight against evil in the home, in labor, in the state, in international relations. Today throughout a cruel and blood-stained age, you have the choice either of remaining silent while this generation goes farther from Christ, more deeply into the horrors of even worse warfare than we have seen, or of praying, "Come, Holy Spirit, help me turn this world of hatred, violence, crime, greed, destruction, upside down through Jesus!"

its increasing lists of suicides feature the folly of outlawing the only God; when — and this is the supreme tragedy — three of every four human beings on the face of the earth do not recognize the Almighty — we, who know the truth, instead of permitting tragedy to triumph, should testify as never before that the one and only Lord is the Father, the Son, and the Spirit, three persons, yet one God.

We denounce the millions of false gods which men have invented: the crude mud idols in Africa, the sacred cows, the Brahmas, Sivas, and Vishnus of India, the laughing Buddhas and the long dead ancestors of China, the emperor of devastated Japan, the Allah of the Mohammedans, the vague, undefined creations of highly cultured men who worship force, light, the Supreme Architect, the Eternal Being, the Infinite Mind, without beginning to know who this highest Lord is, or — and this is the most prevalent idolatry — who actually bow down before themselves. The doctrine of the Trinity is not a theological invention; it is a Bible-based, Scripture-sealed, Heaven-revealed truth. Hundreds of passages of Holy Writ testify to the three powerful Persons — each called, described, and worshiped as God; and a dozen other passages state or imply that these three are One. Therefore, when the early Christians sought a short, simple statement of their faith — we call it the Apostles' Creed — they declared on the basis of clear-cut Holy Writ, "I believe in God the Father . . . and in Jesus Christ, His only Son, our Lord . . . and . . . in the Holy Ghost."

Mere human reason cannot understand the Trinity, but that is no cause for rejecting its reality. Every moment you live you are surrounded by marvels of nature far too intricate for you to analyze; yet you never question their reality. Why, then, should mere mortal man be brash and blasphemous enough to insist, "If you cannot explain the Trinity, I will certainly not believe it"? Can you explain how one ray of sun brings light, heat, and power? Yet you do not deny that the sun shines upon us. Why, then, question the Trinity, when minds, far mightier than yours, have gratefully bowed before its blessing? For example, Murillo, the world-renowned artist, whose canvases are worth fortunes, stated, that he believed, "firmly and truly in the divine mystery of the Holy Trinity — Father, Son, and Holy Ghost, three persons, really distinct, and yet one true God." With ten thousand times more such testimony, why should you refuse to worship the Triune God?

Regrettably many American churches have pushed the Trinity out of their pulpits and thus robbed themselves of the triple comfort this divine doctrine offers. If you want to know why certain churches, including particularly some of the oldest, wealthiest, most fashionable, are decreasing in membership and influence, show no conversions to Christ, no rebirth through the Holy Spirit, you can discover the cause in the shocking fact that they deliberately bar the Triune God. Let me prove this to you! We have in our country two denominations definitely opposed to accepting the Trinity. How have they fared? In 1906 one of them had 435 churches, but at the last religious census in 1936 only 305, a loss of 130, while the membership dropped from 70,000 to 59,000 during the same period. The story of the other group is worse. In 1906 it had 811 congregations; in 1936 it listed fewer than half, only 339, and a 65-per-cent decrease in Sunday schools. When the 1946 religious census appears, it will show still further decrease. If you want to stop American churches from declining in influence and disintegrating altogether, stop the preachers in your own denomination from denying the Trinity! Silence the modernist, Scripture-rejecting pulpiteer who sneers at this truth!

Our Trinity Sunday text starts with the Savior, as the Apostle writes, *"The grace of the Lord Jesus Christ . . . be with you all."* Saint Paul may have had our own age in view when he chose this order and put Christ first, for today in opposition too many speak of God, call Him "the Spirit," but stubbornly refuse to admit that Jesus is, as an early creed declares, "very God of very God." Christ is the name political figures often studiously omit from their public prayers, their addresses, their conversation — except, of course, in profanity. I tell you plainly (so that you cannot face me and say: "You sidestepped the issue." "You never warned me." "You could have helped me, but you did not"): if you reject Jesus as your God, no matter whom you worship, you have a false God, for our Lord Himself declared, *"If ye believe not that I am He, ye shall die in your sins."*

Now, the Apostle wishes the Corinthians, as I wish for you, *"the grace of the Lord Jesus Christ."* What a wondrous, marvelous meaning His *"grace"* has! It describes the highest love, the deepest devotion, the widest compassion, the most magnificent mercy, heaven itself could offer. It tells every one of you — and how I thank the Lord that during this hard year of broadcasting He gave me the privilege to bring you the message of glorious grace every Sunday — that Jesus, the Son of God, knew you before you were born; that He loved you when you hated Him, sought you when you spurned Him, yearned to save you for eternity, while others, your own flesh, the devil, the human agents of hell, cunningly tried to destroy you. He offered you life, when you were *"dead in trespasses and sin."* He opens the gates of Paradise, when the doors of perdition swung closed behind you. He did more than seek you, call you, love you. From all eternity He had a hallowed, heavenly design of salvation, and no matter how your color, creed, or condition, financial or social, may seek to contradict this, He has a place for you in those everlasting plans of pardon and peace. Every time you sin, you drift farther from Him; every time you refuse the invitation of His outstretched arms and His appeal, *"Come unto Me,"* you drop deeper toward hell; every time you blaspheme His holy name, the devil's clutches tighten about you. No priest or preacher, no holy man or martyr, no saint or select leader, can rescue you from ruin. No pious mother can scrub your sins away, no devoted daughter pray them away; no host of God-fearing friends, relatives, neighbors, associates, can atone for them. Angel hosts may carol divine praise, destroy mighty armies, lead believers out of prison; yet even the cherubim and the seraphim cannot save you. Praise the Lord with me, however — Jesus not only *can* deliver you from death and hell, He has. If only all of you would believe His glorious *"grace"!*

Fellow sinners and fellow redeemed, your deliverance cost Him dearly — how dearly you will never know until either in hell, seeing the horror of your transgressions, or in heaven, where mysteries like the marvel of the Trinity will be understood by the fuller celestial knowledge, you learn to measure the heightless, depthless, breathless love of God's Son. He had to be lashed until His back ran bloody; He had to be beaten, spit upon, crowned with a circle of cutting thorns, burdened by the heavy timbers of His own cross until He collapsed. Enduring soul-deep agony a million times more crushing than this anguish of body, He had to be nailed to the accursed cross and to fulfill God's holy Law in your stead, remove your sins, forever defeat death for you. And now comes the fullest, most blessed meaning the word *"grace"* can ever have. What price does Jesus demand in return for all this? What must we pay to secure His blood-bought pardon? Oh, it cost Him His life and far more, the horror of being forsaken by His Father, the terror of enduring the woe and weight of human transgressions; but by the Gospel of His grace it costs you nothing. You need only believe that Jesus is your personal Savior, confess your crimson crimes, cling tightly to His matchless, mighty mercy, and then you are saved for eternity.

That *"grace of the Lord Jesus Christ . . . be with you all"!* It is offered to every one of you here and now. You cannot have transgressed God's Law too frequently, blasphemed too brutally to be pardoned by His mercy. Yet remember: you cannot be saved until you know that you need to be saved, until you realize that your sins rise up to accuse you and cast you into hell. That is why I plead with particular appeal to those in this mission of the air who for years have listened to the broadcast, yet have stubbornly continued in their evil ways. Out in Los Angeles a thief stole radium from the office of a cancer specialist, and the police broadcast a warning that the radium was not in its usual lead case and hence could destroy the person who had it. In a much more important message I am broadcasting to you that your neglect of Jesus can help destroy both body and soul in hell.

With heaven at stake, why do masses in America close their eyes, ears, mind, and heart to Christ's appeal? Musgrove Reade was a prominent atheist for twenty years, but after much inner trouble he found Christ as his Savior, and with Him, peace and happiness. Years later he wrote: "Having tasted that the Lord was good, I yearned to let other blind souls know this great joy; but I soon found out that they did not want to know. . . . I marveled greatly that . . . the blessed news of Christ's love to sinful men should meet with such a cold response; but I remembered my own sad case, how blind and perverse I had been for twenty years" — and how thankless, how ungrateful men are, we add. Recently the newspapers mentioned the fact that a Milwaukee man remembered in his will a woman who once, fifty years ago, as a young girl, had kissed him; but if we would worthily pay tribute to Jesus, who loved us with the intensity of a devotion which cost His life, we would gladly give all we have and are for His holy cause. Every year before I return to the air after the summer, hundreds in this radio mission have been called away by death. Because in life's uncertainty I may never again have the privilege of inviting and urging you to come to the Savior, I earnestly ask you to write, phone, wire, radio, or cable that you want the *"grace of the Lord Jesus Christ"* to abide with you.

His mercy is unfailing. Its promises are sure. Men,

even the greatest, may be false prophets. A hundred years ago Lord Shaftesbury declared, "Nothing can save the British empire from shipwreck"; but that empire enjoyed great growth after his time. Sir Humphrey Davey, one of the outstanding scientists of his day, asserted, "It would be as easy to bring down a bit of the moon as to light London with gas"; but London was lit with gaslight. Bismarck prophesied, "Russia can never join France against Germany"; but it did, twice in twenty-five years. Similarly when you read the glowing reports of the good times ahead of us, put a question mark behind them! Politicians and experts gave us the same roseate forecasts at the end of the last war. So much the more, however, trust Christ to keep His word! He will never fail; He can never fail! His grace be with you alway!

II

"THE LOVE OF GOD . . . BE WITH YOU ALL"

Our Trinity Sunday text continues to ask that *"the love of God,"* the Father, *"be with you all."* True, in the intoxication of victory, millions are not worried about God. World figures leave Him out of their plans for the new age. Builders of our cities cut Him out of their programs. In New York, for example, a life insurance company is spending $50,000,000 to tear down eighteen blocks of buildings, on which modern apartments will be built. A church in this locality for sixty-two years will be destroyed, and the whole area left without a house of worship. The members of that congregation rightly declare, "America cannot afford to have its housing projects planned without God." More than half of our 138,000,000 citizens have only pennies for the Savior, at best; yet the average liquor bill last year was $54 for every man, woman, and child in the United States. Our country lists two taverns for every church, five taverns for every schoolhouse. With our national income last year reaching the record figure of $150,000,000,000, multitudes think that they do not need the Lord. But what of the future? When Napoleon was at the pinnacle of his power, his mother said that everything in his empire was splendid, but she added, "provided it lasts." Our age, more than any other, should know that nothing except God lasts, and that the day of reckoning, national and individual, cannot be avoided. The Lord is so just and holy that He keeps His word, and on the basis of Scripture, I tell you that multitudes in America, prosperous, yet forgetful of God, self-confident, but not penitent, cannot go on indefinitely, without having divine retribution overtake them. If our nation was shaken by the consequences of the First World War, how great will be the convulsions following this second, far more destructive, upheaval? Therefore, America needs a penitent return to the Almighty. God give each of you real sorrow over your sins, a genuine determination to walk in His way, to set your house, your finances, your affairs in order for the days ahead after the flush of postwar prosperity has subsided! With our casualty list now close to one million, and experts asserting that the total will exceed that figure, how many more afflictions do we need to arouse us from our complacency? The newspapers this spring brought the picture of a woman in a flood area as she was leaving her home for the fifty-eighth time in as many years. "Why," you ask, "did she not move away after the second or third flood?" Prob-

God Be with You!

ably because she wanted to stay just where she was. Why, we ask, do some of you, driven away from the Lord by your sin for more than fifty-eight years, always return to the favorite but fatal follies of your smart, yet suicidal unbelief?

If only you could realize God's power and the help He can give you! What are the mighty oceans to Him if not merely what drops of water are to us? What are the wide continents to the Almighty if not smaller than grains of sand to us? What is this globe to the Lord? Less than what a ball is to us! And what to Him are men — proud, boastful, blasphemous men — who sullenly shake their fists against Him, if not as ants to us?

Therefore, ask your heavenly Father for Jesus' sake to forgive you, accept you, restore you, as I plead that in Christ *"the love of God . . . be with you"* to direct your life, to provide you with food, clothing, shelter, to guard you in days of peril, to comfort you in times of grief, to defend you against your enemies, and to give you peace, calm, quiet, in the Lord. During the height of the blitz in London, while the restless masses stayed awake, fearing the terrors that might come at night, an elderly woman said her prayers, turned out the light, and went calmly to bed. "For," she said, "I have put everything in the hands of my God, who neither slumbers nor sleeps; and there is no point in both of us staying up." By faith in your Savior you can have the same courageous confidence.

Don't let the sorrows in your life, particularly the woes of this war, prevent you from clinging to your gracious Lord! — "Where was God when my son was killed in battle?" a bereaved father demanded of a

Christian pastor. Slowly he replied, "Where was God when His own Son was crucified at Calvary?" To the believer, through Christ, God is always in the right place, even through the darkest difficulties and the bitterest bereavements. At the cross we understand that *"all things work together for good to them that love God"*; that our heaviest afflictions are the deepest evidences of His mercy, designed as they are, to keep us close to our Father, loyal to the Savior, firm in the faith. Remember that, you the shut-in, the invalids, the aged, to whom the Lord has permitted me to speak these many years! Pray that this *"love of God . . . be with you all"* and remain with you always! You have often read, I am sure, of atheists and scoffers who, tortured on their deathbed by the enormity of their sins, have cried out, "Oh, that I had never been an unbeliever!" But I ask you pointedly, have you ever heard of anyone who in his last moments regretted that he had been a believer?

III

"THE COMMUNION OF THE HOLY GHOST BE WITH YOU ALL"

Now, to live for Christ, to die in Christ, and then to be resurrected by Christ, we need, besides the Father and the Son, the Holy Spirit. Therefore Saint Paul prays in our text, *"The communion of the Holy Ghost be with you all!"* We are still in the shadow of Pentecost and feel keenly what the Apostle means by this word *"communion."* It is the fellowship with the Holy Spirit or, even more directly, His presence in our hearts and lives, when we commune with Him, pray to Him, and in return receive from His indwelling, rebirth into the new life, comfort, strength, guidance, instruction.

Without the Holy Spirit's blessing you cannot know God, come to the Savior, and receive His redemption; but when you have the communion of the Spirit, you are born again into a new existence, in which you hate sin, love Jesus, find courage even in the darkest moments, joy in the deepest sorrow, direction in testifying to the cross, strength to fight temptation, and in your Father's good time, heaven as the blessing of your faith.

I pray today, *"The communion of the Holy Ghost be with you,"* because you need heavenly help in battling against sin. How treacherously evil spreads and multiplies its ruin! In 1869 at Medford, Massachusetts, a French scientist was experimenting with silkworms. To carry out his research, he had brought from Europe an interesting brown moth, otherwise unknown in this country, called the gypsy moth. As he sat before the open window, the wind blew the pasteboard box with the eggs of the gypsy moth out the window. They were scattered over the ground. He notified Massachusetts officials of the incident and told them that he had been unable to recover the eggs. Ten years passed and nothing happened. But five years later people in the vicinity of Boston began to notice enormous caterpillars. In a year or two they swarmed by the billions, and we are told: "Villages were overrun. Sidewalks were slippery with their crushed bodies. They crawled into houses." They caused millions of dollars' loss, and it required more millions to fight them. — So it is with sin. It starts small and unnoticed. People refuse to pay any attention to it; some even think it attractive; but when years later sin comes back with its curse as a punishing, pestilential evil, the single transgression which seems insignificant is multiplied beyond counting, as one satanic spirit has returned with seven others to ruin your life and destroy your soul. You need divine help. And here it is, in the sanctifying Spirit. If you want to walk in your Savior's footsteps; if you want to lead clean, courageous lives; if you want to break off evil, ugly habits; if you want to tear selfish, revengeful desires from your heart, then beseech God daily in Jesus' name for the Holy Spirit!

How our hate-filled age needs His peace and love! An American missionary doctor in the Philippines was imprisoned and persecuted by the Japanese; but the first thing he did when freed was to perform an operation which saved the life of his archenemy in that torture camp. A Dutch doctor locked behind the walls of the atrocious Siegburg prison in Germany, when released, stayed there in its squalor to help fight typhoid fever. We must have this humane spirit of love for our postwar world, no matter how loudly the advocates of force and annihilation scream for total destruction and curse the Christ who says, *"Love your enemies!"* That love comes when the Spirit controls and directs our souls. Therefore I pray that the *"communion"* of God *"the Holy Ghost be with you all,"* to show you your sins, their fearful, eternal consequences; to lead you to your Savior, who has promised, *"Him that cometh to Me I will in no wise cast out";* to cleanse your life, direct your afflictions to your advantage; to help you triumph over temptation and remain loyal to Jesus until the end.

Pray also that *"the communion of the Holy Ghost,"* His blessed presence, may rest upon this broadcast! By divine grace — and by that benediction alone — the forward march of "Bringing Christ to the Nations" con-

God Be with You! 309

tinues. Listen to these points of progress within the last few days: Advance Number One: three new frequency-modulation stations added! Advance Number Two: six new and larger regular stations in various parts of the country added! Advance Number Three: nine new Spanish broadcasts added along the Mexican border! Advance Number Four: an invitation from a Lisbon, Portugal, long- and short-wave station, to use its facilities — our first official invitation into Europe! Pray that no barriers of bigotry will keep us from accepting! Advance Number Five: negotiations with stations in Holland for Dutch broadcasts! Advance Number Six: constantly more Government-controlled stations added in military and naval areas as in veterans' hospitals! Advance Number Seven: an invitation to fly to Africa and Australia in behalf of our broadcast and its expansion! Advance Number Eight: this week the first meeting to consider the establishment of a European radio station from which 400,000,000 people can hear the story of Christ's love in their own language!

I thank you for the outpouring of your letters endorsing the proposal of bringing Christ to war-torn Europe, if possible, from the place where Martin Luther translated the New Testament. Stand by us with your fervent, effectual prayers! Help us change the title of our program from "Bringing Christ to the Nations" to "Bringing Christ to the World"!

Thus God in His infinite grace has permitted me to complete my part in the twelfth season of our broadcasting. The program continues as usual, and I ask your prayers in behalf of the men who will stand before this microphone in my place. As I praise God for His unspeakable grace in enabling me, unworthy as I am, to proclaim the Savior's love, I also thank you from the bottom of my heart for all your interest, support, and prayer. If only I could shake hands with every one of you, especially those who by the Holy Spirit have come to Christ through these broadcasts! But one promise is sure: Loyal to the Savior, though we may never see each other on earth, we shall meet one blessed day before the Throne. What unspeakable joy then! Above all, I wish that it were possible for me to speak directly to you who are close to the Kingdom, almost persuaded and still not definitely decided for Jesus. Will you not — and this is my parting plea with you — stop postponing and make Christ yours today? Until next October, then, if in all the uncertainty of life and the growing opposition to our faith, God gives me the opportunity to broadcast to you again, I close (thinking particularly of you the sick, the invalid, the imprisoned, the persecuted, the aged, the dying) with the concluding words of Saint Paul to his Corinthian Christians, *"The grace of the Lord Jesus Christ, the love of God the Father, and the communion of the Holy Ghost be with you all,"* until we meet again. Amen!

BX 8066 .M25 R38
Maier, Walter Arthur,
  1893-1950.
Rebuilding with Christ

DATE DUE

BX 8066 .M25 R38
Maier, Walter Arthur,
  1893-1950.
Rebuilding with Christ

DATE DUE	BORROWER'S NAME

Concordia College Library
Bronxville, NY 10708